Democratic Citizenship Education in Non-Western Contexts

This book examines the issues of theorizing citizenship education research in non-Western societies that have embarked on democratic development after the fall of authoritarianism and colonialism.

Despite a proliferation of studies on citizenship and citizenship education in non-Western contexts, there has been limited theorization of this research and little discussion of the applicability to such contexts of Western theoretical frameworks. This volume addresses these issues through empirical case studies of citizenship conceptions, practices, and education in South and West Africa, Latin America, Central Europe, and the Middle East. The contributors to the volume call into question the uncritical application of Western theoretical frameworks to non-Western societies and advocate for the development and wider application of new paradigms rooted in local processes and indigenous knowledge to better understand and theorize citizenship and citizenship education in such societies.

This volume will be of interest to scholars, researchers, and practitioners working in the field of comparative and international citizenship education.

This book was originally published as a special issue of *Compare: A Journal of Comparative and International Education*.

Serhiy Kovalchuk is a Research Associate and Lecturer at the University of Toronto, Canada. His research interests include democratic citizenship education, comparative and international education, and qualitative research methods. His work has appeared in *Compare: A Journal of Comparative and International Education*, *European Education: Issues and Studies*, and the *Journal of Ukrainian Politics and Society*. He is a co-editor of *Reimagining Utopias: Theory and Method for Educational Research in Post-Socialist Contexts* (2017).

Anatoli Rapoport is an Associate Professor of Curriculum and Instruction at Purdue University, USA. He is editor of the *Journal of International Social Studies* and past Chair of the Citizenship and Democratic Education Special Interest Group of the Comparative and International Education Society (CIES). His research interests include global aspects of citizenship education, comparative education, and constructivist theory. He is the author of *Fields Unknown: Russian and American Teachers on Their International Exchange Experiences* (2007), co-author of *Civic Education in Contemporary Global Society* (in Russian, 2009), and editor of *Competing Frameworks: Global and National in Citizenship Education* (2018).

Democratic Citizenship Education in Non-Western Contexts

Implications for Theory and Research

Edited by
Serhiy Kovalchuk and Anatoli Rapoport

LONDON AND NEW YORK

First published 2019
by Routledge
2 Park Square, Milton Park, Abingdon, Oxon, OX14 4RN

and by Routledge
52 Vanderbilt Avenue, New York, NY 10017

Routledge is an imprint of the Taylor & Francis Group, an informa business

© 2019 British Association for International and Comparative Education

All rights reserved. No part of this book may be reprinted or reproduced or utilised in any form or by any electronic, mechanical, or other means, now known or hereafter invented, including photocopying and recording, or in any information storage or retrieval system, without permission in writing from the publishers.

Trademark notice: Product or corporate names may be trademarks or registered trademarks, and are used only for identification and explanation without intent to infringe.

British Library Cataloguing in Publication Data
A catalogue record for this book is available from the British Library

ISBN 13: 978-0-367-26449-9

Typeset in Minion Pro
by RefineCatch Limited, Bungay, Suffolk

Publisher's Note
The publisher accepts responsibility for any inconsistencies that may have arisen during the conversion of this book from journal articles to book chapters, namely the inclusion of journal terminology.

Disclaimer
Every effort has been made to contact copyright holders for their permission to reprint material in this book. The publishers would be grateful to hear from any copyright holder who is not here acknowledged and will undertake to rectify any errors or omissions in future editions of this book.

Contents

Citation Information	vii
Notes on Contributors	ix

1. Democratic citizenship education in non-Western contexts: implications for theory and research
   Serhiy Kovalchuk and Anatoli Rapoport — 1

2. Exploring Western and non-Western epistemological influences in South Africa: theorising a critical democratic citizenship education
   Patricia K. Kubow — 11

3. Remembering West African indigenous knowledges and practices in citizenship education research
   Laura Quaynor — 24

4. Wait-citizenship: youth civic development in transition
   Michelle J. Bellino — 41

5. Obstacles and opportunities for global citizenship education under intractable conflict: the case of Israel
   Heela Goren and Miri Yemini — 59

6. Reframing approaches to narrating young people's conceptualisations of citizenship in education research
   Bassel Akar — 76

7. Citizenship education discourses in Latin America: multilateral institutions and the decolonial challenge
   Diego Nieto — 94

8. Rendering technical the responsible citizen: implementing citizenship education reform in Kosovo
   Jennifer Otting — 113

Index — 129

Citation Information

The chapters in this book were originally published in *Compare: A Journal of Comparative and International Education*, volume 48, issue 3 (May 2018). When citing this material, please use the original page numbering for each article, as follows:

Chapter 1
Democratic citizenship education in non-Western contexts: implications for theory and research
Serhiy Kovalchuk and Anatoli Rapoport
Compare: A Journal of Comparative and International Education, volume 48, issue 3 (May 2018), pp. 339–348

Chapter 2
Exploring Western and non-Western epistemological influences in South Africa: theorising a critical democratic citizenship education
Patricia K. Kubow
Compare: A Journal of Comparative and International Education, volume 48, issue 3 (May 2018), pp. 349–361

Chapter 3
Remembering West African indigenous knowledges and practices in citizenship education research
Laura Quaynor
Compare: A Journal of Comparative and International Education, volume 48, issue 3 (May 2018), pp. 362–378

Chapter 4
Wait-citizenship: youth civic development in transition
Michelle J. Bellino
Compare: A Journal of Comparative and International Education, volume 48, issue 3 (May 2018), pp. 379–396

Chapter 5
Obstacles and opportunities for global citizenship education under intractable conflict: the case of Israel
Heela Goren and Miri Yemini
Compare: A Journal of Comparative and International Education, volume 48, issue 3 (May 2018), pp. 397–413

Chapter 6
Reframing approaches to narrating young people's conceptualisations of citizenship in education research
Bassel Akar
Compare: A Journal of Comparative and International Education, volume 48, issue 3 (May 2018), pp. 414–431

Chapter 7
Citizenship education discourses in Latin America: multilateral institutions and the decolonial challenge
Diego Nieto
Compare: A Journal of Comparative and International Education, volume 48, issue 3 (May 2018), pp. 432–450

Chapter 8
Rendering technical the responsible citizen: implementing citizenship education reform in Kosovo
Jennifer Otting
Compare: A Journal of Comparative and International Education, volume 48, issue 3 (May 2018), pp. 451–466

For any permission-related enquiries please visit:
http://www.tandfonline.com/page/help/permissions

Notes on Contributors

Bassel Akar is Director of the Center for Applied Research in Education at Notre Dame University – Louaize, Lebanon.

Michelle J. Bellino is an Assistant Professor of Educational Studies in the School of Education at the University of Michigan, USA.

Heela Goren is a PhD candidate at the University College London Institute of Education, UK.

Serhiy Kovalchuk is a Research Associate and Lecturer at the University of Toronto, Canada.

Patricia K. Kubow is Professor of International Comparative Education in the School of Education at Indiana University-Bloomington, USA.

Diego Nieto is a PhD candidate in Curriculum Studies and Teaching Development at the Ontario Institute for Studies in Education, the University of Toronto, Canada. He is also a Professor in the Department of Political Studies at the Universidad Icesi, Colombia.

Jennifer Otting is a doctoral student in Education Policy Studies in the School of Education at the University of Wisconsin-Madison, USA.

Laura Quaynor is an Assistant Professor in the Division of Foundations, Leadership and Literacy in the College of Education at Lewis University, USA.

Anatoli Rapoport is an Associate Professor of Curriculum and Instruction at Purdue University, USA.

Miri Yemini is a Lecturer in the School of Education at Tel Aviv University, Israel.

Democratic citizenship education in non-Western contexts: implications for theory and research

Serhiy Kovalchuk and Anatoli Rapoport

Until recently, despite growing empirical research, the field of comparative education rarely offered a comprehensive, theoretically substantiated ontological approach to understanding education developments and transformations in post-authoritarian, post-colonial, and post-socialist societies (or 'non-Western' societies). The topic discussed in this Special Issue, namely how to theorise democratic citizenship education research in non-Western contexts, presents an even more challenging task by engaging contested concepts such as democracy and citizenship.[1]

Recent decades have witnessed a proliferation of studies on citizenship and citizenship education in post-authoritarian, post-colonial, and post-socialist societies, many of which have embarked on a transition to democracy (Stevick and Levinson 2007; Tobin 2010; Vickers and Kumar 2015). Yet there has been limited discussion in these studies about the theorisation of citizenship education research, and particularly about the applicability to non-Western societies of Western theoretical paradigms that dominate citizenship education research. Many scholars point to the limitations of Western conceptual lenses in capturing and interpreting the realities of non-Western societies as well as to the absence of alternative contextually relevant frameworks for studying citizenship and citizenship education beyond the West (Chua and Sim 2017; Moland 2015; Williams 2013). Observers have also noted that transitioning non-Western societies continue to be recipients of, rather than contributors to, citizenship education theories. However, as Haste, Bermudez, and Carretero note (2017), the emerging research on citizenship education around the globe is 'beginning to challenge the hegemony of Euro-American theorising, and giving us new ways to think about many aspects of civic life and systems, which might enlighten everyone' (12).

We conceive this Special Issue as a contribution to the discussion on researching and theorising democratic citizenship education in non-Western contexts with the aim of using such research and theorisation to cross-culturalise the field of comparative and international citizenship education (see Takayama 2018). We pursue that aim by examining conceptions and practices of citizenship and citizenship education in non-Western contexts, challenging the applicability of Western theoretical frameworks to such contexts, and presenting theoretical and methodological approaches to studying citizenship and citizenship education in these contexts. In the Special Issue, we use the terms 'Western' and 'non-Western' in two ways. On the one hand, we use the former to refer to Western Europe and North America, or the Global North, and the latter to refer to post-authoritarian, post-colonial, and post-socialist societies of the Global South and East. This usage allows us to acknowledge asymmetrical power relations between epistemological and methodological traditions of the West and non-West, which resulted in the dominance of Western theoretical frameworks in the field of citizenship education research. As Connell (2007) notes, while alternative ways of thinking about the world exist in the Global South, they have been marginalised by the hegemonic knowledge of the Global North as a result of colonial and imperial processes. On the other hand, we use the West and non-West as ideological concepts, or rhetorical devices, to distinguish more individualistic societies from their less individualistic counterparts (Dunn 1996). For this approach, as for any socially constructed reality, the West and non-West exist only as interpretive metaphors of specific sets of ideas, values, and practices. We do not view the concepts of West and non-West as homogeneous or binary, for they represent diverse and complex histories, disparate political and economic systems, and, notably in the context of this Special Issue, divergent models of citizenship education (Hahn 2016; McCowan 2009; Quaynor 2012).

This Special Issue speaks to a wider conversation in the field of comparative education about the dominance of Western theoretical frameworks in understanding the world, the flow of knowledge from North to South and West to East, and the marginalisation of epistemological and methodological orientations generated beyond Western scholarship (Silova, Millei, and Piattoeva 2017; Takayama, Sriprakash, and Connell 2017). Despite the rise of alternative epistemological and methodological orientations such as Africanist ethnography and epistemology, Latin American legalist epistemology, Indian subaltern studies, southern theory from the Commonwealth South, and Asia-centric research methodology (Park 2017, 760), the field of comparative education continues to be dominated by Western epistemological and methodological orientations (Takayama, Sriprakash, and Connell 2017). However, as Sobe et al. (2017) note, 'a reliance on Western-centric theoretical frameworks and methodological approaches may result in devaluing epistemic differences and subsequently leading to the displacement of alternative worldviews and interpretations in education research' (302). An uncritical reliance on such frameworks can result in an inaccurate, oversimplified and distorted understanding of phenomena investigated in non-Western contexts. In order to address these issues, critical scholars in the field of comparative education recommend not viewing theories and concepts generated in the West as universal and thus as readily transferrable across cultural contexts and national boundaries. They also advocate studying and deploying epistemological and methodological orientations produced in non-Western contexts (Takayama 2018). They further suggest appropriately incorporating local knowledge and traditions into research undertaken in non-Western contexts in order to better understand local realities rather than viewing such knowledge and traditions as primitive or insufficiently scientific, or as obstacles to the processes of modernisation (Sobe et al. 2017).

Like the larger field of comparative education, the field of comparative and international citizenship education has been dominated by Western theoretical frameworks informed mainly by liberal-democratic principles. As Haste, Bermudez, and Carretero (2017) observe with regard to the research on civic engagement, 'the history of writing and research on civic participation and competences has been heavily Euro-American, often in fact just North American' (12). However, in comparison to the broader field of comparative education, there has been little discussion in the area of citizenship education about the dominance of Western theoretical frameworks and the appropriateness of their application to post-authoritarian, post-colonial, and post-socialist societies that differ qualitatively from those in which such frameworks originated.[2] When it comes to the use of theoretical lenses and the consideration of context in researching citizenship and citizenship education in non-Western contexts, studies in the field of comparative and international citizenship education can be divided roughly into three large groups: (1) those that mechanically apply Western theoretical frameworks to non-Western contexts and do not attend to the specifics of the context, particularly during the data analysis; (2) those that deploy Western theoretical frameworks but consider the realities of non-Western contexts during the data analysis and challenge and extend such frameworks; and (3) those that draw on context-specific, indigenous concepts of citizenship and citizenship education.

While studies from the first group may contribute to our understanding of citizenship and related education in non-Western contexts, they run the risk of painting an oversimplified, incomplete, or distorted picture by mechanically applying Western frameworks of citizenship education and not attending to the specifics of context in interpreting the social phenomena under investigation. For such studies, context is 'a matter of fact' rather than 'a matter of concern'; that is, while they may situate their research subject in particular political, economic, social, and cultural contexts, they do not necessarily consider the relationality between the subject and the context or the ways in which the context shapes the subject (Sobe and Kowalczyk 2013). In contrast, studies from the second and third groups use context as one of their interpretive tools. Although studies from the second group rely on Western theoretical frameworks, their consideration of context allows them to discern the hybridity of global and local citizenship discourses (e.g. Dull 2012; Sim, Chua, and Krishnasamy 2017). They recognise the challenges and limitations of applying such frameworks to non-Western contexts (e.g. Chua and Sim 2017; Moland 2015) and highlight ways in which these frameworks can acquire different meanings and significance in post-authoritarian, post-colonial, and post-socialist societies (e.g. Kovalchuk 2015; Williams 2013). Like studies from the second group, those from the third group also challenge and extend Western theoretical frameworks. Their distinctive feature is that they draw on context-specific indigenous concepts when examining citizenship and its education in non-Western societies (e.g. DeJaeghere 2017; Kubow 2007). Studies from the last two groups have the potential to produce contextually relevant frameworks for studying citizenship and its education in non-Western contexts and new ways of thinking about it, thereby challenging the hegemony of Euro-American theorising.

Attention to context and consideration of indigenous knowledge will help to produce contextually and culturally relevant theoretical frameworks and avoid the marginalisation of local knowledge and traditions. As numerous scholars note, when post-authoritarian, post-colonial, and post-socialist societies embarked on a transition to democracy, their knowledge, traditions and histories were seen in many cases as obstructive to the transition process and there were calls to replace them with Western knowledge and values. For instance, in their reflection on education transformations in post-Soviet countries, Silova, Millei, and Piattoeva (2017) note that 'socialist pedagogy was constructed [by Western development agencies] as authoritarian and serving a totalitarian state, concluding that it needed to be eradicated in order to become truly modern and (ultimately truly Western)' (81). According to them, this view of local knowledge, traditions, and histories led to their marginalisation in the knowledge hierarchy; they ceased to be 'sources of intellectual authority in the present' (Connell 2007, xi). However, despite being discarded by international development actors, local knowledge, traditions, and histories continue to influence the beliefs, values, and practices of people (see Silova 2010) and thus should be considered in the study of citizenship and its education in non-Western contexts.

The examination and theorisation of citizenship and citizenship education in both Western and non-Western contexts is partially an outcome of the research methodologies used. The methodological issues of conducting research on citizenship and its education in non-Western contexts are beyond the scope of this issue, but it should be noted that the methodologies, especially the qualitative ones, commonly taught and applied in Western contexts may be met with suspicion and resistance in non-Western contexts, thus ultimately affecting the process of knowledge production and theorisation. Such suspicion and resistance can be attributed to multiple factors ranging from context-specific research traditions and negative historical legacies to cultural nuances and current societal issues. For instance, numerous scholars have reported challenges in conducting qualitative research in post-Soviet countries because of the prevalence of the positivist psychological and quasi-experimental design of most education and social science research in the region (DeSoto and Dudwick 2000; Sobe et al. 2017). Their study participants did not always consider their qualitative research methods to be serious and were not accustomed to providing interviews or participating in classroom observations. Some study participants were also reluctant to engage in formal interviews because of the fragile state of freedom of expression in their countries and the Soviet legacy of reporting dissent. These issues ultimately affected the quality of the data that the researchers were able to collect. While the wider field of comparative education has become more conscious and critical about the implications and limitations of applying Western research methodologies to non-Western contexts (Silova et al. 2017; Zhang, Chan, and Kenway 2015), very little has been written on this topic in the field of comparative and international citizenship education. We do not know much, for instance, about how researchers in non-Western contexts go about researching topics of democracy and citizenship that could be perceived by study participants as 'politically provocative' (see Kovalchuk 2015).

This Special Issue is the outcome of a symposium that took place during the 2016 Comparative International Education Society annual conference in Vancouver, Canada, which brought together emerging and established scholars in the field of comparative and international citizenship education. The contributors to the Issue discuss the hybridity of citizenship in non-Western contexts, focusing on the interaction between global and local discourses in relation to citizenship. They reflect on the benefits of using indigenous knowledge in the study of citizenship and citizenship education and of considering the role of political, social, and cultural contexts in interpreting them. They point to the challenges of implementing Western-based models of citizenship education in post-authoritarian, post-colonial, and post-socialist societies and propose alternative theoretical and methodological approaches by drawing on their research in Guatemala, Colombia, South Africa, West Africa, Lebanon, Israel, and Kosovo. Overall, the Special Issue contributes to various aspects of citizenship education theory and research, including conceptions of democracy and citizenship, civic values and practices, pedagogies, and theories and methodologies for studying citizenship and its education in non-Western contexts.

This Special Issue opens with an article by Patricia K. Kubow, *Exploring Western and Non-Western epistemological influences in South Africa: theorising a critical democratic citizenship education*, which puts forward a new framework of critical democratic citizenship education informed by cultural values and cultural hybridity. Kubow developed this framework on the basis of her research in post-apartheid South Africa, where she explored the convergence and divergence of Western and indigenous knowledge in the construction of democratic citizenship. Her empirical work reveals that while her study participants' conceptions of democracy and citizenship resembled those of the West, they also reflected local understandings of democracy and citizenship rooted in *Ubuntu*, a sub-Saharan African approach to morality. Kubow suggests considering the hybridity of different citizenship discourses in theorising democratic citizenship education in contexts such as South Africa. For her, the idea of hybridity allows us to better capture the cultural flows and interactions between globalism and nationalism and tradition and modernity in transitioning societies. Her empirical work also reaffirms the importance of culture in shaping understandings of democracy and citizenship. Kubow's article demonstrates how a consideration of indigenous knowledge can extend existing conceptions of democracy and citizenship and help to formulate more culturally responsive conceptions of them.

Laura Quaynor, in her article *Remembering West African indigenous knowledge and practices in citizenship education research*, argues that existing citizenship frameworks fail to account for actual conceptions and practices of citizenship in both African and African Diasporic societies, which results in an incomplete understanding of citizenship in such contexts. Quaynor draws on post-colonial theory, which takes into consideration indigenous knowledge and practices, the ways in which they relate to other discourses, and flows of knowledge and capital between the centre and the periphery. She demonstrates the application of post-colonial theory to citizenship education research by presenting two indigenous West African systems related to political participation and belonging. In particular, she examines how two historical and indigenous African texts address the relationship between the individual and the community and, more broadly, unity and diversity. Quaynor also demonstrates the uses of post-colonial theory in citizenship education research by incorporating information about indigenous systems of justice co-existing with Western-style government bodies in her study of citizenship beliefs and practices among young people in Liberia. She notes that traditional courts play an important role in solving community problems and concerns in countries such as Liberia and suggests that ignoring these and other indigenous practices results in an incomplete understanding of how young people enact their civic agency. Overall, Quaynor argues that African societies have rich traditions of citizenship and its education and that indigenous knowledge and practices can be a source of useful alternative theories in these areas.

In *Wait-citizenship: youth civic development in transition*, Michelle J. Bellino theorises the concept of 'wait-citizenship' on the basis of her ethnographic research in post-war Guatemala. In a society of fragile democracy, criminal violence, and economic instability, Bellino finds, Guatemalan youth have been instructed by school teachers, families, and society not to make demands but instead to wait for peace, stability, opportunity, and inclusion – they are assured that change will come with time and patience, and not as a result of civic demand and disruption. While some youth engage in protests, demonstrations, and other forms of active citizenship under such conditions and instructions, others withdraw from the public sphere and exhibit a disinterest in politics that could be interpreted as passive citizenship. However, Bellino argues that in the context of Guatemala such withdrawal and disinterest can, in fact, be indicative of youth's critical awareness of societal issues, a lack of confidence in their capacity to enable change, and distrust in unaccountable institutions. The expression and enactment of civic agency by wait-citizens differs from Western, liberal conceptions of engaged and active citizenship. As well as reminding us to attend to the specifics of context in interpreting citizenship and its practices, Bellino's article demonstrates what active citizenship engagement might look like in areas such as Guatemala and points to the need to develop theoretical tools to accurately capture the civic experiences of youth in societies transitioning to democracy.

Heela Goren and Miri Yemini investigated teachers' perceptions of global citizenship education (GCE) in Israeli schools. Their article, *Obstacles and opportunities for global citizenship education under intractable conflict: the case of Israel*, reports the many challenges faced by GCE in conflict-ridden societies where national or nationalistic and ethno- or culture-centric narratives usually play a dominant role in curricula. The Israeli-Palestinian conflict creates specific political, ideological, social, and cultural contexts similar in ways to other conflict-ridden societies, such as Cyprus, Northern Ireland, or Catalonia. The study reveals that an 'us versus them' narrative, with its emphasis on particularistic rather than universalistic ideas, and its negative public perception of immigrants, overshadows GCE, and impedes its open introduction in curricula. Goren and Yemini argue that in order to be incorporated into the Israeli education system, or that of any conflict-ridden society, the ideas of global citizenship need to be articulated as supplementary to national citizenship rather than as clashing with it as an alternative model of identity. Goren and Yemini's article highlights the challenges that GCE can face in conflict-ridden societies and points to the inapplicability of its dominant model to such societies. The authors conclude that these societies need new models of GCE, distinct from those that are practised in conflict-free societies.

Drawing on his own qualitative work in Lebanon and other qualitative studies across the globe, Bassel Akar, in *Reframing approaches to narrating young people's conceptualizations of citizenship in education research*, proposes a social constructivist methodology for comparative and international research on citizenship and citizenship education. This approach is a critical response to international quantitative citizenship studies that utilise instruments with specifically defined indicators of citizenship informed by Western European and North American theoretical constructs. According to Akar, these analyse young people's understandings of citizenship in different parts of the world with measurements constructed by someone else and do not allow us to capture those understandings, or the ways in which they are shaped by their context. He suggests a social constructivist approach to learning how young people conceptualise citizenship. This would involve applying wide-ranging citizenship frameworks to interpret their conceptions, delineating culturally specific characteristics of citizenship, and empowering young people by engaging them in the reflection and construction of the meanings of citizenship. Akar demonstrates how such an approach would work by presenting and discussing the findings of his own research on teachers' and students' understandings of citizenship in Lebanon. The article demonstrates the strengths and weaknesses of different epistemological and methodological orientations to studying citizenship in diverse contexts.

In *Citizenship education discourses in Latin America: multilateral institutions and the decolonial challenge*, Diego Nieto critically examines some of the global discourses that shape citizenship education policies and practices across Latin America and he presents indigenous-based pedagogical approaches as alternatives to these discourses. Drawing on his analysis of selected policy documents, Nieto argues that the dominant discourses, which are rooted in Western conceptions of democracy and citizenship and disseminated by multilateral organisations, portray young people in the region as deviant, passive, and apathetic, and provide a set of curricular prescriptions on how to resolve this problem. Citizenship education framed by such discourses takes on a 'civilisatory' role, that of trying to construct a modern, rational citizen. As Nieto points out, multilateral organisations disregard longer traditions of popular education, political participation, and political struggle in the region, which can be used as culturally appropriate sources for educating young people about citizenship and democracy. In addition to his discussion of citizenship education in Latin America, Nieto presents a methodological framework that draws on decolonial theory, political discourse analysis, and vertical comparisons for analysing the movement and dissemination of dominant global discourses of democracy and citizenship in contexts such as Latin America. Overall, the article demonstrates how multilateral organisations that disregard local knowledge and traditions transmit dominant, Western-based discourses of citizenship, and argues that decolonial theory can be used to uncover the operation of such discourses.

In the last article of this special issue, *Rendering technical the responsible citizen: implementing citizenship education reform in Kosovo*, Jennifer Otting examines how educational actors make sense of citizenship education within the economic, political, and social conditions of the fragile state of Kosovo. The intention of Kosovo citizenship education was to focus on issues of human rights, democratic processes, and general public issues as part of peace-building and nation-building efforts. Through interviews with education stakeholders and classroom observations, Otting demonstrates a schism between the intentional design of the educational policy and its actual implementation. Citizenship learning embodied technical processes that replaced the substantive content material critical for mediating issues of fragility. The implementation of citizenship education focused on technocratic elements – standards and measurements that ignored conversations about content in addressing the social, economic and political issues causing fragility. Otting concludes that curriculum training should not focus exclusively on standards and measurements, disregarding the knowledge and experiences of educators. Designing a curriculum in fragile contexts requires the inclusion of multiple voices so that contrasting views of what creates conditions of fragility can be understood.

Taken together, the articles featured in this Special Issue represent a critical approach to studying citizenship and citizenship education in post-authoritarian, post-colonial, and post-socialist societies that have embarked on a transition to democracy. They remind us to attend to the specifics of context in defining and interpreting democracy, citizenship, values, identity and the practices associated with them. They highlight the importance of considering indigenous knowledge and practices related to democracy, citizenship, and citizenship education in designing research studies and analysing the data. They point to the ways in which such knowledge and practices can serve as alternatives or complements to dominant Western theoretical frameworks that often fail to adequately capture the realities of post-authoritarian, post-colonial, and post-socialist societies. They illuminate the issues associated with implementing Western-based models of citizenship education in non-Western contexts and disregarding local dynamics and voices. Lastly, the articles provide theoretical and methodological approaches, rooted mainly in post-colonial, decolonial, and social constructivist theories, to studying citizenship and citizenship education in non-Western contexts. We hope that the contributions to the Special Issue will generate an engaging conversation in the field of comparative and international citizenship education about theoretical and methodological dilemmas of conducting research in non-Western contexts and that they will facilitate discussion about the need to theorise democratic citizenship education research in such contexts, thus moving the field beyond the dominance of Western theoretical frameworks.

Notes

1. As editors of this special issue, we recognise that democracy, citizenship, and citizenship education are complex and contested terms. We believe that different types of democracy are reflected in different types of citizenship; that they put different demands on citizens (Cunningham 2002; McLaughlin 1992). We view citizenship in very broad terms – as membership in a political community (Delanty 2000; McCowan 2009). We also subscribe to a broad view of citizenship education that encompasses all forms and levels of education through which individuals are taught to function in a democratic society (Audigier 1998). Given that the contributors to this special issue discuss wide-ranging conceptions of democracy and citizenship, we decided not to examine these in this introduction; our main goal here is to point to a lack of theorising and conceptualising of democratic citizenship education in non-Western contexts in the field of comparative and international citizenship education and to encourage discussion of this topic.
2. As we examine the applicability of Western theoretical frameworks to the study of citizenship and citizenship education in non-Western contexts in this Special Issue, our intent is not to discard existing citizenship education research or theories that have proven their relevance. Instead, we question the adequacy of using Western-centric interpretive tools to study social phenomena in the realm of democracy, citizenship, and education in non-Western contexts; we challenge the universality of such interpretive tools and encourage researchers to be critical and reflective in using them.

Acknowledgements

This Special Issue would not have been possible without the Compare editorial board, contributors and the generous support of the James F. Ackerman Center for Democratic Citizenship (College of Education, Purdue University). We would like to thank to the editorial board for expressing an interest in our Special Issue proposal. We also would like to thank each symposium participant and Special Issue contributor, as well as express our gratitude to the James F. Ackerman Center for supporting the symposium

Disclosure statement

No potential conflict of interest was reported by the authors.

References

Audigier, François. 1998. *Basic Concepts and Core Competencies for Education for Democratic Citizenship*. Strasbourg: Council of Europe.

Chua, Shuyi, and Jasmine B.-Y. Sim. 2017. "Postmodern Patriotism: Teachers' Perceptions of Loyalty to Singapore." *Asian Education and Development Studies* 6 (1): 30–43.

Connell, Raewyn. 2007. *Southern Theory: The Global Dynamics of Knowledge in Social Science*. Malden, MA: Polity Press.

Cunningham, Frank. 2002. *Theories of Democracy: A Critical Introduction*. New York: Routledge.

DeJaeghere, Joan. 2017. *Educating Entrepreneurial Citizens: Neoliberalism and Youth Livelihoods in Tanzania*. New York: Taylor & Francis.

Delanty, Gerard. 2000. *Citizenship in a Global Age: Society, Culture, Politics*. Buckingham: Open University Press.

DeSoto, Hermine G., and Nora Dudwick. 2000. *Fieldwork Dilemmas: Anthropologists in Post-Socialist States*. Madison, WI: University of Wisconsin Press.

Dull, Laura J. 2012. "Teaching for Humanity in a Neoliberal World: Visions of Education in Serbia." *Comparative Education Review* 56 (3): 511–533.

Dunn, Elizabeth. 1996. "Money, Morality and Modes of Civil Society among American Mormons." In *Civil Society: Challenging Western Models*, edited by Christopher Michael Hann and Elizabeth Dunn, 27–49. New York: Routledge.

Hahn, Carole L. 2016. "Pedagogy in Citizenship Education Research: A Comparative Perspective." *Citizenship Teaching & Learning* 11 (2): 121–137.

Haste, Helen, Angela Bermudez, and Mario Carretero. 2017. "Culture and Civic Competence: Widening the Scope of the Civic Domain." In *Civics and Citizenship: Theoretical Models and Experiences in Latin America*, edited by Benilde García-Cabrero, Andrés Sandoval-Hernández, Ernesto Treviño-Villareal, Silvia Diazgranados Ferráns, and María Guadalupe Pérez Martínez, 3–15. Amsterdam, The Netherlands: Sense Publishers.

Kovalchuk, Serhiy. 2015. "Teacher Education for Democracy in Post-Soviet Ukraine." PhD dissertation, Ontario Institute for Studies in Education, University of Toronto, Toronto, Canada.

Kubow, Patricia K. 2007. "Teachers' Constructions of Democracy: Intersections of Western and Indigenous Knowledge in South Africa and Kenya." *Comparative Education Review* 51 (3): 307–328.

McCowan, Tristan. 2009. *Rethinking Citizenship Education: A Curriculum for Participatory Democracy*. New York: Continuum.

McLaughlin, Terence H. 1992. "Citizenship, Diversity and Education: A Philosophical Perspective." *Journal of Moral Education* 21 (3): 235–250.

Moland, Naomi A. 2015. "Can Multiculturalism Be Exported? Dilemmas of Diversity on Nigeria's Sesame Square." *Comparative Education Review* 59 (1): 1–23.

Park, Jae. 2017. "Knowledge Production with Asia-Centric Research Methodology." *Comparative Education Review* 61 (4): 760–779.

Quaynor, Laura J. 2012. "Citizenship Education in Post-Conflict Contexts: A Review of the Literature." *Education, Citizenship and Social Justice* 7 (1): 33–57.

Silova, Iveta. 2010. "Rediscovering Post-Socialism in Comparative Education." In *Post-Socialism is Not Dead: (Re)Reading the Global in Comparative Education*, edited by Iveta Silova, 1–24. Bingley, UK: Emerald Group Publishing Limited.

Silova, Iveta, Zsuzsa Millei, and Nelli Piattoeva. 2017. "Interrupting the Coloniality of Knowledge Production in Comparative Education: Post-Socialist and Postcolonial Dialogues after the Cold War." *Comparative Education Review* 61 (S1): S74–S102.

Silova, Iveta, Noah W. Sobe, Alla Korzh, and Serhiy Kovalchuk. 2017. *Reimagining Utopias: Theory and Method for Educational Eesearch in Post-Socialist Contexts*. Amsterdam, The Netherlands: Sense Publishers.

Sim, Jasmine B.-Y., Shuyi Chua, and Malathy Krishnasamy. 2017. "'Riding the Citizenship Wagon': Citizenship Conceptions of Social Studies Teachers in Singapore." *Teaching and Teacher Education* 63: 92–102.

Sobe, Noah W., and Jamie Kowalczyk. 2013. "The Problem of Context in Comparative Education Research." *Journal of Educational, Cultural and Psychological Studies* 3 (6): 55–74.

Sobe, Noah W., Iveta Silova, Alla Korzh, and Serhiy Kovalchuk. 2017. "(Re)Imagining Utopias." In *Reimagining Utopias: Theory and Method for Educational Research in Post-Socialist Contexts*, edited by Iveta Silova, Noah W. Sobe, Alla Korzh, and Serhiy Kovalchuk, 301–315. Amsterdam, The Netherlands: Sense Publishers.

Stevick, Doyle E., and Bradley A. U. Levinson. 2007. *Reimagining Civic Education: How Diverse Societies Form Democratic Citizens*. Lanham, MD: Rowman & Littlefield.

Takayama, Keita. 2018. "Towards a New Articulation of Comparative Educations: Cross-Culturalising Research Imaginations." *Comparative Education* 54 (1): 77–93.

Takayama, Keita, Arathi Sriprakash, and Raewyn Connell. 2017. "Toward a Postcolonial Comparative and International Education." *Comparative Education Review* 61 (S1): S1–S24.

Tobin, Kerri. 2010. "Civic Education in Emerging Democracies: Lessons from Post-Communist Poland and Romania." *Journal of Research in International Education* 9 (3): 273–288.

Vickers, Edward, and Krishna Kumar. 2015. *Constructing Modern Asian Citizenship*. New York: Routledge.

Williams, Dierdre. 2013. "When 'Minimalist' Conceptions of Citizenship Reveal Their Complexity." *Citizenship Teaching & Learning* 8 (3): 357–369.

Zhang, Hongzhi, Philip Wing Keung Chan, and Jane Kenway. 2015. *Asia as Method in Education Studies: A Defiant Research Imagination*. New York: Routledge.

Exploring Western and non-Western epistemological influences in South Africa: theorising a critical democratic citizenship education

Patricia K. Kubow

ABSTRACT
My decade-long research on democracy and schooling in a Xhosa township has led to an examination of epistemological influences on democratic citizenship from Western and non-Western (i.e. African) perspectives. While Max Weber advanced the notion of an autonomous citizen within Western democratic states, different philosophical and cultural assumptions operate in South Africa, where the individual is viewed as not separate from, but rather embedded in, the community into which one is born. This theoretical position – a person is a person through other people (isiXhosa proverb) – serves as a thoughtful starting point for theorising a critical democratic citizenship education. This article explores Western and non-Western influences through scholarly literature and practitioner perspectives. The goal is to consider the convergences and divergences between Western and indigenous knowledge with *ubuntu* (humanness), an African moral ethic, as its key construct.

Introduction

My decade-long empirical research on schooling and democracy in 12 primary and secondary schools in a Xhosa township outside Cape Town's city centre has led to theoretical insights about the influences and intersections of democratic citizenship from Western and non-Western (in this case, African) perspectives. While German sociologist Max Weber advanced the notion of an autonomous citizen within Western democratic states, different philosophical and cultural assumptions operate in South Africa, where the individual is not separate from, but, rather, embedded in, the community into which one is born. This theoretical position – *Umuntu ngumuntu ngabantu* (A person is a person through his or her relationship to others: isiXhosa proverb) – serves as a thoughtful starting point for a comparative study of citizen identity to conceptualise anew a critical democratic citizenship education informed by cultural values and cultural hybridity. This article explores Western binaries and non-Western influences 'from above' through the scholarship of policy makers and academics in Western and non-Western contexts to consider constructions of democratic citizenship, as well as 'from below' through the voices of Xhosa teachers in the South African township's schools where I conducted my qualitative case study. This policy-practitioner exploration aids my theorisation work by illuminating some divergences and convergences between Western and non-Western thought regarding ideal constructions of 'democratic citizen' in South Africa.

Because democracy is constructed and shaped by the understandings and interpretations that people hold about their world, democracy is more than a political concept or system of governance, but also extends to the social and cultural systems that inform democracy's meanings. Nóvoa and Yariv-Mashal (2003) contend that democracy entails both material and immaterial space. Material space denotes people's lived experiences within particular physical locales, whereas immaterial space refers to the imaginations and memories formed through associated living with people similar or dissimilar to their selves. Comparative education research therefore offers new assessments of the seemingly familiar in terms of the less familiar (Kubow and Fossum 2007). Examining democracy's material and immaterial spaces within non-Western contexts, and from the perspectives of educators themselves, represents an epistemological and contextual shift that privileges indigenous knowledge and people's lived experiences from below as opposed to solely state definitions of democratic citizenship from above. My intent as a researcher is to not restrict democracy to a 'culture of science' (Baez and Boyles 2009) or to view citizenship solely from Western perspectives, but to consider the ways that democracy is constructed through the epistemological premise of *ubuntu* (humanness) in a South African context.

Understanding indigenous perspectives on 'democracy' and 'citizen' – with *ubuntu* as the African epistemological core – is the stance from which theoretical intersections and departures from Western conceptions of democratic citizenship are examined. Can *ubuntu*, which speaks to a morality of compassion, communalism and collectivism, be appropriate for democratic citizenship in South Africa? What might comparative educators in the Global North and Global South gain from an examination of Western and non-Western perspectives on democracy? How might that learning inform a critical discourse on democratic citizenship education? The goal of my work is to begin to develop a culturally relevant theoretical framework to consider the convergence and divergence of Western and non-Western thought as applied to democratic conceptualisations of citizen and citizenship education for democratic life.

Historical colonial influences: epistemological binaries in Western constructions of democracy

Previously I have examined Western constructions of democracy and citizenship and contrasted those informed by African indigenous knowledge (IK). Because the West has played a major role in shaping understandings about and discourses of democracy beyond its borders, it is important to explore how democracy is conceived by those in non-Western, postcolonial contexts. In the West, democracy is understood as a system of government in which power is vested in people who directly or indirectly exercise that power through a system of representation. Democratic citizenship in the Western tradition refers to the spirited contribution to public problem solving that is grounded in the institutional environments that people inhabit (Boyte 1993). Citizenship education, then, is the processes and experiences by which individuals learn about their rights and responsibilities in a democratic society.

In Western thought, the concept of 'citizen' is associated with the public realm and the individual with that of the private sphere. This public-private epistemological binary stems from a liberal tradition that envisions society as affording individuals opportunities to fulfill their goals through individual freedom, property ownership and privatisation with minimal governmental interference (Cohen 1982). Max Weber, for example, advanced the notion of citizen as an autonomous political subject and linked democracy to individual freedom and civility (Kubow 2007). Weber, however, was concerned that the development of a professional class of politicians might negatively transform public service into a means for private enrichment rather than civic duty (Bellamy 2008).

In his historical analysis of Western perspectives on democracy and citizenship, Bryan Turner (1990) argued that German philosophical orientations linked social rights of citizenship with the development of the democratic civil society *(die bürgliche Gesellschaft)*. The citizen is envisioned as one who leaves the rural area for the urban setting and whose membership to the state (a political space associated with 'the historical embodiment of reason') (204) subordinates, or in some cases even eradicates, *gemeinschaft* membership within an ethnic group *(ethnie)* (Kubow 2007; Smith 1986; Turner 1990). This Western construction of citizen was applied in colonial South Africa as well. Drawing upon the work of Chatterjee (1993), researchers Garuba and Raditlhalo (2008) have explained how Dutch and British colonisers created an outer-inner dichotomy in South Africa whereby the 'outer domain' constituted civil society from which the colonised were excluded and an 'inner domain' into which indigenous culture and tradition were inserted (41). Rural African populations were viewed as ethnic subjects, while those in urban areas were associated with liberal individualist conceptions of citizen (Mamdani 1996). 'Defined officially as subjects of culture, not yet ready for civil society, the colonized began to see "culture" as the domain over which they could claim sovereignty and thus convert into a site of resistance' (Garuba and Raditlhalo 2008, 41).

As I argued in Kubow (2007), 'conceptions of liberal democracy developed in the West often portray democracy in dichotomous terms (e.g. autonomy/authority, opportunity/equity individual rights/cultural group rights)' (312). Within these binaries, tensions between cultural preservation and national interest, personhood and the collective, diversity and commonality are fashioned (Barber 2004). Debates about conceptions of citizenship from liberal individualist notions and from collectivist cultural understandings are ongoing (Cowan, Dembour, and Wilson 2001). Ethnographic studies (see, for instance, von Lieres 2005; Werbner 2002) have shown that 'the conception of the citizen as an atomised and autonomous rights-bearing subject is generally at odds with African realities where intersubjectivity and interconnectedness are highly valued' (Robins 2008, 187).

Thus, urban-rural and citizen-subject binaries do not adequately address 'the complex, hybrid and situated subjectivities of postcolonial citizen-subjects' in present-day South Africa (Robins 2008, 187). 'Hybridity' in general refers to the creation of new transcultural forms produced by colonial contact (Ashcroft, Griffiths, and Tiffin 2007). Hybridity describes the cultural flows and interactions between nationalism/pluralism and traditionalism/modernity. For hybridity theorist Homi Bhabha (2006), cultural difference is the construction of systems of cultural identification whereby 'the cultural' holds distinctive meanings and values and signifies the boundaries of cultures. Both hybridity and fluidity characterise the ways in which indigenous populations live and engage in politics at the local and national levels. 'What appears to be an autonomous rights-bearing citizen in one setting may, in another context, morph into an "ethnic" subject invoking indigenous values, traditional beliefs and forms of sociality based on family, clan and community' (Robins 2008, 187). Consequently, as Catherine Odora Hoppers (2000, 2002) has asserted, it is problematic to accept the Western liberal democratic tradition as noncontroversial; attention therefore must be given to indigenous knowledge systems.

African IK and non-Western democratic constructions

Indigenous knowledge in general refers to the epistemologies, values and practices of indigenous groups (Kubow 2007). Developed in local settings, IK systems are based on particular orientations to life, ethics, human development and social relations (Kubow 2007). A sub-Saharan African approach to morality, *ubuntu* (humanness) is an African philosophical tradition based on 'a morality of compassion, communalism, and concern for the interest of the collective' (Kubow 2007, 313). The isiXhosa proverb, *Umuntu ngumuntu ngabantu* signifies that a person's humanity is defined through sociability. From this stance, the individual is linked to the collective through brotherhood or sisterhood (Swanson 2014). Metz (2015) refers to *Ubuntu* as an 'Other-regarding ethic' because to become a genuine human being requires one to engage in respectful relations with other people. Humanness, therefore, is developed in togetherness with (rather than isolation from) others. Fundamental to African sociological thought, *Ubuntu* illuminates 'the communal rootedness and interdependence of persons', which serves 'as an important measure of human wellbeing or human flourishing in traditional African life' (Letseka 2000, 179; see also Venter 2004).

Distinct from scientism premised on objectivity, IK's epistemological assumptions about reality embrace the sacred as well as the empirical and include ways of knowing based on intuition, experience, inspiration and revelation (Bhola 2002). Those embracing the IK tradition contend that practical, everyday issues cannot be separated from the philosophical. Practical cultural knowledge, however, has often been marginalised in discourses on democracy and democratic citizenship. Increasingly, globalisation has contributed to the perception that knowledge championed by powerful nations, or even by elites in less powerful countries, is of higher value than knowledge produced in particular cultural communities and/or by those with less voice and prominence. In their discourses about democracy and education, policymakers and other global elites fashion conceptions of democratic identity and citizenship that serve the interests of the most powerful at the expense of the less powerful, thereby actualising Weber's greatest fear. Academic researchers in the field of comparative and international education have given attention to the intellectual and political contexts of knowledge production and legitimation and some have focused on the deconstruction of dominant worldviews to examine the relationships among knowledge, politics and power (Crossley 2009). The intent of such inquiries, Crossley has asserted, is to understand 'the world from the perspective of the South, the formerly colonized, the marginalized, from their own distinctive vantage points – and informed by their own political and contextual sensitivities' (1177).

At the policy level in South Africa, former presidents Nelson Mandela and Thabo Mbeki called for an African Renaissance as a means to build democratic unity, to counter the devaluing of indigenous knowledge and to advocate for 'imaginative alternatives beyond limit-experiences' (Swanson 2014, 51). Dalene Swanson (2014) has argued that colonialism depicted Africa in terms of 'limit-experiences' that have shaped African social imaginaries from the perspective of 'inferiorities, oppressions, essentialisms, deficits, and human and spiritual disinvestments' (51). *Ubuntu*, however, is an epistemological concept with the potential to challenge these limit-experiences. Defined as 'a spiritual way of being in the broader sociopolitical context of Southern Africa' (Swanson 2014, 56), *ubuntu* refers to the journey toward 'becoming human' (Vanier 1998) or that 'which renders us human' (Tutu 1999).

'*Ubu*' signifies a process or state of perpetual becoming, while '*ntu*' refers to human beings (Mkhize 2008). Taken together, *Ubuntu* denotes a being that is constantly in the process of becoming. In essence, as Swanson argued at the 2015 Annual Meeting of the Comparative and International Education Society, *ubuntu* is a democratic ecology of being – a lived expression, a transcendent ethicality and a relationality that stands in contrast to a detached view of self. Desmond Tutu (1999) powerfully describes the internalisation of the African worldview of *ubuntu* as a way to nurture democratic behavior through social belonging and connection:

> It is not, 'I think therefore I am.' It says rather: 'I am human because I belong. I participate, I share.' A person with *ubuntu* is open and available to others, affirming of others, does not feel threatened that others are able and good, for he or she belongs in a greater whole and is diminished when others are humiliated or diminished, when others are tortured or oppressed or treated as if they were less than who they are. (31)

It is important to recognise that indigenous knowledge is dynamic and has taken shape in South Africa within a context of struggle against political domination, during and after apartheid. Thus, as Green (2008) has aptly noted, 'the mobilization of the idea of "indigenous knowledge" is itself a vehicle of modernity, and a political instrument in the era of globalization' (133). In some ways, indigenous knowledge can be considered a kind of hybrid creation that has emerged from a more static and bounded view of culture (Thornton 1988). It is to a discussion of culture and globalisation and their implications for democracy that I now turn.

Culture, globalisation and shifting democratic identities

According to Ngũgĩ wa Thiong'o (1986), people's cultural values constitute 'the basis of their world outlook, their collective and individual image of self, their identity as a people who look at themselves and to their relationship to the universe in a certain way' (cited in Odora Hoppers 2000, 105). The importance of culture in shaping democratic constructions of citizenship cannot be denied. Cultural dimensions have become more important than grand economic ones due to the failure of the Enlightenment project of modernity, which was premised on a construction of the democratic society as harmonious, hegemonic, rights-based and socially equitable (Garuba and Raditlhalo 2008). However, there is also a danger in conceiving of culture as stable and shared by all of its cultural members because such a formulation can readily mutate to a view of culture as homogenous and static, wherein the Western coloniser armed with 'rationality' and 'science' transforms non-Western societies and peoples into 'anthropological objects ruled by their culture' or tradition (Boonzaier and Spiegel 2008, 198).

Influenced by Weberian theory, cultural identity is largely associated with ethnicity or the ethnic group which, within this tradition, is explained by two epistemes, namely primordialism (a shared biology or ancestral origin) and instrumentalism (a social construction created in light of threats to the ethnic group's self-determination) (Comaroff and Comaroff 2008). The colonised in South Africa used culture as a tool of struggle and a form of political resistance. In the present age, culture or indigeneity has also been used as a mechanism to construct a new citizen identity. South African policy makers' call for an African Renaissance is simultaneously a means of cultural preservation and cultural self-definition. While Kai Horsthemke (2008) asks, 'What is the emphasis on indigenous knowledge meant to achieve?' (129), the response is found in the ideas offered by IK advocates (see, e.g. Higgs et al. 2004; Odora Hoppers 2002; Semali and Kincheloe 1999), which include: decolonising thoughts and minds; reclaiming cultural values and traditional heritages; validating indigenous epistemologies; protecting against new forms of colonisation and exploitation (i.e. globalisation); and promoting the sacred and spiritual as valid ways of knowing (Semali and Kincheloe 1999).

Two polar opposites, therefore, are often used to frame indigenous knowledge, namely relativism and universalism (Green 2008). Politics at local and global levels are increasingly being seen as a struggle for recognition of identity (Taylor 1994). Likewise, the denial of identity is also seen as a cruel act of exclusion (van Binsbergen 2004). Unequal power relations between the Global North and Global South have also contributed to culture becoming 'central to thinking about forms of subjectivity and sociality, social life and agency, knowledge and knowledge systems, and the very nature of our being-in-the-world' (Garuba and Raditlhalo 2008, 37). Indigenous knowledge, however, is not uniform, and different IKs exist. It is dangerous, therefore, to label the West as bad and what is African as good (Green 2008) because exploitation exists in cultural communities as well as within and between societies at large. But to ignore or disregard the knowledges of cultural communities denies the ways that postcolonialism and globalisation implicate the daily lives of indigenous peoples.

Thus, democracy is located within, and implicated by, 'the global and local, time and space, power and boundaries, embeddness and distanciation' (Arthur, McNess, and Crossley 2016, 12). For Homi Bhabha (1994), 'the very concepts of homogenous national cultures, the consensual or contiguous transmission of historical traditions, or "organic" ethnic communities – *as the grounds of cultural comparativism* – are in a profound process of redefinition' (7, emphasis in original). Increasingly, traditional conceptualisations such as 'national identity' and 'culture' are being questioned and problematised (Arthur, McNess, and Crossley 2016). Values birthed in Western and non-Western contexts interact in ways that shape democracy's meanings and create hybrid citizen identities. Therefore, 'democracy is enlarged and constrained by both global and local influences' (Kubow 2008, 162). Economic interdependence and convergence of institutions, including schools, toward similar aims and operating structures (Astiz, Wiseman, and Baker 2002) are but two instances of the intensifying effects of globalisation that shape democratic citizenship education.

Comparative educators and social science researchers should increasingly learn from the interactions among culture, indigenous knowledge and globalisation and how they imagine and implicate democracy in non-Western settings. Researchers should also be aware of how Western and non-Western states appropriate their own definitions of citizenship, which often limit the opportunity 'for redefinitions of citizenship "from below"' (von Lieres and Robins 2008, 55–56). Globalisation and knowledge transfer make it increasingly difficult to identify what counts as 'Western' and what might be considered 'non-Western'. Greater attention is needed as to how globally shifting identities and cultural values shape democratic citizenship. Moreover, the challenges of understanding the epistemologies influencing such democratic conceptualisations are made more complex 'when dealing with two or more cultural and/or linguistic communities' (Arthur, McNess, and Crossley 2016, 11). Because a global hierarchal structure of democracy exists with Western views of democracy overshadowing non-Western ones, there is growing recognition that various ontological and epistemological boundaries are regularly encountered and negotiated by teachers who assume responsibility for formal citizenship education in their classrooms and schools. Struggles over whose knowledge should be taught and valued in the school curricula remain an area of contention for democratic citizenship education policy and practice, especially in postcolonial African contexts.

Divergences and convergences in Xhosa teachers' constructions of democracy

While it can be argued that modernist and colonialist perspectives have no doubt informed democratic citizenship in South Africa, in my research I wanted to know how indigenous knowledge was manifested in discourse on democracy and citizenship education in a particular setting (namely 12 schools in a Western Cape township), from a particular cultural tradition (Xhosa) and in light of particular social and historical conditions (a postcolonial environment). I also wondered about the understandings that Xhosa primary and secondary teachers hold about democracy and how these knowledge perspectives might inform Western discourses on democracy and democratic citizenship education in South Africa.

The Xhosa township, the setting for this case study, is located 20 km outside Cape Town's city centre. Xhosa constitute South Africa's second largest indigenous group. The township – the country's first created during the apartheid era – has approximately 50,000 Xhosa residents and numerous undocumented individuals who reside in squatter camps within and outside the township. With approval for my qualitative case study obtained from the Western Cape Education Department, I then met with each school principal to ask if his or her respective teachers would be interested. The principals announced the study to their respective faculty, and a total of 87 primary and secondary teachers (57 female, 30 male) participated, representing approximately one-fourth of the teaching population from all 12 schools in the township. The teachers' ages ranged from 20 to 69 years and their teaching experience varied from 1 to 30 years. Their teaching subjects included: languages (Afrikaans, English, Xhosa); art and culture; social studies (economics, geography, history); life orientation; mathematics; and technology.

The focus-group interviews provided a forum for the teachers to share their views on the meanings they assigned to democracy, the values and skills they considered essential for democratic citizenship and insights as to how their schools might develop democratic dispositions and actions. The interviews lasted from 45 to 75 minutes, were audio recorded and transcribed verbatim. The interview transcripts were then imported from Microsoft Word documents into NVivo 10, a software package for computer-assisted qualitative data analysis that facilitates open coding. The thematic coding was organised by the research questions to ascertain the Xhosa teachers' meanings of democracy, values/skills associated with democratic citizenship and roles that formal schooling might play in fostering democratic dispositions. The teachers opening up to me (as researcher) and each other (as peers) through semi-structured focus-group discussions is equivalent to what Maxine Greene (1995) calls sharing with each other 'the texts of our lived lives' (116). My findings emphasise the cultural contours of democracy and the ways in which teachers reaffirm *and* question a narrative of democracy premised upon Western-oriented assumptions and beliefs.

The Xhosa teachers did describe democracy in terms of political practices involving rights and duties, such as freedom of choice, speech and movement. This construction of democracy is aligned with the political form of citizenship emphasised in Western countries, whereby citizen participation in voting and abiding by democratically passed laws is characteristic of political citizenship (Bellamy 2008). The participants also spoke of their rights to education, shelter, safety, security, healthcare and sanitation as markers of economic and cultural and racial equality. Though deplorable conditions of poverty, crime and high drop-out rates challenge the degree to which the Xhosa teachers believe their rights have been realised in terms of economic benefit and cultural or racial justice.

While a great deal of discourse on democracy in Western settings focuses on 'rights and responsibilities', the results from my case study reveal movement towards a 'rights, responsibilities and respect' discourse. The most cited meaning given to democracy by the teacher participants was respect for different races, cultures, languages and generations. As a moral theory, *ubuntu* speaks to the interconnectedness of human beings and the responsibility that flows from that connection (Letseka 2012). This was evidenced in the following comment from a male (3), grade 5 teacher:

> I think basically we need to inculcate a sense of responsibility in our kids. To start it and to teach them to develop a self-respect that which, at the end of the day, result in people being able to respect the people around you – these people, peers or other, or elders.

The epistemic orientation of person as embedded in society and not separate from it means that *how* one relates to others is of utmost importance. Respect for other human beings is a central premise of *ubuntu* because, as Mfuniselwa John Bhengu (1996) has explained, 'through respect an individual is given his or her status of being human' (6). A female teacher (5) from School 3 reported that democracy as practiced in South Africa departs from an *ubuntu*-inspired conception. Similar to some of her peers, the teacher expressed concern that some citizens have appropriated rights for themselves individually without considering the rights of the collective or whole: 'Such disdain for self-interest is linked to a distrust of Western-centric, rights-oriented conceptualizations of democracy, which often prioritize the individual over others' (Kubow and Min 2016, 7). *Ubuntu* (humanism) therefore is a theoretical concept with practical value. This moral ethic was demonstrated in the following comment from a female (6), grade 2–8 teacher in the township:

> I say to my learners that you might have the highest degree, but if you don't have certain values you are a hollow man. Whereby if you want to be involved with other people, always look at the people with respect.

Ubuntu is also viewed as a path to guide national development. According to Bhengu (1996), 'For democracy to survive, its roots have to sink deeply into the minds and hearts and souls of the people' (32). The best way to accomplish this, as Bhengu (1996) has argued, is 'to teach future citizens the habits and attitudes and character traits of democracy' and 'a subject that stands a good chance of achieving this, is Ubuntu' (32). The Xhosa teachers in my study cited colonialism and apartheid as having contributed to a decline in *ubuntu* and to a present Western form of democracy in postcolonial South Africa that is not culturally relevant to an African population. A grade 7–8 male teacher (2) in one of the township's schools was adamant that the democracy practiced in contemporary South Africa diverges from an indigenous form of democracy as practiced in the past:

> This [current] democracy doesn't go in line with our lifestyle, you know. But the people of South Africa want the policies and our lifestyle and our customs and we slaughter cows, sheep, goats. We did not slaughter with foreigners calling their democracy. What I want to say is that we did have our democracy before 1652. This [current] democracy came along with the West. We do what they want us to do. There is no promotion of black culture in the Constitution, in curricular books such as textbooks, no promotion of our lifestyle.

Other Xhosa teachers also expressed that democracy was practiced prior to its Western formulation in South Africa. Drawing a parallel between traditional African kings and counselors and that of contemporary democratic committees and cabinets, a grade 5 male teacher (3) expressed at length about how South Africa's present democracy deviates from *Ubuntu*:

> It [democracy] has been in Africa for a very long time, you know. There were no counselors or mayors or presidents or prime ministers of any sort. But it is very interesting to note that long ago they [Westerners] killed off chiefs, kings, queens …. The king or the queen or the chief used to [give] control to the people, and the people at the end of the day [would] come up with some suggestions and come [to some] decisions …. The king or the counselors, they and the people, would form a committee, today called a cabinet …. Those people used to act as the advisor to the king. That alone was quite explicit that the king did not just impose the ideas in their head and whatever he thought was okay for the people. He would respect the people and listen to them and actually hear how they feel about every issue on the table. That is why I am saying that it [democracy] is not a new concept. Even in homes, parents used to consult their kids in a manner that would today qualify as democratic. We [Xhosa] are finding that definition of the word [democracy]; we don't have to take it from the textbook. The definition differs maybe from place to place, from town to town, or even maybe from continent to continent.

The failure of modernity to advance human flourishing for indigenous groups was evident in the Xhosa teachers' discourse about the need for the state to align economic wellbeing with democratic political structures to better meet the needs of South Africa's indigenous citizens. While the Xhosa teachers did describe democracy as freedom of speech, choice and movement (much the same as the West), as well as citizens having the right to education, shelter, safety, security, sanitation and healthcare, the present democratic state, in their estimation, has fallen short of realising economic and racial equality for all South Africans. Teacher concern for the lack of respect for different generational, cultural and linguistic communities was also prominent in the school findings. For example, a grades 6–8 male teacher (4) at a secondary school in the township said that his generation's experience with both the apartheid and post-apartheid era has provided unique insight into teaching students democratic values and encouraging them to use democratic processes to foster social change. However, he noted that, 'there are still portions of people disrespecting others in terms of culture.'

Critical democratic citizenship education

My work in the Xhosa township has raised many important and pressing questions: Do epistemological boundaries exist in relation to democracy? In what ways do these epistemologies diverge or converge? Can *ubuntu* and Western constructions of democracy inhabit a shared space or discourse? And, specifically, how might *ubuntu* – an African indigenous knowledge system and social ethic to guide interaction – be used to theorise a critical democratic citizenship to guide educational research and practice? Recognizing that both researchers and participants move between positions as insiders and outsiders (Arthur, McNess, and Crossley 2016), greater attention must be given to the epistemologies and assumptions guiding conceptualisations of democracy.

I have argued that *ubuntu* contributes to a theoretical base to inform discourses about democratic citizenship within and outside Southern African contexts. Respect, as the Xhosa teachers readily pointed out, is central to a culturally relevant theorisation of the democratic South African citizen. In their view, respect – a central tenet of *ubuntu* – must be made a part of formal citizenship education. As Yusef Waghid (2015) has explained, *ubuntu* is not simplistic caring but, rather, holds the potential to evoke the potentialities of others. 'People show respect for one another when they consider their judgements to have value' (Waghid 2010, 65). In the Western tradition, Kant equates respect for all persons with human dignity regardless of social standing. According to Thomas Hill (2000), this means that people are to be understood 'as worthy of respect as human beings, regardless of how their values differ and whether or not we disapprove of what they do' (69). Although both Western and non-Western conceptualisations of democratic citizenship have a shared concern for the worth of human beings, from the epistemological position of *ubuntu*, the notion of respect is a precondition to democratic practice and group belonging.

Citizenship in South Africa, therefore, 'has come to signify both an affirmation of the democratization project and also a critique of it' (von Lieres and Robins 2008, 47–48). Although there is disagreement among scholars as to whether *ubuntu* allows individuals to be critical of their own indigenous communities, there has been a resurgence of culture as an authority for behaviour and practice and as an explanatory concept in educator practitioner discourse. The citizenship discourse that emerges in postcolonial South Africa is a citizenship 'defined by highly localized processes of identification and political mobilization and not only by the claims of the rights-bearing citizen vis-à-vis the state' (von Lieres and Robins 2008, 49).

An examination of epistemological influences has helped to reveal the extremes of ideal-type characterisations of democratic citizenship from both Western and non-Western perspectives. These dualisms (e.g. modernity/traditionality, urban/rural, autonomous citizen/ethnic subject, individualist/collectivist) help us to understand that contestations over citizenship education are actually epistemological debates that inform the meanings of democratic citizenship that people hold. These epistemologies are part of modern life and global reality. They occupy both a material and immaterial space with defined and imagined boundaries. They mark differences and identify who is included and excluded from democratic citizenship. The kind of democratic citizen identity that has emerged in South Africa is neither solely traditional nor Western but, rather, a hybrid identity composed of a complex set of identity markers. Hybridity helps to more accurately describe the cultural flows and interactions between globalism and nationalism and tradition and modernity in South Africa. This hybridity, then, must be considered in theorisations of a critical democratic citizenship education.

Critical democratic citizenship education is a formulation of citizenship that will nurture *ubuntu* and democratic behaviour through social belonging and connection. Because humanity is defined through sociability, formal citizenship education in South Africa should help develop in students an Other-regarding ethic and draw upon knowledge and content that is sacred and empirical and philosophical and practical. A critical democratic citizenship is one that recognises that teachers negotiate for themselves and with their students the epistemological binaries and boundaries presented by Western and indigenous influences. Nurturing a rights-based citizenship alongside respect is a conceptualisation of democratic citizenship that is culturally relevant and responsive. This critical democratic citizenship, premised on a democratic ecology of being, requires that schools help students to view democratic life as both a lived expression and a transcendent ethicality that is developed through relationality.

Conclusion

The overall implication of my decade-long research on democracy and schooling in a Xhosa township is that formal citizenship education must help students address the complex, hybrid and situated subjectivities they experience as postcolonial citizens. A critical democratic citizenship education will enable children and youth to recognise that human flourishing is not an individual endeavour but a result of communal rootedness and interdependence. Students' identities as citizens are located within and transformed by intersections among global and local factors, time and space, and cultural embeddedness and distanciation. As such, constructions of citizenship in South Africa and elsewhere are always in the process of being remade and are shaped by the epistemologies on which they are grounded.

The theorisation of a culturally relevant, critical democratic citizenship education that emerges from the Xhosa practitioner data 'from below' can help expand Western researchers' perspectives on democracy and citizenship, while also informing policy makers 'from above' in South Africa and elsewhere. Political resistance to historical colonial influences have mixed with African indigenous knowledge systems and epistemologies to form a construction of democracy based not only on rights and responsibilities, but also on a moral ethic of *ubuntu* whereby respect is central to democratic citizenship, and interconnectedness and embeddedness of the person within society is undisputed. For the Xhosa teachers, a citizen is not only a rights-bearer of the state forged through a political orientation to citizenship, but also a values-bearing citizen whose deference to respect for self and others is observed through habits, attitudes and character traits founded on relationality. Western constructions of democratic citizenship that view the individual as an autonomous citizen-subject divorced from culture and community do not resonant with the Xhosa participants in this study, for they assert that one's humanity is based on, and developed through, sociability. From this epistemological stance, the moral ethic of *ubuntu* speaks to the cultural side of a hybridised democratic citizenship, where indigenous values mix with rights-oriented discourses to fashion the kind of democratic citizenship to be cultivated in the township's schools.

Disclosure statement

No potential conflict of interest was reported by the author.

References

Arthur, Lore, Elizabeth McNess, and Michael Crossley. 2016. "Introduction: Positioning Insider-Outsider Research in the Contemporary Context." In *Revisiting Insider-Outsider Research in Comparative and International Education*, edited by Michael Crossley, Lore Arthur and Elizabeth McNess, 11–20. Oxford: Symposium Books.

Ashcroft, Bill, Gareth Griffiths, and Helen Tiffin. 2007. *Post-Colonial Studies: The Key Concepts*. 2nd ed. London: Routledge.

Astiz, M. Fernanda, Alexander W. Wiseman, and David P. Baker. 2002. "Slouching towards Decentralization: Consequences of Globalization for Curricular Control in National Education Systems." *Comparative Education Review* 46 (1): 66–88.

Baez, Benjamin, and Deron Boyles. 2009. *The Politics of Inquiry: Education Research and the 'Culture of Science'*. Albany: State University of New York Press.

Barber, Benjamin. 2004. *Strong Democracy: Participatory Politics for a New Age, Twentieth-Anniversary Edition, with a New Preface*. Berkeley: University of California Press.

Bellamy, Richard. 2008. *Citizenship: A Very Short Introduction*. Oxford: Oxford University Press.

Bhabha, Homi K. 1994. *The Location of Culture*. New York: Routledge.

Bhabha, Homi K. 2006. "Cultural Diversity and Cultural Differences." In *The Post-Colonial Studies Reader*, edited by Bill Ashcroft, Gareth Griffiths and Helen Tiffin, 155–157. New York: Routledge.

Bhengu, Mfuniselwa John. 1996. *Ubuntu: The Essence of Democracy*. Cape Town: Novalis Press.

Bhola, Harbans Singh. 2002. "Reclaiming Old Heritage for Proclaiming Future History: The Knowledge-for-Development Debate in African Contexts." *Africa Today* 49 (3): 3–21.

van Binsbergen, Wim M. J. 2004. "Challenges for the Sociology of Religion in the African Context: Prospects for the Next 50 Years." *Social Compass* 51 (1): 85–98.

Boonzaier, Emile, and Andrew D. Spiegel. 2008. "Tradition." In *New South African Keywords*, edited by Nick Shepherd and Steven Robins, 195–208. Johannesburg: Jacana.

Boyte, Harry C. 1993. "Why Citizenship: A Project Perspective." *Public Life* 1–2, 4–7.

Chatterjee, Partha. 1993. *The Nation and Its Fragments*. Princeton, NJ: Princeton University Press.

Cohen, Carl. 1982. *Four Systems*. New York: Random House.

Comaroff, John L., and Jean Comaroff. 2008. "Ethnicity." In *New South African Keywords*, edited by Nick Shepherd and Steven Robins, 79–90. Johannesburg: Jacana.

Cowan, Jane K., Marie-Bénédicte Dembour, and Richard A. Wilson, eds. 2001. *Culture and Rights: Anthropological Perspectives*. Cambridge: Cambridge University Press.

Crossley, Michael. 2009. "Rethinking Context in Comparative Education." In *International Handbook of Comparative Education*, edited by Robert Cowen and Andreas M. Kazamias, 1173–1187. London: Springer.

Garuba, Harry, and Sam Raditlhalo. 2008. "Culture." In *New South African Keywords*, edited by Nick Shepherd and Steven Robins, 35–46. Johannesburg: Jacana.

Green, Lesley J. F. 2008. "Indigenous Knowledge: Part II." In *New South African Keywords*, edited by Nick Shepherd and Steven Robins, 132–142. Johannesburg: Jacana.

Greene, Maxine. 1995. *Releasing the Imagination: Articles on Education, the Arts and Social Change*. New York: Jossey-Bass.

Higgs, Philip, Sølvi Lillejord, Queeneth Mkabela, Yusef Waghid, and Lesley Le Grange, eds. 2004. "Indigenous African Knowledge Systems and Higher Education." *South African Journal of Higher Education* 18 (3): 40–45.

Hill, Thomas E. 2000. *Respect, Pluralism, and Justice: Kantian Perspectives*. Oxford: Oxford University Press.

Horsthemke, Kai. 2008. "Indigenous Knowledge: Part I." In *New South African Keywords*, edited by Nick Shepherd and Steven Robins, 129–132. Johannesburg: Jacana.

Kubow, Patricia K. 2007. "Teachers' Constructions of Democracy: Intersections of Western and Indigenous Knowledge in South Africa and Kenya." *Comparative Education Review* 51 (3): 307–328.

Kubow, Patricia K. 2008. "Developing Citizenship Education Curriculum Cross-Culturally: A Democratic Approach with South African and Kenyan Educators." In *Advancing Democracy through Education? U.S. Influence Abroad and Domestic Practices*, edited by E. Doyle Stevick and Bradley A. U. Levinson, 159–178. Charlotte, NC: Information Age Publishing.

Kubow, Patricia K., and Paul R. Fossum. 2007. *Comparative Education: Exploring Issues in International Context*. 2nd ed. Upper Saddle River, NJ: Merrill Prentice Hall, Pearson Education.

Kubow, Patricia K., and Mina Min. 2016. "The Cultural Contours of Democracy: Indigenous Epistemologies Informing South African Citizenship." *Democracy & Education* 24 (2): 1–12.

Letseka, Moeketsi. 2000. "African Philosophy and Educational Discourse." In *African Voices in Education*, edited by Philip Higgs, Ntombizolile Vakalisa, Thobeka Mda, and N'Dri Thérèse Assié-Lumumba, 179–193. Lansdowne: JUTA.

Letseka, Moeketsi. 2012. "In Defence of Ubuntu." *Studies in Philosophy of Education* 31: 47–60.

von Lieres, Bettina. 2005. "Marginalisation and Citizenship in Post-Apartheid South Africa." In *Limits to Liberation after Apartheid: Citizenship, Governance and Culture*, edited by Steven Robins, 22–32. Oxford: James Currey.

von Lieres, Bettina, and Steven Robins. 2008. "Democracy and Citizenship." In *New South African Keywords*, edited by Nick Shepherd and Steven Robins, 47–57. Johannesburg: Jacana.

Mamdani, Mahmood. 1996. *Citizen and Subject: Contemporary Africa and the Legacy of Late Colonialism*. Princeton, NJ: Princeton University Press.

Metz, Thaddeus. 2015. *Meaning of Life*. Philosopher's Zone. Podcast of the Australian Radio National Broadcast on 18 October 2015. www.abc.net.au/radionational/programs/philosopherszone

Mkhize, Nhlanhla. 2008. "*Ubuntu* and Harmony: An African Approach to Morality and Ethics." In *Persons in Community: African Ethics in a Global Culture*, edited by Ronald Nicolson, 35–44. Scottsville, South Africa: University of KwaZulu-Natal Press.

Nóvoa, António, and Tali Yariv-Mashal. 2003. "Comparative Research in Education: A Mode of Governance or a Historical Journey?" *Comparative Education* 39 (4): 423–438.

Odora Hoppers, Catherine A. 2000. "Globalization and the Social Construction of Reality: Affirming or Unmasking the 'Inevitable'?" In *Globalization and Education: Integration and Contestation across Cultures*, edited by Nelly P. Stromquist and Karen Monkman, 101–118. Lanham, MD: Rowman and Littlefield.

Odora Hoppers, Catherine A. 2002. *Indigenous Knowledge and the Integration of Knowledge Systems: Towards a Philosophy of Articulation*. Claremont: New South Africa Books.

Robins, Steven. 2008. "Rights." In *New South African Keywords*, edited by Nick Shepherd and Steven Robins, 182–194. Johannesburg: Jacana.

Semali, Ladislaus M., and Joe L. Kincheloe, eds. 1999. *What is Indigenous Knowledge? Voices from the Academy*. New York: Falmer Press.

Smith, Anthony D. 1986. *The Ethnic Origins of Nations*. Oxford: Blackwell.

Swanson, Dalene. 2014. "Frames of Ubuntu: (Re)Framing an Ethical Education." In *Framing Peace: Thinking about and Enacting Curriculum as 'Radical Hope'*, edited by Hans Smits and Rahat Naqvi, 49–63. New York: Peter Lang.

Taylor, Charles. 1994. *Multiculturalism and 'the Politics of Recognition'*. Princeton, NJ: University of Princeton Press.

wa Thiong'o, Ngũgĩ. 1986. *Decolonising the Mind: The Politics of Language in African Literature*. Portsmouth, NH: Heinemann.

Thornton, Robert. 1988. "Culture: A Contemporary Definition." In *South African Keywords: The Uses and Abuses of Political Concepts*, edited by Emile Boonzaier and John Sharp, 18–29. Cape Town: David Philip.

Turner, Bryan S. 1990. "Outline of a Theory of Citizenship." *Sociology* 24 (2): 189–217.

Tutu, Desmond. 1999. *No Future without Forgiveness*. New York: Doubleday.

Vanier, Jean. 1998. *Becoming Human*. Series: CBC Massey Lectures. Toronto: Anansi.

Venter, Elza. 2004. "The Notion of Ubuntu and Communalism in African Educational Discourse." *Studies in Philosophy of Education* 23 (2): 149–160.

Waghid, Yusef. 2010. *Education, Democracy and Citizenship Revisited: Pedagogical Encounters*. Stellenbosch: SUN MeDIA Stellenbosch under the imprint SUN PReSS.

Waghid, Yusef. 2015. "On the (Im)Potentiality of an African Philosophy of Education to Disrupt Inhumanity." *Educational Philosophy and Theory* 47 (11): 1234–1240.

Werbner, Richard P. 2002. *Postcolonial Subjectivities in Africa*. London: Zed Books.

Remembering West African indigenous knowledges and practices in citizenship education research

Laura Quaynor

ABSTRACT
Democratic citizenship education is of key concern in many societies, particularly with the adoption of global citizenship education in the United Nations' Education First Initiative. There have been particular critiques that current frameworks for understanding citizenship fail to account for civic understandings and practices in both African and African Diasporic societies. In this paper I share examples of indigenous civic knowledges and practices from societies within West Africa, the main nexus of the African diaspora. To illustrate the rich contexts societies have related to rights and political participation, I examine Adinkra symbols from the Akan in Ghana, and the Mande Charter of 1222, from what is now Mali. I then illustrate including indigenous knowledges in empirical research via a study of citizenship education in Liberia that included questions about traditional justice in a survey instrument, demonstrating varying access to traditional justice systems by gender.

Introduction

Democratic citizenship education is often posited as the central goal of schooling, and is a focus of international, national, and non-governmental organizations worldwide. With the adoption of global citizenship education as a key goal in the United Nations' Education First initiative (Tawil 2013), democratic citizenship education will have an increased presence in global education agendas. In this historical moment, it is critical to consider the theories used to conceptualise, plan, evaluate, and research democratic and global citizenship education worldwide. There have been particular critiques that current frameworks for understanding citizenship fail to account for civic understandings and practices in both African and Afro-Diasporic societies (Kubow 2007; Williams 2013). In this paper I share examples of civic knowledge and practices from societies within West Africa, often considered the main nexus of the African diaspora (Falola and Childs 2004). These examples provide rich philosophies and ideas regarding civic participation that might generate alternate theories of contemporary citizenship. I then describe one way that including such indigenous civic practices within empirical research in West Africa provided for a more nuanced understanding of citizenship.

In the current global landscape, scholars raise concerns that citizenship education initiatives and analyses might prioritise conceptions of democracy and citizenship created and propagated by Western cultural institutions, assuming the universality of ideas such as the separation of the public and private sphere and a focus on individual rights over community concerns (Kubow 2007; Mookherjee 2005; Mutua 2008). To expand and nuance theories of citizenship, post-colonial theorists suggest attention to context and power in recognition of hybrid identities; the importance of indigenous languages, knowledge, and practices; the use of periphery and center flows of knowledge and capital, and attention to the ecological dimensions of concepts, constructs, and material reality (Patel 2015; Dimitriadis and McCarthy 2001; Bhabha 1994; Ngũgĩ wa Thiong'o 1986; Said 1978; Spivak 1988). However, as indigenous practices may be marked by secrecy and specificity (Nooter 1993), they are sometimes glossed over in international discussions of citizenship (UNESCO 2014). This paper highlights indigenous knowledges from one region often missing from civic education research (Schulz et al. 2017) in order to foster appreciation for the span and depth of indigenous civic practices within one region and to generate theories of citizenship that are more relevant to particular contexts.

The need for new paradigms

Relying solely on frameworks developed from Eurocentric concepts of citizenship and democracy to research citizenship education in non-Western[1] contexts is problematic on both conceptual and practical levels. Citizenship and citizenship education are by definition sites of political struggle (Hahn 1998; Starkey 2012; Waghid and Davids 2013). Defining citizenship from a historical perspective based in Europe, such as that found in the United Nations Charter of Human Rights, runs the risk of losing conceptions of rights and participation important in a particular place. For example, there are differences between the United Nations Convention on the Rights of the Child and the African Charter on the Rights and Welfare of the Child (Harris-Short 2003; Kaime 2011) related to children's responsibilities and appropriate discipline for children (Adu-gyamfi and Keating 2013). These differences, as well as Eurocentric notions of human rights, are sometimes cited by community workers in African contexts as barriers to the acceptance of children's rights among communities (Afua Twum-Danso 2008). For legitimate and popular forms of democracy and democratic education to flourish, they must be integrated into local traditions, epistemologies, and realities (Na'im 1995, 2003). Understanding alternate epistemologies related to rights and citizenship strengthens the efforts of citizenship education. As Mutua claims (2008), 'The universalization of human rights cannot succeed unless the corpus is moored in all the cultures of the world. Ideas do not become universal merely because powerful interests declare them to be so' (156).

Within West Africa and the African diaspora, scholars have noted that using Western democratic frameworks to research citizenship education appears to lead to incomplete information regarding the strengths and functions of citizenship education; for example, in Jamaica, Williams (2013) notes that teachers' conceptions of citizenship would be classified by theroretical frameworks developed in the USA and Europe as minimalist, as teachers focused on embodying national rights and responsibilities and volunteerism related to charity rather than justice. However, when these foci are interpreted in the context of Jamaican political violence and poverty levels, Williams argues that they become complex attempts to help students understand their local codes of power and counter challenges in their national context created in part by globalisation and neo-liberal policies. In this way, incorporation of contextual information changes the way scholars might understand democratic citizenship education in practice.

Contextual information may also change the way researchers understand political participation. For example, despite the widespread consensus among Western democracies that voting is a defining characteristic of a democracy, in countries transitioning from conflict or political upheaval, the notion of voting as democratic participation can be largely symbolic and does not actually confer agency on citizens to elect their political leaders, as noted in scholarship from different African societies (Moran 2006; Moshi and Osman 2008); decision-making via consensus rather than majority rule is an alternate democratic paradigm (Arthur 2001; Mutua 2008; Samassékou 2011). Privileging the one-man-one-vote principle in post-conflict Liberia was associated with threats and fear of election-related violence (Moran 2006). In Bleck's (2015) recent study of citizenship in Mali, democratic participation was expressed through religion, a cultural preference for democracy by consensus, and civic networks than a focus on an individual's vote. Citizenship education and related research must be aware and responsive to these differences.

Including indigenous knowledges and practices in citizenship education research

Contemporary discourses of citizenship, statehood, democracy, and rights have been fundamentally shaped by global contact involving imperialism and colonisation from the fifteenth century through to the present (Aminzade 2013). Indeed, the contemporary African diaspora was created via colonialism and imperialism (Falola and Childs 2004; Bay 2000). Given this historical location, I draw on post-colonial theory to frame this inquiry into alternate paradigms for research within West Africa and the African Diaspora. The regional focus of this paper allows for a focus on indigenous civic practices in a region that is more often seen as a place of state fragility in international discourse (Economic Commission for Africa 2012).

A post-colonial theoretical framework requires the inclusion and interrogation of localised knowledge (Patel 2015). Localised or indigenous knowledge are considered in this paper to be community understandings developed in relationship to a particular ecology and environment (Semali and Kincheloe 2002). Despite debates about the origins of the word indigenous and the relationship between indigenous and Western knowledges, indigenous knowledge as a common social resource has transformative potential both for insiders and outsiders to those communities (Freire and Faundez 1989).

In the sphere of citizenship, many societies have rich civic traditions that may not be included in school-based citizenship education due to the colonial development of schools (Antal and Easton 2009). At the heart of the civic enterprise are universal tensions between unity and diversity and between the individual and the community. Historically, communities have different ways of dealing with these tensions and the ways to incorporate these concepts into decision-making. The goal of considering indigenous knowledges about these ideas is not to romanticise any of these indigenous or indigenised ideas or suggest that they might describe an ideal democratic society (Temu and Swai 1981). Rather, the inclusion of indigenous practices and languages in theoretical work elucidates rich ways that concepts of participatory societies and individual liberties have been taken up in a society of interest over time.

In the West African region, many indigenous cultures and worldviews use communalist rhetoric around rights (Wingo 2015). However, in the contemporary moment, all communities exist in conversation between local and global ideas, interacting with globalisation of business and government, international rights documents and multiple local ideas about rights and citizenship (Abramowitz 2014). Post-colonial theory highlights both the consideration of indigenous knowledge as well as the use of hybridity as an organising concept:

> Within us are contradictory identities, pulling in different directions, so that our identifications are continuously being shifted about. If we feel we have a unified identity from birth to death, it is only because we construct a comforting story or 'narrative of the self' about ourselves. (Hall 2011, 598)

Cultures and individuals, through personal and communal interactions, are linked, combined, and recreated in deep and meaningful ways (Hall 2011; Spivak 1988; Gilroy 1993). This hybridity may be a space for both liberation or oppression, but is an unavoidable fact (Bhabha 1994). In this vein, then, Western and non-Western ideas about citizenship are influenced by their relationship to each other (Gilroy 1993); this hybridity should be incorporated in citizenship education research. The reason this hybridity is important to consider in citizenship education research in non-Western contexts is that often research on citizenship and democracy draws on normative, Western definitions of citizenship practice (Kubow 2007). In the following section I share ways that the relationship between unity and diversity and the individual and the community are taken up in two West African historical and indigenous texts that reference political participation and belonging.

Adinkra symbols and political knowledge

The first tradition comes from the Adinkra symbols of the Akan: these symbols have historically been used as funeral garb, and date in use to at least the early-eighteenth century (Arthur 2001; Fortune 1997; Willis 1998). In contemporary culture, Adinkra symbols are used as images on T-shirts and cars as well as in more formal arenas (Blay 2009). Ideas related to citizenship, cooperation and power are evident in many symbols; here, I highlight three: *funtunfunefu denkyemfunefu*, *wonsa*, and *kurontire ne Akwamu*.

Figure 1 displays the symbol *funtunfunefu denkyemfunefu*. In this symbol two crocodiles have separate mouths but the same stomach: this image seems to indicate that individualism is but an illusion – in the end, we are nourished not only by what we 'eat' but by what others 'eat' as well (Arthur 2001; Quarcoo 1971). The symbol seen in Figure 2, entitled *wonsa*, is from the proverb '*Wo nsa da mu a, wonni nnya wo*', translated as 'If your hands are in the dish, people do not eat everything and leave you nothing' (Arthur 2001, 76). This image provides a different balance between individualism and communalism than *funtunfunefu denkyemfunefu*; the *wonsa* symbol emphasises communal resources but individual action. An individual has to have their hands in the communal dish in order to ensure they are individually nourished (Arthur 2001). Although traditional Akan kingdoms were limited monarchies, a leader required broad public support and the need for balance in government and judicial affairs is represented by the symbol in Figure 3, *kurontire ne Akwamu*

Figure 1. funtunfunefu denkyemfunefu.

Figure 2. wonsa.

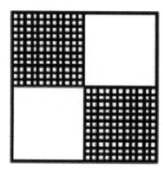

Figure 3. kurontire ne Akwamu.

(Nascimento and Gá 2009). This symbol, also written *Kronti ne Akwamu*, indicates that one head does not constitute a council nor a jury, and symbolises complementary branches of the states (Arthur 2001). A multitude of other symbols represent interdependence and the need for communal decision-making.

Wiredu and Gyekye (1992) discuss the ways that Akan philosophies of personhood mirror these symbolic tensions between the individual and the community. Both of these thinkers agree that among the Akan, each human being has inherent dignity and respect based on the possession of a divine spark, *okra*, itself separate from an individual's heart/will and mind/reason. However, Wiredu posits, based on proverbs, statements, and customs that human beings can become *persons (onipa)* through doing their part in social relations: marrying, taking care of kin, assisting the community as a whole, and participating in community development. Gyakye holds that each human being is a person *(onipa)*, although those who do not fulfill their social duties may be referred to as *onipa hun* (a useless person). Ajume Wingo (2008) describes how the person-human duality is connected to the democratic enterprise:

> … the Akan notion of personhood helps to support social cooperation and provides a framework superbly suited to resolving collective action problems. The Akan have fashioned a means of motivating individuals to contribute to the social good while still insuring that the moral value of even the most unproductive individual is retained. For the Akan, personhood is the reward for contributing to the community and the basis of the individual's moral worth is located in an independent source – a common humanity. (6)

This type of personhood is embedded in the concept of relational freedom, or being free in society, as opposed to the Western concept of a person being free from society, or personal freedom. For example, the fundamental Western right is the right to be left alone; the fundamental African right is the right to be helped (Wingo 2010).

Taken together, these diverging messages in symbols and sayings are helpful in highlighting the balance of ideas about citizenship and participation existing within the same society. These two symbols show visual representations of communalism and individualism originating from Akan society. Researchers focusing on citizenship and democracy in nations with Akan ethnic groups might consider using concepts of community and individuality from Adinkra symbols as a framework for their investigations.

The Mande Charter of 1222

The second example of indigenous knowledge and traditions related to citizenship and democracy shared here is from the thirteenth century Malian empire, during the reign of Sunjata Keita. This oath, often called the Mande charter, was written by a men's group and named specific liberties and rights important to human beings (Diagne 2009). This oath has often been compared with the Magna Carta of 1215, although the Magna Carta was specifically focused on the freedom of privileged landlords to control their own property (Wingo 2010). Unlike the positive rights and duties prioritised in Adinkra symbols, this oath is an example of negative rights – rights of an individual to be free from societal constraints. Although the entire oath has seven articles (Diagne 2009), the following excerpts are especially helpful for the development of non-Western frameworks for studying citizenship education:

> Article 1: Every human life is a life…It is true that a life comes into existence before another life…But no life is more 'ancient', more respectable than any other…In the same way no one life is superior to any other.
>
> Article 7: But his 'soul', his spirit lives on three things…He must see what he wishes to see…He must say what he wishes to say…And do what he wishes to do…If one of these things were to miss from the human soul…It would suffer and would surely become sick…In consequence the hunters declare…Each person from now on is free to dispose of his own person…Each person is free to act in the way he wishes…Each person disposes of the fruit of his labour from

now on…This is the oath of the Manden…For the ears of the whole world. (Chanthalangsy and Crowley 2014, 39)

Those investigating citizenship education in Mali might consider modern interpretations of this historic knowledge. Furthermore, organisations and initiatives wishing to promote citizenship education in Mali might consider drawing on these historical traditions. These examples demonstrate the richness of citizenship and rights discourse indigenous to one regional context. As citizenship education researchers seek to make their research valid and applicable in non-Western contexts, they can consider local civic traditions and conceptions in order to capture the meaning of the civic enterprise in a particular place and time. The indigenous practices shared here are not intended to circumscribe possibilities for civic education in West Africa, but rather as contextual information that can inform theory, design, and analysis. In the subsequent section I illustrate this suggestion via an empirical research project focused on citizenship education in West Africa that incorporated indigenous practices and attention to relationships in the collection and analysis of data.

Incorporating Liberian traditional justice systems in citizenship education research

Working with currently available theoretical frameworks, a post-colonial approach is one of the most expansive regarding the incorporation of indigenous or localised knowledges into empirical research (Patel 2015). The post-colonial approach also considers the ways that these localised knowledges relate to other discourses and realities in a particular moment. This ecological or relational model helps researchers to consider what ideas and practices are fixed and fluid; some power structures remain over time, while others are renegotiated in different historical moments.

In relationship to rights and citizenship education, the tenet of post-colonial theory related to power asks: What is important to individuals regarding security and basic needs? How does citizenship integrate into this? In the post-conflict period in Liberia, as well as in other nations, it is common to talk about the right to clean water without universal access to clean water (Quaynor 2015); a right to education but no universal access to education; a right to freedom of speech but detainment for libel for political reasons. A post-colonial approach to citizenship education asks: What do these contradictions do to citizenship education for young people? How is citizenship education related to the educational ecology of the country?

In a 2011 study of citizenship education in Liberia, I incorporated post-colonial theory via attention to context and power. To consider context, when surveying students about citizenship practices, I included items about indigenous civic institutions in Liberia. To consider power and relationships in the analysis, I considered whether groups with differing access to social capital have differing responses to questions about citizenship practice.

The theoretical framework for this highlighted study combined post-colonial theory (Kubow 2007; Dimitriadis and McCarthy 2001) and Osler and Starkey's (2005) three dimensions of citizenship – status, feeling, and practice – to understand citizenship education in a post-conflict and post-colonial context. In this model, status refers to the political and legal status conferred to citizens of a state in terms of rights and duties; feeling refers to the sense of belonging to a community of citizens; practice invokes the idea of active citizenship upholding democracy and human rights. Osler and Starkey (2005) argue that individuals hold citizenship in different communities in terms of these three dimensions. Students might express a belief in rights (status), feel connected to people elsewhere because of common humanity (feeling), and post advocacy articles on social media (practice). In this paper, I focus on beliefs and practices.

Post-colonialism is a fitting lens for studying citizenship education in Liberia due to the particular historical legacies of colonialism related to both citizenship and the state. Although Liberia was settled by individuals of African descent from the USA, these settlers established a nation and a schooling structure in opposition to indigenous structures. Indeed, the national project of Liberia from its founding in 1821 through to the 1950s was to civilize, control, and exploit indigenous people (Cassell 1970; Library of Congress 1998). Today's political realities in Liberia are shaped by this historical context, and issues of Americo-Liberian and indigenous ethnicity continue to be relevant politically and socially (Bohrer 1999). Combining post-colonial theory and Osler and Starkey's citizenship framework acknowledges that young people experience citizenship status, feeling, and practice in the context of power inequities and local contexts. For example, young people with citizenship status in one country who experience ethnic discrimination may establish feelings or practices of citizenship that do not align with their citizenship status. This lens provides recognition that students develop as citizens in a world where historical contexts and power differentials can shape a student's identity, opportunity, and schooling.

Traditional justice systems and citizenship

From the beginning of the colonial project, people have used colonial courts and judges strategically in tension with indigenous forms of justice (Mann and Roberts 1991; Roberts 2013). In a post-colonial context, citizenship education research should consider the knowledge and skills around the use of both systems. Indigenous systems of justice may be of particular interest to citizenship education researchers, as they are one manifestation of systems of political participation. This importance is widely documented in development studies: as part of rule-of-law initiatives in post-conflict, non-Western contexts, strengthening judicial institutions is key; development reviews have found that focusing on strengthening traditional institutions rather than only supporting formal judicial institutions is more helpful locally and is correlated with an increase in gross domestic product (Browne 2013).

In Liberia, the strengthening of the rule of law and judicial systems has been a major focus of international donors (Weah 2012); between 2000 and 2010, over 600 million dollars in development aid from USAID and the EU focused on this topic (Jaye 2009). Furthermore, surveys in both rural and urban areas indicate that most of the population does not make use of the formal judicial system, with only 3% of reported disputes being adjudicated in the formal system and 38% via traditional courts (Isser, Lubkemann, and N'Tow 2009). International studies of citizenship education, however, do not focus extensively on skills, attitudes, and practices related to the judicial system, nor on differences within systems. In the IEA 1999 Civic Education Study and 2009 International Civic and Citizenship Study, the questions in Figure 4 were two of four items that addressed the judicial system.

The relationship between youth and the judicial system is an incredibly personal and often daily citizenship experience for young people. This is particularly true in post-conflict nations (Finkel, Sabatini, and Bevis 2000; Quaynor 2014) and communities experiencing conflict (Carr, Napolitano, and Keating 2007; Fine et al. 2003; Sewell et al. 2016). Approaching this study through a post-colonial lens, I asked: What types of justice systems do students think are an

How much of the time can you trust each of the following institutions?

Consider each of these institutions and select the box in the column which shows how you feel you can trust them.

	never	only some of the time	most of the time	always	don't know
	1	2	3	4	0
D3 Courts[e]	☐	☐	☐	☐	○
D4 The police[e]	☐	☐	☐	☐	○

Figure 4. IEA CivEd and ICCS items. (Schulz and Foy 2004; Schulz 2011).

important part of citizenship? Are there class or gender differences in the ways students understand their access to different judicial systems?

Empirical research and traditional justice systems

This 2011 multi-site study in Liberia included a quantitative survey distributed to students in four lower-secondary schools, individual interviews with teachers and administrators, and focus-group interviews with students (Quaynor 2015). In the examples below I focus on data collected via the survey. Via purposive sampling, I selected four lower-secondary schools to invite to participate in the study: two government and two non-government schools. Overall, data included an 82-item survey from 286 8th grade students; interviews with social studies teachers ($n = 6$) and administrators ($n = 4$), including one or two teachers and one administrator at each school; student focus-group interviews ($n = 53$), involving two groups of six or seven students at each school for interviews lasting 30–45 min each; and an analysis of the main textbook. All schools were located in Greater Monrovia and served low- and middle-income students.

In the survey, students were asked to rate the likelihood of particular actions they thought were representative of good citizenship. They then rated how likely they were to take these actions, or how likely they would be to take these actions in the future. For this paper, I am focusing on the response to six of the survey questions centred around students' practices about resolving community problems or concerns. These questions are listed in Figure 5.

For these questions I investigated differences across gender groups as well as groups based on levels of parental education. Mean responses among students in these different groups varied at times. Responses by gender are presented in Table 1. When asked if, as a youth, they were likely to take community problems or concerns to a judge and to a traditional leader, there were some differences in the patterns of responses of young men and young women. Both groups of students were equally likely to say they would take problems to a judge, with mean responses falling between two, rarely, and three. However, the mean response from young men was higher than the mean response for young women regarding the likelihood of taking community problems/concerns to a traditional leader. This difference did not apply in the response to the question about future behaviour; the mean response for young men and women was not significantly different regarding their plans in the future to take community problems or concerns to a traditional leader.

Some statistically significant differences were also present in the responses of students when placed in groups based on parental education, shown in Table 2. Students whose

1	2	3	4
Never	Rarely	Sometimes	Often

Good citizens....
　___ take community problems or concerns to a traditional leader
　___ take community problems or concerns to a judge

As a student, I …
　___ take community problems or concerns to a traditional leader
　___ take community problems or concerns to a judge

In the future, I plan to....
　___ take community problems or concerns to a traditional leader
　___ take community problems or concerns to a judge

Figure 5. Selected survey questions.

parents had a university or high school education expressed a higher mean response to the

Table 1. Responses by gender.

Survey item	Girls	Boys	Statistical significance
Good citizens take community problems/concerns to a traditional leader	2.77	2.93	
Good citizens take community problems/concerns to a judge	2.86	2.85	
I take community problems/concerns to a traditional leader	2.47	2.91	**
I take community problems/concerns to a judge	2.55	2.51	
I plan to take community problems/concerns to a traditional leader	2.91	2.97	
I plan to take community problems/concerns to a judge	2.97	3.34	

Note: Response by gender is a number. This number is an average score from a survey instrument with a Likert Scale from 1–4. $*p < .1$, 2-tailed t-test; $**p < .05$.

Table 2. Responses by parental education level.

Parent education	Some or no school	University or highschool	Significance
Good citizens take community problems/concerns to a traditional leader	2.51	2.89	**
Good citizens take community problems/concerns to a judge	2.71	2.9	
I take community problems/concerns to a traditional leader	2.62	2.72	
I take community problems/concerns to a judge	2.43	2.61	
I plan to take community problems/concerns to a traditional leader	2.75	2.98	
I plan to take community problems/concerns to a judge	2.68	3.37	*

$*p < .1$, 2-tailed t-test; $**p < .05$.

statement 'Good citizens take community concerns to a traditional leader' than students whose parents had not completed high school. The mean response for students whose parents had a university or high school education was also higher for the statement 'Good citizens take community concerns to a judge', and this difference was statistically significant at a lower level.

These results raise issues around access to both traditional and formal courts for students from different backgrounds. First, this study found differences in civic participation between men and women, although not always in predictable ways. Although young women were less likely to say that they consulted traditional leaders for problem resolution, they expected to do so in the future at the same rates as young men. In addition, there were no statistically significant differences between young men and women regarding current or future plans to consult judges regarding community problems. This does not necessarily mean that there will not be gendered differences in future behaviour, but that there are no differences in expectations of future behaviour.

This study also notes the ways that social status may influence perceptions of citizenship and the judicial system. Students whose parents had more formal education were more likely to say that good citizens take problems to traditional leaders than students with less formal education. These students were also more likely to say that they themselves would take problems to a judge. Students with a higher parental-educational background have higher expectations of accessing both indigenous and judicial systems; higher amounts of this type of social capital seem to be associated with greater access to both formal and indigenous systems of justice. Although it is important to refrain from extending generalisations from these findings to other regions of Liberia without corresponding investigations, this data raises important issues related to gender, class, and citizenship education. Aligning with work in transitional justice (Chopra and Isser 2012), this data indicates that indigenous systems of justice in Liberia are not only for those without access to formal systems of education. For the most part, students participating in the survey study rated engagement with traditional leaders as equally important as engagement with the formal judicial system.

Conclusion

This paper discusses indigenous knowledges and practices related to citizenship within West Africa. This region is central to critiques of Western citizenship ideas and yet often absent from international discussions about citizenship education (Adu-gyamfi and Keating 2013; Schulz et al. 2017). In response, I have discussed two indigenous knowledge systems from the region related to citizenship: the Adrinkra tradition and the Mande Charter. These systems demonstrate a value of individual action for the common good, as seen in the *funtunfunefu denkyemfunefu* symbol, which shows two individual animals sharing a stomach, and the concept of the fundamental right to be helped. At the same time, they show consideration of individual action for personal benefit, as in the *wonsa* symbol, which emphasises the importance of an individual taking what he or she needs, and in the Mande Charter, which discusses the importance of individual expression and self-determination. As global attention to citizenship education as a central purpose of schooling continues and even increases (Tawil 2013), it is important to consider that indigenous knowledges and practices have rich traditions regarding citizenship and education.

Empirical evidence, indeed, points to the power of incorporating indigenous knowledges such as *Adinkra* for student learning (Babbit et al. 2015). In order to connect the theoretical and practical incorporation of indigenous knowledges, I have discussed the civic institution and practice of traditional judicial systems in Liberia, and how this important civic practice can be incorporated into empirical civic education research. Civic participation in the Liberian context can involve the navigation of multiple civic spheres – both Western-style government bodies and traditional government. Focusing on only one of these spheres provides an incomplete understanding of how youth participate in issues at local and national levels as responsible and responsive citizens, which is one of the learning objectives prioritised by UNESCO (2015).[2] In addition, analysing the participation patterns of students by gender and social capital attends to equitable access to citizenship education and citizenship processes. In this case, the empirical study shared here notes that young men report higher access to the traditional justice system than young girls. Students with parents who completed high school also report higher plans to access the Western-style judiciary system than students whose parents did not complete high school.

In the above example, I show that using a theoretical framework that necessitates the incorporation of historical, cultural, political, and social contexts has a direct impact on the types of questions researchers are able to ask in their work. I share indigenous knowledges and practices from one region in order to include indigenous knowledges in contemporary initiatives related to global citizenship education. This is one way to speak to the limitations of theoretical frameworks that prioritise voting and individual rights as the most important civic practices and knowledges in a society (Moran 2006).

Another important conversation that intersects with indigenous knowledges is the concept of youth civic funds of knowledge. The key element of funds of knowledge (González, Moll, and Amanti 2005) is that researchers study the knowledge and practices different students and their families bring in order to make recommendations for how educational institutions might help convert what students bring to the school to the social and cultural capital valued in their society. These funds of knowledge would include but not be limited to historical indigenous knowledges, perhaps involving knowledge of how to engage in activism via social networking sites, an important youth civic action in the current era (Ratto and Boler 2014).

This contextual, strengths-based approach guards against one of the difficulties in engaging in democratic citizenship education research in non-Western contexts, which is to avoid evaluating the success of democratic citizenship education in one context based on a measure or concept developed in another context (Vavrus and Bartlett 2013). Without such attention, Western researchers risk inscribing a narrative of deficit and difference in regards to non-Western democracies (Williams 2013). The indigenous knowledges and practices shared here serve as a counter-narrative to normative international research information by including contextually specific citizenship information as a major research focus.

The incorporation of indigenous knowledges requires attention to the role of power in the study itself and in the concepts under study (Semali and Kincheloe 2002). This type of analysis is evident in frameworks from fields as diverse as critical studies (Apple 2010; Giroux 2013), critical race theory (Ladson-Billings and Tate 1995; Parker and Lynn 2002), post-colonial studies (Patel 2015; Dimitriadis and McCarthy 2001; Spivak 1988), and feminist studies (Moraga 2015; Villaverde 2008), which seek to make visible the ways that power works in the world. Scholars can attend to power with the use of the conceptual frames of webs and flows. These might include the structural relationship of the centre and the periphery seen in post-colonial frameworks, or a situated learning model founded in Lave and Wenger's (1991) work, used in IEA studies of civic education (Schulz et al. 2017). A web-like model is incomplete without attention to the interactional patterns between the relationships. For example, the study described in this paper notes the possibility of power differentials between young men and women as relates to citizenship (Lukose 2009). These power differentials are historically and culturally inscribed, but change over time. The empirical example shared here demonstrates that indigenous courts, a locally-generated space for fostering democratic dialogue, may at the same time be a place where gender roles are redefined and contested, and where powerful political individuals reassert their authority.

This paper is part of a conversation for investigating possible theoretical frameworks for democratic citizenship education in a world with global attention directed to this contextual practice. As the UN advocates for a focus on the values of peace, human rights, respect, cultural diversity, and justice within schools (Tawil 2013), it is essential to consider how the enactment of these values might differ across contexts. With or without researchers, young people and their many teachers – inside and outside of schools – will experience and create democratic citizenship education that is meaningful to them. In order to both understand and support this activity, the research community should consider including indigenous knowledges in the process of democratic citizenship education.

Notes

1. Although the terms are complex, for the purpose of this paper, the terms Eurocentric and Western are used interchangeably to indicate ideas or practices originating in Europe and spreading throughout the globe via imperialism and colonisation (Pieterse 2009).
2. Local civic practices also include learning and activism via cyber and mobile technologies, an important part of youth practice that is discussed in more detail in other scholarly work (Ratto and Boler 2014).

Acknowledgements

I would like to thank Serhiy Kovalchuk and Anatoli Rappoport for feedback on this work.
An earlier version of this paper was presented at the 2016 Comparative and International Education Society (CIES) Conference in Vancouver, B.C.

Disclosure statement

No potential conflict of interest was reported by the author.

Funding

The research discussed in Liberia was supported by Open Society Foundations through the Privatization in Education Research Initiative.

References

Abramowitz, Sharon Alane. 2014. *Searching for Normal in the Wake of the Liberian War*. 1st ed. Pennsylvania Studies in Human Rights. Philadelphia, PA: University of Pennsylvania Press.
Adu-gyamfi, Jones, and Frank Keating. 2013. "Convergence and Divergence between the UN Convention on the Rights of the Children and the African Charter on the Rights and Welfare of the Child." *Sacha Journal of Human Rights* 3 (1): 47–58.
Afua Twum-Danso, Afua. 2008. "A Cultural Bridge, Not an Imposition: Legitimizing Children's Rights in the Eyes of Local Communities." *The Journal of the History of Childhood and Youth* 1 (3): 391–413. doi:10.1353/hcy.0.0023.
Aminzade, Ronald. 2013. *Race, Nation, and Citizenship in Post-Colonial Africa: The Case of Tanzania*. Cambridge Studies in Contentious Politics. New York: Cambridge University Press.
Antal, Carrie, and Peter Easton. 2009. "Indigenizing Civic Education in Africa: Experience in Madagascar and the Sahel." *International Journal of Educational Development* 29 (6): 599–611. doi:10.1016/j.ijedudev.2008.10.004.
Apple, Michael W., ed. 2010. *Global Crises, Social Justice, and Education*. New York: Routledge.
Arthur, Kojo. 2001. *Cloth as Metaphor: (Re)Reading the Adinkra Cloth Symbols of the Akan of Ghana*. Legon, Ghana: Centre for Indigenous Knowledge Systems.
Babbitt, William, Michael Lachney, Enoch Bulley, and Ron Eglash. 2015. "Adinkra Mathematics: A Study of Ethnocomputing in Ghana." *Multidisciplinary Journal of Educational Research* 5 (2): 110. doi:10.17583/remie.2015.1399.
Bay, M. 2000. *The White Image in the Black Mind: African-American Ideas about White People, 1830–1925*. New York: Oxford University Press.
Bhabha, Homi. 1994. *The Location of Culture*. New York: Routledge.
Blay, Yaba. 2009. "Adinkra." In *Encyclopedia of African Religion*, edited by Molefi Kete Asante and Ama Mazama, 6–10. Thousand Oaks, Calif: SAGE.

Bleck, Jaimie. 2015. *Education and Empowered Citizenship in Mali*. Baltimore, MD: Johns Hopkins University Press.

Bohrer, Kevin. 1999. "'It's Hard to Be a Refugee': Cultural Citizenship and the Experience of Modernity among Urban Liberians in Exile." Dissertation, University of Wisconsin.

Browne, Evie. 2013. *Evidence on 'Rule of Law' Aid Initiatives (GSDRC Helpdesk Research Report 1008)*. GSDRC: University of Birmingham. http://www.gsdrc.org/docs/open/hdq1008.pdf

Carr, Patrick J., Laura Napolitano, and Jessica Keating. 2007. "We Never Call the Cops and Here Is Why: A Qualitative Examination of Legal Cynicism in Three Philadelphia Neighborhoods?" *Criminology* 45 (2): 445–480. doi:10.1111/j.1745-9125.2007.00084.x.

Cassell, C. A. 1970. *Liberia: History of the First African Republic*. New York: Fountainhead publishers.

Chanthalangsy, Phinith and John Crowley. 2014. *Philosophy Manual: A South-South Perspective*. UNESCO: King Abdullah bin Abdulaziz International Programme for a Culture of Peace and Dialogue, Unesco, and South-South Co-operation Programme.

Chopra, Tanja, and Deborah Isser. 2012. "Access to Justice and Legal Pluralism in Fragile States: The Case of Women's Rights." *Hague Journal on the Rule of Law* 4 (2): 337–358. doi:10.1017/S187640451200019X.

Diagne, Souleymane Bachir. 2009. "Individual, Community, and Human Rights." *Transition*, 101 (103): 8–15.

Dimitriadis, Greg, and Cameron McCarthy. 2001. *Reading and Teaching the Postcolonial: From Baldwin to Basquiat and beyond*. New York: Teachers College Press.

Economic Commission for Africa. 2012. *Fragile States and Development in West Africa. United Nations Economic Commission for Africa: Sub-Regional Office for West Africa*. a/SRO-WA. Niamey, Niger.

Falola, Toyin, and Matt D. Childs, eds. 2004. *The Yoruba Diaspora in the Atlantic World. Blacks in the Diaspora*. Bloomington: Indiana University Press.

Fine, Michelle, Nick Freudenberg, Yasser Payne, Tiffany Perkins, Kersha Smith, and Katya Wanzer. 2003. "'Anything Can Happen with Police Around': Urban Youth Evaluate Strategies of Surveillance in Public Places." *Journal of Social Issues* 59 (1): 141–158. doi:10.1111/1540-4560.t01-1-00009.

Finkel, Steve E., Christopher A. Sabatini, and Gwendolyn G. Bevis. 2000. "Civic Education, Civil Society, and Political Mistrust in a Developing Democracy: The Case of the Dominican Republic." *World Development* 28 (11): 1851–1874. doi:10.1016/S0305-750X(00)00067-X.

Fortune, Leasa Farrar. 1997. "Adinkra: The Cloth That Speaks." National Museum of African Art.

Freire, Paulo, and Antonio Faundez. 1989. *Learning to Question: A Pedagogy of Liberation*. New York: Continuum.

Gilroy, Paul. 1993. *The Black Atlantic: Modernity and Double Consciousness*. Nachdr. Cambridge, Mass: Harvard Univ. Press.

Giroux, Henry A. 2013. *Youth in Revolt: Reclaiming a Democratic Future*. Boulder: Paradigm Publishers.

González, Norma, Luis C. Moll, and Cathy Amanti. 2005. "Introduction: Theorizing Practices." In *Funds of Knowledge: Theorizing Practice in Households, Communities, and Classrooms*, edited by González, Norma, Luis C. Moll, and Cathy Amanti, 1–28. Mahwah, N.J: L. Erlbaum Associates.

Hahn, Carole. 1998. *Becoming Political: Comparative Perspectives on Citizenship Education*. Albany: State University of New York Press. SUNY Series, Theory, Research, and Practice in Social Education

Hall, Stuart, ed. 2011. *Modernity: An Introduction to Modern Societies*. Malden, Mass.: Blackwell.

Harris-Short, Sonia. 2003. "International Human Rights Law: Imperialist, Inept and Ineffective? Cultural Relativism and the UN Convention on the Rights of the Child." *Human Rights Quarterly* 25 (1): 130–181. doi:10.1353/hrq.2003.0004.

Isser, Deborah, Stephen Lubkemann, and Saah N'Tow. 2009. "Looking for Justice: Liberian Experiences with and Perceptions of Local Justice Options." United States Institute of Peace. http://www.usip.org/sites/default/files/liberian_justice_pw63.pdf

Jaye, Thomas. 2009. "Transitional Justice and DDR: The Case of Liberia." International Center for Transitional Justice. https://www.ictj.org/sites/default/files/ICTJ-DDR-Liberia-CaseStudy-2009-English.pdf

Kaime, Thoko. 2011. *The Convention on the Rights of the Child: A Cultural Legitimacy Critique*. Groningen: Europa Law Publishing.

Kubow, Patricia K. 2007. "Teachers' Constructions of Democracy: Intersections of Western and Indigenous Knowledge in South Africa and Kenya." *Comparative Education Review* 51 (3): 307–328. doi:10.1086/518479.

Ladson-Billings, Gloria, and William F. Tate. 1995. "Toward a Critical Race Theory of Education." *Teachers College Record* 97 (1): 47–68.

Lave, Jean, and Etienne Wenger. 1991. *Situated Learning: Legitimate Peripheral Participation*. New York: Cambridge University Press. Learning in Doing. Cambridge [England].

Library of Congress. 1998. "History of Liberia: A Time Line." author. http://memory.loc.gov/ammem/gmdhtml/libhtml/liberia.html

Lukose, Ritty A. 2009. *Liberalization's Children Gender, Youth, and Consumer Citizenship in Globalizing India*. Durham [NC]: Duke University Press. http://public.eblib.com/choice/publicfullrecord.aspx?p=1170615

Mann, Kristin, and Richard L. Roberts, eds. 1991. *Law in Colonial Africa*. Social History of Africa. London: Portsmouth, NH: Heinemann Educational Books ; James Currey.

Mookherjee, Monica. 2005. "Affective Citizenship: Feminism, Postcolonialism and the Politics of Recognition." *Critical Review of International Social and Political Philosophy* 8 (1): 31–50. doi:10.1080/13698230042000335830.

Moraga, Cherríe. 2015. "Catching Fire: Preface to the Fourth Edition." In *This Bridge Called My Back: Writings by Radical Women of Color*, edited by C. Moraga and G. Anzaldúa, 4th ed, xv–xxvi. Albany: State University of New York Press.

Moran, Mary H. 2006. *Liberia: The Violence of Democracy*. The Ethnography of Political Violence. Philadelphia, PA: University of Pennsylvania Press.

Moshi, Lioba J., and Abdulahi A. Osman. 2008. "Democracy and Culture: An African Perspective." In *Democracy and Culture: An African Perspective*, edited by Moshi, Lioba J., and Abdulahi A. Osman, 17–22. London: Adonis & Abbey.

Mutua, Makau. 2008. *Human Rights: A Political and Cultural Critique*. Pennsylvania, Pa: Univ of Pennsylvania Pr. Pennsylvania Studies in Human Rights.

Na'īm, 'Abd Allāh Aḥmad, ed. 2003. *Human Rights under African Constitutions: Realizing the Promise for Ourselves*. Pennsylvania Studies in Human Rights. Philadelphia, PA: University of Pennsylvania Press.

Na'īm, 'Abd Allāh Aḥmad an-, ed. 1995. *Human Rights in Cross-Cultural Perspectives: A Quest for Consensus*. 1. Paperback Printing. Pennsylvania Studies in Human Rights. Philadelphia, PA: Univ. of Pennsylvania Press.

Nascimento, Elisa Larkin, and Luiz Carlos Gá. 2009. *Adinkra: sabedoria em símbolo africanos = African wisdom symbols = Sagesse en symboles africains = Sabiduría en símbolos africanos*. Rio de Janeiro: Pallas.

Ngũgĩ wa Thiong'o. 1986. *Decolonising the Mind: The Politics of Language in African Literature*. London: Portsmouth, N.H: J. Currey; Heinemann.

Nooter, M. 1993. "Introduction: The Aesthetics and Politics of Things Unseen." In *Secrecy: African Art That Conceals and Reveals*, edited by Mary, Nooter. New York: Museum for African Art.

Osler, Audrey, and Hugh Starkey. 2005. *Citizenship and Language Learning*. London: Trentham Books.

Parker, Laurence, and Marvin Lynn. 2002. "What's Race Got to Do With It? Critical Race Theory's Conflicts With and Connections to Qualitative Research Methodology and Epistemology." *Qualitative Inquiry* 8 (1): 7–22. doi:10.1177/107780040200800102.

Patel, Leigh. 2015. *Decolonizing Educational Research: From Ownership to Answerability*. Series in Critical Narrative. New York: Routledge.

Pieterse, J. N. 2009. *Globalization and Culture: Global Mélange*. Lanham, MD: Rowman & Littlefield.

Quarcoo, A. K. 1971. *The Language of Adrinkra Patterns*. Legon, Ghana: Institute of African Studies, University of Ghana.

Quaynor, Laura. 2014. "'I Do Not Have the Means to Speak:' Educating Youth for Citizenship in Post-Conflict Liberia." *Journal of Peace Education* 1–22. July, doi:10.1080/17400201.2014.931277.

Quaynor, Laura. 2015. "Liberia: Citizenship Education in the Post-Conflict Era." In *Education in West Africa*, edited by Emefa Amoako, 283–296.

Ratto, M., and M. Boler, eds. 2014. *DIY Citizenship: Critical Making and Social Media*. Cambridge Massachusetts: The MIT Press.

Roberts, Richard L. 2013. "Law, Crime and Punishment in Colonial Africa." In *The Oxford Handbook of Modern African History*, edited by John Parker and Richard Reid, 171–188. Oxford: Oxford University Press. http://www.oxfordhandbooks.com/view/10.1093/oxfordhb/9780199572472.001.0001/oxfordhb-9780199572472

Said, E. W. 1978. *Orientalism*. New York: Pantheon Books.

Samassékou, A. 2011. "From Eurocentrism to a Polycentric Vision of the World: Advocacy for a Paradigm Shift." *Diogenes* 58 (1-2): 147–158. doi:10.1177/0392192112448295.

Schulz, Wolfram, ed. 2011. *ICCS 2009 Technical Report*. Amsterdam: International Association for the Evaluation of Educational Achievement.

Schulz, Wolfram, and Pierre Foy, eds. 2004. *IEA Civic Education Study Technical Report*. Amsterdam: IEA.

Schulz, W., J. Fraillon, G. Agrusti, J. Ainley, B. Losito, and T. Friedman. 2017. *Becoming Citizens in a Changing World: IEA International Civic and Citizenship Education Study 2016 International Report*. Amsterdam: IEA.

Semali, Ladislaus, and Joe Kincheloe. 2002. *What is Indigenous Knowledge? Voices from the Academy Indigenous Knowledge and Schooling*. New York: Routledge.

Sewell, Whitney, Christina E. Horsford, Kanisha Coleman, and Charity S. Watkins. 2016. "Vile Vigilance: An Integrated Theoretical Framework for Understanding the State of Black Surveillance." *Journal of Human Behavior in the Social Environment* 26: 1–16. doi:10.1080/10911359.2015.1127735.

Spivak, G. C. 1988. "Can the Subaltern Speak?" In *Marxism and the Interpretation of Culture*, edited by Cary Nelson and Lawrence Grossberg, 271–313. Champaign-Urbana: The University of Illinois Press.

Starkey, Hugh. 2012. "Education, Social Cohesion and Human Rights." In *Rethinking Education for Social Cohesion: International Case Studies*, edited by Maha Shuayb, 37–49. Basingstoke: Palgrave Macmillan.

Tawil, Sobhi. 2013. *Education for 'Global Citizenship': A Framework for Discussion*. Paris: UNESCO.

Temu, Arnold, and Bonaventure Swai. 1981. *Historians and Africanist History: A Critique; Post-Colonial Historiography Examined*. London: Zed Pr.

United Nations Educational, Scientific and Cultural Organization. (2015). *Global Citizenship Education Topics and Learning Objectives*. Paris: UNESCO.

Vavrus, Frances Katherine, and L. Bartlett. 2013. *Teaching in Tension International Pedagogies, National Policies, and Teachers' Practices in Tanzania*. Rotterdam [u.a.]: SensePublishers.

Villaverde, Leila E. 2008. *Feminist Theories and Education Primer: Primer*. New York: Peter Lang. Peter Lang Primer

Waghid, Yusef, and Nuraan Davids. 2013. *Citizenship, Education and Violence: On Disrupted Potentialities and Becoming*. http://search.ebscohost.com/login.aspx?direct=true&scope=site&db=nlebk&db=nlabk&AN=683989

Weah, A. 2012. "Hopes and Uncertainties: Liberia's Journey to End Impunity." *International Journal of Transitional Justice* 6 (2): 331–343. doi:10.1093/ijtj/ijs007.

Williams, Dierdre. 2013. "When 'Minimalist' Conceptions of Citizenship Reveal Their Complexity." *Citizenship Teaching & Learning* 8 (3): 357–369. doi:10.1386/ctl.8.3.357_1.

Willis, W. Bruce. 1998. *The Adinkra Dictionary: A Visual Primer on the Language of Adinkra*. Washington, D.C: Pyramid Complex.

Wingo, Ajume H. 2008. "Akan Philosophy of the Person." In *Stanford Encyclopedia of Philosophy*, edited by Edward N. Zalta. http://plato.stanford.edu/archives/fall2008/entries/akan-person/

Wingo, Ajume H. 2010. "The Odyssey of Human Rights." *Transition* 102: 120–138.

Wingo, Ajume H. 2015. "The Immortals in Our midst: Why Democracies in Africa Need Them." *The Journal of Ethics* 19 (3-4): 237–255. doi:10.1007/s10892-015-9209-2.

Wiredu, Kwasi, and Kwame Gyekye, eds. 1992. *Person and Community: Ghanaian Philosophical Studies I. Cultural Heritage and Contemporary Change*, vol. 1. Washington, D.C: Council for Research in Values and Philosophy.

Wait-citizenship: youth civic development in transition

Michelle J. Bellino

ABSTRACT
This paper builds a theory of wait-citizenship, wherein the lack of opportunities for structural inclusion has contributed to young people's liminal positioning in society and their struggles to become social adults while seeking equality, democratic freedoms, and a sense of belonging. Two decades after civil war, Guatemalan youth are routinely reminded of the fragility of their democracy and instructed not to make demands for inclusive and transformative citizenship. As young people become 'wait-citizens' they develop strategies for navigating precarious openings between dangerous actions and coercive structures, often in ways that do not conform to Western, liberal expectations. The paper argues for broader conceptions of civic agency to account for how young people make decisions about exercising their civic voice, particularly in settings where legacies of authoritarianism constrain long-awaited democratic freedoms.

Guatemala's better future

The bulletin board in Profe Castillo's room is decorated with colourful paper notes scattered under the question, 'What do you promise to do to make Guatemala a better country?' Eleventh and twelfth grade students posted promises to abide by laws, stop littering, create jobs, and vote 'for the president who will make Guatemala succeed'. An elite-serving school, students here focused on how they could wield their economic power to improve national security and development. Paper did not stick to the walls of the humid rural classrooms, or even the cement walls of the school catering to working-class students several kilometers away, but this same question emerged in every classroom I entered in 'post-war' Guatemala, a fragile democracy suffering high rates of violence. Teachers across diverse communities actively communicated that Guatemala was in dire need of change, and that youth had a role to play. Through the formal and hidden curriculum, strong messages of youth empowerment were paired with caution and concern about the parameters of good citizenship in a fragile democracy, and the obligations of the post-war generation to contribute to the better future.

In a state with a long history of authoritarian governance, inequality, ongoing popular resistance struggles – and today, experiencing a violent aftermath of civil war – I expected particular communities to guide young people either toward civic compliance or resistance.

In particular, I anticipated that marginalised communities such as rural indigenous and urban working-class populations would privilege transformative civic stances with goals of reallocating wealth and power, preparing young people to join ongoing struggles for justice and equity. Instead, I found that young people's impressions of their role in shaping Guatemala's better future were, in many cases, profoundly passive and complacent. Young people on the margins voiced frustrations and desires for change, before falling into fatalistic stances that over time little had changed through collective action. For many, desires to bring about change sat uneasily alongside hopelessness that Guatemala had not changed, could not change, and that ordinary citizens could not be effective agents of change. To make Guatemala 'a better country', they set their goals on taking care of their families, staying out of trouble, advancing their education, and securing employment. At the other extreme, young people explained that they had to put everything on the line for a better Guatemala. They recognised that the state would not take care of people 'like them' and that it fell to the most marginalised to achieve social justice for themselves. When questions about changing Guatemala emerged, these young people insisted that they could not sit idle and wait for the government to act, as time had proven that change only came from the people and not the state. They spoke about the risks endured by those who took action to shift the status quo, the high rates of violence targeting change agents, the narrowing space for dissent, and the need to move cautiously into unconventional spaces to be seen and heard. I was left with an unsettling question: which of these young people were more poised to engage in their post-war democracy: those willing to join high-risk resistance movements, or those valuing patience for the sake of stability?

Drawing on Victor Turner's (1967) accounting of liminality as a transitional phase in which identities and social values undergo radical transformation, I conceive of post-war generations as structurally positioned in a liminal stage. Societies in transition shape citizens in transition, who anticipate transformations embedded in democratisation processes, but remain wary of authoritarian legacies and conflict structures from the past that survive transitions and undermine democratic reform (Holston and Caldeira 1998). The transition itself thus comprises a liminal condition between *Guatemala at war* and *Guatemala after war*, though all citizens appear to be entrapped by the violent present, 'no longer' at war and 'not yet' at peace (96). The rules of the authoritarian past do not fully apply, nor do the rules of the elusive democratic future, yet elements of both coexist, simultaneously expanding and constraining opportunities for civic participation. How, then, should citizens engage in the civic life of a not-yet democracy when they desire change: should they embrace security and conform to the boundaries of the authoritarian past, when collective organising was 'tantamount to a death sentence' (Grandin, Levenson, and Oglesby 2011, 361), or should they take on the risks necessary to make public demands, accessing newfound freedoms of expression to insist on the democracy they were promised?

Youth civic development in post-war Guatemala is influenced by legacies of the past and their undercurrents in the present. In effect the legacy of the loyal, 'apolitical' citizen who strategically survived the war through wilful non-involvement, intersects with the transitional state's call for patient citizens who acquiesce to positions of 'waithood' during times of uncertainty. Together these conditions contribute to young people's liminal positioning in society and their struggles to become social adults while pursuing equality, democratic freedoms, and a sense of belonging. On issues of collective organising, popular resistance, and political involvement, Guatemalan youth are routinely reminded of the fragility of their democracy and instructed not to make demands but instead to *wait* – for peace, stability, opportunity, voice, inclusion; to wait for the changed nation they were promised at the end of the conflict; to 'wait … for returns on their investments of hope' (Burrell 2013, 165). In postponing their demands for inclusive and transformative citizenship, young people in this society become 'wait-citizens'.

This article builds a theoretical argument based on 14 months of ethnographic data gathered from 2010–2012 in four school-community sites, two in the urban setting of Guatemala City and two rural villages in the province of Izabal. In each setting, I spent 6–12 weeks attending secondary school classes and accompanying focal students from their schools to their homes and communities. Semistructured and unstructured interviews complement observations, centering on how young people make meaning of their educational encounters with injustice and develop a sense of civic agency. I maintained contact with a number of participants and, in 2015, conducted individual and group interviews remotely with several high school graduates, now working or attending college and some heavily immersed in youth activist movements. Throughout the research process, I conceived of citizenship as rooted in youth's daily experiences with the civil contract within and outside of schools, rather than rely on pre-existing theoretical constructs or adult-constructed projections of what young people should know. Long-term ethnographic immersion allowed for the documentation of everyday civic experiences and youth interpretations.

Elsewhere I describe in more detail the research design, methods, and findings particular to each community (Bellino 2015, 2016, 2017). Here I draw on data from youth participants across rural and urban contexts to highlight the resonance of the construct of wait-citizenship in emergent democracies such as Guatemala, and the ways that young people – particularly members of historically oppressed groups – develop a sense of civic identity and agency in a society they consider 'not yet' a democracy. I demonstrate that nonparticipation in issues of civic significance and professed disinterest in politics can, at times, be indicative of young people's critical awareness of inequity, deep distrust in corrupt institutions, and lack of confidence in their capability to penetrate an unjust system. The strategies youth develop as wait-citizens navigate precarious openings in the spaces between dangerous actions and coercive structures – often in ways that do not conform to Western, liberal expectations for engaged and active citizenship. I link these findings to the shifting nature of youth transitions in an era of globalisation, as young people increasingly endure protracted periods of 'waithood', unable to meet cultural and societal expectations to become socially recognised adults. I close with implications for future research, arguing for expanded conceptions of youth civic agency to better account for how young people make decisions about exercising their civic voice, particularly in settings where they are taught that their agency lies not in shaping the better future but in waiting for it to arrive.

Democratic disjuncture and citizenship in a not-yet democracy

From 1960–1996, Guatemala experienced one of the most brutal civil wars in Latin America's history. Nearly two decades after peace negotiations, Guatemala's post-war society is hardly at peace. The work of human rights advocates, lawyers, judges, activists, journalists, and forensic scientists seeking truth, justice, and reparations for the past; indigenous communities resisting mega-development projects; and even community leaders with local aims such as organising rural peoples has generated a new wave of repressive and violent responses aimed at discrediting the activist voice and the act of collective organising as a valid mechanism of social change. In other words, Guatemala's authoritarian practices are not past, but present 'in the form of new victims' (Grandin 2004, 171).

Amidst a host of post-war challenges, Guatemala is experiencing a severe 'youth problem' (Burrell 2013, 20). Reflective of the global youth bulge, nearly 40% of Guatemalans are younger than age 15. A recent World Bank report (de Hoyos, Rogers, and Székely 2015) documents a growing population of *ninis* – youth who neither (*ni*) attend school nor (*ni*) work – across Latin America. The report identifies a relationship between the growth rate of *ninis*, particularly the increased proportion of male youth (ages 15–24) out of school and out of work, and the rise in violence across Central America. Among the many shortcomings placed on the shoulders of young Guatemalans, ranging from their disregard for the past to their alleged absence of moral values, the 'youth problem' faults young people for not embracing their roles as citizens in a democracy. On cross-national measures of citizenship such as the International Civic and Citizenship Education Study, Guatemalan youth expressed support for dictatorships and authoritarian governments over democracy when they stood to bring about 'order and safety' and 'economic benefits.' Meanwhile, they reported significantly lower trust in their national government, political parties, courts of justice, police, and people in general than their Latin American peers (Schultz et al. 2011, 42–43). More worrying, these studies demonstrate that youth do not trust in fellow citizens or their country's democratic institutions to resolve the challenges they face. Instead, these structural challenges fall to individuals to surmount on their own.

Once envisioned as the ambassadors of the post-war democracy and peaceful future, youth's role in society has shifted from 'a solution to be cultivated' to 'a problem to be resolved' (Dryden-Peterson, Bellino, and Chopra 2015, 636). A United Nations Development Program representative (2012) noted that youth, 'are not the future but the present of Guatemala', conveying a generation so burdened by the challenges of the present that they are unable to think or act beyond them (para 4). Meanwhile, growing numbers of criminal youth and climbing rates of youth homicides have provoked, and been provoked by, the grim reality that 'young people [are] locked into a dead end future' (Adams 2011, 45). On a societal level, many adults have come to fear and pity young people rather than support and empower them.

In and outside of schools, young people have daily experiences with civic agents and institutions that shape their understanding of the social contract, fairness and justice, and individual and collective roles within a democratic society (Flanagan et al. 2010, Levinson 2012). Young people in all societies come to understand democracy and the civil contract through experiences with their weaknesses and 'disjunctures', as well as their strengths and 'convergence' with democratic ideals (Rubin 2012). Particularly in transitional democracies, the deficiencies and exclusions evoked through 'democratic disjuncture' (Holston and Caldeira 1998) powerfully resonate with historical injustice and the illusory promises of the better future. For many Guatemalans living the violent aftermath of war, these breaches imply more than the failures of a fragile post-war state. Gaps in the civil contract evoke the deception and corruption embedded in the promises made to transform Guatemalan society. They signify unresolved authoritarian legacies, remnants of the authoritarian past that 'lie in the fissures between formally democratic institutions and the institutionalization of undemocratic practices' (Cesarini and Hite 2004, 5). They signify that Guatemala remains *not yet* a democracy. Democratic transitions thus promise to expand opportunities for civic participation, while legacies of authoritarianism produce democratic disjunctures, simultaneously subverting these opportunities.

Guatemala is not alone in its uneven transition from war to war's violent aftermath, with post-war citizens caught in between, wondering whether and when they might characterise their society as 'post'. South Africa's 'born free' generation faces ongoing racism, inequality, segregation, and a lack of opportunities for social advancement. Set against the optimism for inclusion in the post-Apartheid 'Rainbow Nation', disenfranchised youth have constructed alternative futures through delinquency (Swartz, Hamilton Harding, and De Lannoy 2012). Youth in post-genocide Rwanda contend with a society so restrictive that they are prohibited from criticising government or speaking openly about ethnicity. Sommers (2012) finds that youth are 'stuck' in 'endless liminality' (3) as they struggle to meet cultural expectations and access opportunities that facilitate transitions to social adulthood. Ignoring the experiences of youth who feel increasingly marginalised, Rwanda has cultivated 'almost an entire generation of failed adults' (193). In post-war El Salvador where contemporary youth violence is on par with neighbouring Guatemala, citizens view their democracy as 'stunted' (2), 'backwards' (163), and 'worse than war' (Moodie 2010). Across these contexts, post-war generations were fated to inherit more inclusive, liberal, and equitable societies than the ones their parents experienced. Instead, their structural exclusion and political alienation are illustrative of a global rise in 'failed citizens' (Zaalouk 2015) and 'failed citizenship' (Banks 2015).

Building on the concept of failed states, Zaalouk (2015) conceptualises 'failed citizens' as 'unable to function as a community and … not capable of fulfilling their obligations to their compatriots' (para. 3). In the absence of opportunities to exercise their civic voice, failed citizens turn 'to brutal violence, total apathy or some form of atomized existence' (para. 3). Coining a similar concept that extends to stable democracies, Banks (2015) identifies citizens who are structurally excluded and politically alienated from the nation-state as 'victims of failed citizenship' (152). Failure is the result of 'social, cultural, economic, and political systems within a nation-state [that] prevent marginalized groups from attaining full structural inclusion into the nation' (152). Consequently these citizens do not internalise the values of the nation-state, develop a sense of identity with it, or cultivate a sense of political efficacy or engagement. Both Zaalouk and Banks seek to understand the experience of citizens who have legal status but are structurally marginalised within democratic states, either because of the state's willful or unwitting denial of the civil contract.

Across diverse contexts, studies find that neoliberal economic reforms mapped onto persistent social inequalities have had made it more difficult for young people to achieve and sustain social adulthood. Theories of waiting, waithood, and 'wait adulthood' (Sommers 2012, 3) seek to understand this 'period of suspension between childhood and adulthood … a prolonged adolescence or an involuntary delay in reaching adulthood' (Honwana 2013, 4). The concept denotes a temporal dimension to waiting for opportunities to emerge, as well as an affective response to the disillusionment that young people internalise when they do not see opportunities to shape viable futures. If waithood derives from unfulfilled expectations in the midst of reconfigured opportunity structures, then democratic transitions surely add to this uncertainty, particularly when reforms are considered partial or inauthentic. How do young people positioned as wait-citizens develop a sense of agency to participate in, and transform, the civic life of their not-yet democracy? To begin to answer this question, we first need to consider what constitutes an expression of civic agency, and according to whose criteria.

Youth agency and apathy

Civic engagement is considered a near-universal dimension of youth development and an essential element of resilient democracies (Flanagan and Levine 2010; Youniss et al. 2002), a particular concern in transitional states where democracy lacks a record of stability. Active citizenship depends on a conviction that one's actions will make a difference, however small the scale and however broad the timeline for change, as well as a predictable logic that actions lead to consequences, however that effectiveness is measured. That is, to be agentic is not simply to act, but 'to intentionally make things happen by one's actions' (Bandura 2001, 2). Civic action also necessitates 'self-esteem and a sense that one is worthy of participation in political life' (Lloyd 2005, 352). Young people's sense of civic efficacy thus mediates their agency and their likelihood to take action in a particular situation. Yet what counts as action is debatable.

In designing measures for civic efficacy, we often embed unexamined assumptions about what kinds of decisions and actions showcase agency and engagement, in contrast to those that signify apathy or disengagement. As Durham (2008) reminds us, ideas about youth apathy are always linked to ideas about how youth agency should be expressed, so that certain actions become labelled agentic while others are dismissed as passive (157). She further argues that Western researchers too easily find agency in acts of refusal and rebellion (164–165), dismissing expressions of agency that might better resonate with local norms and values. Relatedly, citizenship education that is transformative in orientation is (often implicitly) valued by researchers studying these contexts as higher impact and more socially conscious, despite awareness that expressions of civic action are contextually variable and culturally, politically, and historically contingent (Levinson and Berumen 2007). What might we miss when we expect youth citizenship to conform to a set of expectations that have been developed largely in the context of stable democratic settings?

Based on findings in Guatemala, I argue that we risk overlooking a complex set of negotiations underlying youth decision-making if we inadvertently limit youth agency to expressions of resistance to dominant structures. Similarly, we risk missing more subtle expressions of resistance if we restrict our analysis to actions that are public, collective, and compliant, as Levinson (2012) notes we already limit conceptions of civic action. Rather than asking why are young people not more engaged or active in national and local politics or community decision-making, we might expand our questions to consider what underlies their decisions to act and not act in particular ways, in particular circumstances, as well as what young people perceive as the forces obstructing their capacity for particular kinds of action.

These questions are worth asking in stable democratic contexts, but they prove particularly important in states emerging from conflict and authoritarianism, where democracy is embraced as key to transforming society. Post-war transitions and peacebuilding efforts depend on active and authentic civic engagement, so that citizens develop a sense of obligation to contribute to democratisation, social cohesion, and violence prevention, goals often imagined to take root in schools. But in post-war societies individuals often learn, through the experience of injustice and its enduring legacies, not to see themselves as the protagonists of their pasts, presents, and futures, but instead to look to intangible forces such as a 'culture of violence' as accountable agents (Oglesby 2007). There is often a sense that both violence and the peace process 'happened *to* us' (Lederach 2005, 60, emphasis added), rather than represent deliberate choices and actions made by civic actors. Perceptions of powerlessness not only lead to individual withdrawal, but also risk becoming a driver of violence.

At the war's end, Guatemala's truth commission noted in their report that the institutionalisation of state violence would have a profound effect on how citizens' perceive and interact with their post-war democracy. The Commission ((CEH, 1996/MoS) wrote:

> the state tried to destroy within people's hearts the potential and will for change, in the present as well as for the future … to make it clear that, regardless of one's actions or intentions, it was impossible to change the established order. (CEH, 1996/MoS, 143)

Real and perceived lack of agency explains why large numbers of Guatemalan youth turn to criminal pathways, even when doing so limits them to 'necroliving', in which they 'control life through their power to take it away' (Levenson 2013, 6).

If powerlessness to affect the course of one's life is a legacy of war, research on youth citizenship in conflict-affected contexts needs to account for how young people develop a sense of civic efficacy and a belief that their actions matter. State repression and complicity in rights abuses degenerate trust between a state and its citizens, as well as interpersonal trust and interdependence within civil society. Under these conditions, how do young people come to see themselves as individual or collective agents of change?

While wait-citizenship structurally positions youth as compliant and patient in the face of incomplete political transitions, it is important to note that waithood does not denote youth 'inactively 'waiting' for their situation to change' (Honwana 2013, 4), although that is sometimes how young people respond to the structural constraints and exclusion they experience (Dhillon and Yousef 2009; Jeffrey 2010). As Auyero (2012) makes clear, emphasising the waiting of subordinated groups in relation to the state is not meant as a deprivation of citizens' agency, but rather a way of capturing one's agency *vis-a-vis* the state. He writes, 'True, they are agents; but *in their interactions with the state*, their sense of agency is minimal to non-existent' (154, emphasis in original). In the following sections, I highlight everyday decisions young people made in the context of schools, homes, and communities to demonstrate the ways that wait-citizenship has led to strategies that are engaged and agentic but could be interpreted as passive and apathetic without a fuller understanding of the context from which they emerge.

Everyday negotiations

In order to showcase the ways that young people's possibilities for taking on engaged and active roles in society are doubted, disrupted, and delayed in everyday spaces, this section is organised around a set of recurrent questions young people ask of civic action and participation. The first concern pertains to the precarity of the present moment, which can function as both a call to action and a constraint limiting one's sense of self-efficacy. Importantly, young people demonstrate that decisions about taking action are weighed against the costs and benefits of both action and inaction, asking themselves: *What will happen if I take action? What will happen if I do not take action?* In the second section, young people question the long-term value of their participation in civil society, raising concerns that powerful structural forces nullify civic action and collective movements. Differentiating between meaningless and meaningful actions, they ask: *If I act, will anything really change?* In the final section, young people interpret democratic advances with scepticism that change is sustainable and responsive to civil society pressure. Guarding against disappointment, they ask: *How do I know change is authentic and enduring?* Across these instances, which take place in schools and in youth-led community spaces, young people are positioned as citizens with agency to invest in civil society, but also cautioned about the coercive structures that will thwart their intended goals. In an effort to identify opportunities for effective, secure, and meaningful participation, young people respond to the structural barriers in their lives occasionally through direct resistance, but also through avoidance, withdrawal, and defeatism.

Navigating precarious openings: What will happen if I act? What will happen if I do not act?

Once a modest fishing village, Río Verde has been profoundly transformed since an international extraction company based a massive mining operation there. Indigenous resistance movements protesting the unauthorised presence and unjust practices of companies engaged in mega-development projects across Guatemala have become critical sites of civic and political conflict. Communities come together to protest and physically blockade entrances to mines for not consulting community members about their development plans, for dispossessing peoples of their ancestral land, for poor working conditions and the withholding of scarce jobs, and for repressing anyone who opposes their presence or practices. In response, the Guatemalan government has instituted martial law and used the military to stabilise communities where companies and local peoples, largely indigenous Maya, are in conflict. When I asked a class of twelfth graders, all of whom expressed concerns about the mine, whether they would consider organising an opposition movement like other villages had, the room fell quiet. Protesting the mine, they explained, was not only a useless exercise at resisting a powerful corporation, but also a death wish. Amílcar explained that he admired other communities' resistance efforts, but the risks of physical retaliation were too high. Moreover, if they opposed the mine, the military – still a feared institution for many whose families were targeted during the civil war – would surely take action to quiet the people. Caught between two powerful forces, neither of which listened to indigenous adults, let alone youths, young people demonstrated the careful ways they negotiated the risk structures in their lives.

Looking ahead to future prospects for employment and local security, young people on the cusp of high school graduation recognised that the mining corporation might be equally, if not more, likely than the state to deliver basic social services. The mine was the purveyor of the new economic order, a symbol of modernisation and national development, and the sole institution in their community promising future employment opportunities. Even those who vehemently opposed the mine were trying to secure jobs there. In this context, the mining company was conceived as a 'para-state' agent, more capable of fulfilling citizens' basic needs than the state itself (Adams 2011). Historically excluded from the benefits of state citizenship, these villagers stood to benefit more from the hopeful possibilities that the mine would open a school and apprentice youth into the relevant knowledge and skill-set required of employees, build infrastructure to link the remote village to other regions, and provide them with electricity and clean water, than the sure repercussions faced by an organised resistance movement. People held onto the potential of these promises, hoping that the mine would become a 'good neighbour', even as their river grew polluted and there remained no signs of infrastructure or local employment. Feelings of exclusion and powerlessness in this community ran deep, and there were abundant examples in the lives of these youth that the choice between participating in high-risk resistance movements, and turning the other way in the face of injustice, was self-evident.

On another occasion, following an instance of mob violence exercised as a form of 'people's justice', these students scrutinised the choices available to them in the face of pervasive criminal violence and impunity on the part of a distrustful state. Rather than intervene or call the police, they explained that the best option was to 'become invisible'. Rosa's comment summarised their view of the ideal response to violent outbreaks, a strategy that was applicable to a number of situations in their lives. Rosa said, 'What you want to do – the only thing you can do – is remove yourself.' Like many conversations at this school, this one gave way to the relative powerlessness students felt over changing the course of their lives and community. These young people wanted their country to improve, but they did not see themselves playing a role in reforming structures that had historically oppressed people like them. Thus without trying, they had already failed. David explained, 'You try to improve your life, you try to escape … and they keep pushing you down, so why try to change anything?' He held out his hands and inched them toward one another, shrinking the space in between: 'You want to stay in the middle.' This theme of 'staying in the middle' by achieving invisibility or neutrality, by distinctly *avoiding* civic issues, ran through many of the conversations during formal class sessions and unstructured time at this school.

From afar, the decision for youth in this community to not act in the face of what are arguably the most critical civic issues in their lives might be interpreted as apathy or a lack of awareness of the larger structural issues at stake, but what underlies their decisions *not* to act is a complex calculation of the risks and benefits of both action and inaction. Moreover, these attitudes were supported by their teachers and other adults in their lives, who frequently emphasised the structural constraints and dangers placed on civic action with transformative aims, often at the expense of their potential contributions. These young people knew well the constraints that would impede their actions and came to see themselves as ineffective agents of change. They further legitimised choices to disengage as markers of mature and responsible citizenship in a fragile state where conflict-avoidance presumably stabilised volatile and unpredictable relationships.

In other instances, the idea that one could only exert agency in invisible and inaudible ways became cause for frustration. For example, Arturo, a youth activist and university student studying in the capital, spoke to the dilemma felt by wait-citizens:

> The situation [today] is the same as the conflict, but what is different is the movement. Do you see how few of us there are [protesting]? Back then, there were many … they had the support of the people. The people gave the guerrilla food. They guided them through the mountains. They wanted the guerrilla to struggle and fight. Today, people call us criminals for what we are doing. They think we carry guns. They think we are terrorists. They do not support us. They call us ugly names, or they pass and say, '*oh look, more protests. Call the police to get those youths out of the way!*' What is happening is that Guatemalans don't see their children in this movement … All those people who don't support us, they are also affected. We are the same. We want the same things. But they think we should just pass time and wait for things to change … without making demands. There is complete *dis*-involvement, and that's what the people want.

Arturo's comment circles between explanations for the lack of public interest in justice movements, ranging from fear and criminalisation, to apathy, overexposure, and inconvenience.

Motivating Arturo's actions is a sense of the disjuncture between idealised democracy and the deficiencies of Guatemala's current democratic arrangements.

Nullified actions: if I act, will anything really change?

Recognizing Guatemala's 'democratic disjunctures', young people consistently questioned their capacity to make a difference, whether participating in the current system or acting against it. Across interviews and focus groups with wealthy and poor, urban and rural, indigenous and non-indigenous youth, the questions I posed that most frequently puzzled them were those that sought to understand where young people in their community felt efficacious and supported. I asked, 'Where do you feel like you can make decisions for yourself? Who are the people you trust? When do adults listen to youth?' These questions were often met with silence, or tentative claims that there were no spaces like that.

Beti, a social studies teacher in an urban and self-described liberal school catering to the working class, explained that civic education was challenging, 'because you have to be honest about the inequality and the violence that we live ... We talk about how the country is, and how we want it to be.' On many occasions, she guided her students through critiques of Guatemala's entrenched inequalities and democratic dysfunction, encouraging them to use their education to create a more just and inclusive society. Simultaneously, a common refrain in this class, 'Our country is military right now', served to remind students of their need to be cautious about what they expected and demanded of their democracy. One afternoon, Beti assigned a set of review questions inquiring about Guatemala's political structure. She was both worried and delighted when students refused to give the textbook answers, explaining that they classified their government not as democratic but as 'corrupt', 'hierarchical', 'oligarchical', 'feudal', 'militaristic', and 'anti-democratic'. One student, Javier, explained that the nature of Guatemala's democracy was hard to pin down: 'We are not at peace. Some say we are still at war .... We are not democratic. Our state is repressive. I don't know what we are. I guess we are something in the middle. Maybe we are both?' Javier's unwillingness to characterise Guatemala's political structure as anything but in-between speaks to the liminality experienced by wait-citizens as they manage the coexistence of freedoms written into formal legislation and the *de facto* reality that legacies of the past continue to undermine those freedoms.

Volunteering in a clean-up project to remove gang graffiti from a local park, Javier and his friends spoke about the power of collective action and the need for local togetherness to overcome division and indifference in a city reeling with violence. After several hours of work, they concluded that the clean-up was a 'publicity stunt' where young people stood alongside adults posing with paintbrushes that they put down the moment the camera was gone. When the event ended, students decided not to volunteer in future projects. Initially, I heard these students asking: why should they help, when others were not? But I later realised that what contributed to their frustration was far more complicated than the idea that collective action without collective participation was unfair. As they discussed amongst themselves, they learned that the park had been cleaned several times before, and each time gangs returned to vandalise it. In their refusal, they asked poignant questions drawing from their experiences with injustice and insecurity: what was the use in repeatedly clearing gang graffiti, when the state was unwilling to protect citizens from the violence caused by gangs? More complicated, the state was complicit in the structural marginalisation that drove youth to join gangs and perpetuate criminal violence, for which working-class youth were blamed. Students' awareness of these contradictions reminded them of the limits on their agency in a state with an inverted civil contract, where citizens were expected to take care of themselves while the state oppressed citizens. They could take action, as long as they did not expect too much, for too long.

Anger and frustration toward the state extended to formal means of democratic participation as well. I met with young people during the 2007, 2011, and 2015 presidential elections, and in each of these election cycles I have been struck by the number of youth who are politically informed and civically engaged in a number of justice issues, but who opt to abstain from voting or choose to vote null in an act of resistance. In each case, youth explained their limited choices for a political leader and refusal to take part in a 'rigged' election, supporting a government that changed names but whose oppressive philosophies remained constant. Preparing to participate in her first election, Paulina, who graduated from Beti's class and is now a university student, explained, 'No matter who wins, Guatemala loses.' She and several of her friends opted instead to exercise their right to vote by voting null, which they saw as distinct from abstaining altogether, since the state was obligated to count these votes and could not attribute them to voter apathy. Her friend elaborated on their limited choices:

> When you vote, you do not vote for the best candidate .... You look at them and say: this one is corrupt and will steal from the people; this one is a soldier and will repress and kill the people; and this one, well maybe he's a puppet controlled by the oligarchy, and will just do what they want. There is no best. You vote for the least worst.

In some cases, these decisions were actively deliberated by youth about how to express their voice as a collective unit. Ironically, even as they rallied collective support to resist the system through null voting, they subjected their actions to their own doubts and scepticism. Ultimately, they understood that their actions would not result in a better president and would be easily interpreted by the state as evidence of illiteracy. Moreover, they would never be able to celebrate the full success of their resistance, because the media would underreport the number of null votes. At the same time, they assured one another that this action was not meaningless. The impact, they believed, would be 'internal', implying that the new regime would have to govern, knowing the extent of people's distrust. This calculation of whether voting, or any civic action for that matter, would make a difference, impacted the decisions young people made as they decided not only whether to vote, but how to participate in what, for many, was their first presidential election as a legal adult.

Maintaining an 'ethos of pessimism': How do I know change is authentic and enduring?

Although Guatemala remains a site of concern for its failures as a democracy (Isaacs 2010), recently it has also been praised for a successful transnational, intergenerational, pluralistic civil society movement that penetrated the state's highest-ranking political office. Frustrated with corruption and violence, Guatemalans organised and strategised on social media, insisting that they would no longer tolerate criminals in both 'state offices and the streets'. Tired of waiting for change, citizens gathered in the streets and demanded the resignation of their president. In September 2015, President Otto Pérez Molina was forced to resign and has since been sent to prison for his involvement in a multimillion-dollar customs scandal. In many ways, Guatemalans had accomplished an impossible feat – through civil society organising, they held public officials accountable for democratic failures. The causal linkages between civil society organising and the outcome of the scandal were praised in media representations of Guatemala's 'anti-corruption spring'.

But inside Guatemala, democratic optimism was met with cautious scepticism and concerns that these high-level changes would have limited impact. Alejandro, studying sociology at an urban university, explained:

> I do not think this is a victory of the people .... The will of the populace is nothing but screams of anger and frustration at closed doors, windows, and walls. Slowly people are starting to become an active part of society, but many do not realize yet that we do not hold the power to lead our country towards what we want.

Meanwhile, Gregorio from Río Verde wrote to tell me that nothing had changed. The scandal in the presidency remained largely irrelevant to villagers' everyday struggles, and everyone was still hoping for a job at the mine.

It initially surprised me that the successes of these recent transformations were so easily reinterpreted as symbolic concessions. Alejandro and his anarchist university student group explained that powerful forces orchestrated these changes, rather than civil society pressure. Pérez Molina was brought down in order to protect other elites, who maintained their power in the shadows. More problematically, many pointed to the newly elected President Jimmy Morales, a comedian with little political experience backed by military hard-liners, as further evidence of the entrenched power of the state military and elite oligarchy. The gap between how these moments are regarded by those observing and those experiencing them evokes questions about whether Guatemalans themselves – or any social group for that matter – are in a position to see change when they are immersed in it. Is change visible without the passage of time? And yet if we ignore their frustrated, sceptical, and at times disinterested reactions, we miss something essential in how young people experience their lives as wait-citizens, where democratic promises are overdue. We miss the ways citizenship, (im)patience, and hope interact in a fragile democracy.

Ideas that change is not happening, is not happening fast enough, or is not authentic are likely common experiences in transitional states. Here we see evidence of how perceptions of change and stasis influence the relationships young people forge with one another, their state, and themselves as they develop a sense of their civic agency. Lederach (2005) identifies an 'ethos of pessimism' (54), which functions as 'hope coupled with indifference' (55). He argues that in societies undergoing transition, judging whether change is authentic and sustainable requires 'a wait-and-see approach' (57), set against the 'continuous and immediate' (58) suspicion that changes are superficial. The authenticity of these changes is measured through everyday experiences with democracy, so that the ongoing exclusion and denial of indigenous rights, persistent conflicts between citizens and global corporate interests, the criminalisation of working-class youth, the narrowing space for dissent, and the privatisation of public goods, contribute to the sense that popular struggles have had limited impact. The nature of these ongoing conflicts '[has] prompted some to ask: Has anything really changed in Guatemala?' (Guatemala Human Rights Commission 2015–2016, 7). Maintaining an 'ethos of pessimism' prevents young people from celebrating incremental and modest successes, but it also guards them against future disappointment when these advances are revealed to be partial, inauthentic, or short-lived.[1]

Postponing democracy

State fragility conveys to young people that the state is unwilling or unable to protect and provide for them, or to uphold their basic rights. Guatemalan youth recognise the narrowing of opportunities to participate in their democracy, and they develop a sense of civic agency in tandem with awareness of constraints. Conventional expressions of democratic citizenship, such as voting in elections, volunteering, and participating in collective action projects, reporting crimes to law enforcement, intervening in local disputes, and advocating for rights and inclusion, are widely perceived to be inhibited by inept and corrupt structures (Isaacs 2010). There is hesitance across classrooms and homes to cast Guatemala as a democratic state, labelling the government 'military' but rhetorically insisting on the political structure of a democracy. The continuation of conflict structures within government and uninterrupted legacies of authoritarianism, including those embedded in the educational opportunity structure, render Guatemala no longer authoritarian, but not yet democratic. The discursive construction of these contradictions – often for the purpose of cautioning young people about the limits on civic action – signifies teachers' and parents' own positioning as wait-citizens, caught between democratic ideals and disjunctive realities. In the absence of security, structural inclusion, and voice, citizens have been forced to '[create] new geographies of political intervention and citizenship' (Honwana 2013, 18) in order to be seen and heard.

Youth voices reveal caution and careful consideration about whether and when to take public action, as well as concerns over being silenced or discredited. While some are empowered to participate and embrace resistance movements, others retreat – on the grounds that personal security, responsible citizenship in a fragile democracy, or both, demand withdrawal from the public sphere. Large numbers of Guatemalan youth have found protective value in strategic withdrawal from collective action, formal participation in political processes, and even from interactions in community spaces (Winton 2005). Structures that fail to integrate and accommodate the perspectives of indigenous, rural, poor, and working-class peoples force youth to rethink where they can be effective and secure, fundamentally altering where they invest effort. Non-participation in this context does not necessarily signify a lack of civic knowledge or empowerment, but speaks to impressions of deeply flawed and untrustworthy institutions, and scepticism that ordinary citizens can steer change. In the process, young people are conditioned to avoid risk and postpone claims on the state, instructed that change will come with time, rather than as an intentional result of civil society demands and disruptions. Arturo captures this tension succinctly when he says that all citizens want peace, stability, and inclusion, but some 'think we should just pass time and wait for things to change, without … making demands.' In his refusal to wait, he is cast as a social agitator, endures physical risks, and contends with his own sense of fatalism.

The irony is that patience and pessimism – stances that do not traditionally come to mind as positive civic attributes – have proven beneficial stances during times of political transition, national reconstruction, and peacebuilding. Hope 'should form a basis for youth to view their own future with positive anticipation … a crucial step toward gaining youth's interest in politics and preserving the civitas' (Youniss et al. 2002, 143). Citizenship in the context of uncertainty, meanwhile, requires patience 'as a long-term political strategy' (Appadurai 2002, 30). Even fatalism has strategic value in this context, in that it provides 'one way of accepting the forces over which one cannot prevail' (Jackson 2007, 39). Although some youth draw a measure of hope from state-level reforms or news of a criminal's capture, others express doubt that the impact will be significant or long lasting, resenting that in Guatemala one is expected to celebrate their state's provision of basic services to citizens. Doubt functions paradoxically as fatalism and hopeful anticipation.

Conclusion

Youth around the world, and particularly in the global South, are increasingly portrayed as in limbo both developmentally and structurally. Aspiring to adulthood, young people are judged against traditional cultural expectations while experiencing rapid and profound societal transformation, in some cases closing conventional pathways to adulthood and leaving youth indefinitely in waithood (e.g.Cole 2004; Dhillon and Yousef 2009; Honwana 2013; Jeffrey 2010; Mains 2012; Sommers 2012). On one hand, we might regard the rise in youth waithood as a largely economic phenomenon. Waithood has largely been described as a consequence of economic globalisation and the spread of neoliberal market-based reforms, structural adjustment policies that reconfigured labour markets and in some cases prompted economic collapse, increased educational access to poor quality institutions coupled with limited growth in employment opportunities, declining state welfare systems, and ongoing poverty and social inequality on local, regional, and global scales. Indeed, the inability for young people to achieve economic adulthood through the imagined progression from school to work has led to profound 'civic disruption' (Youniss et al. 2002, 135), as youth-led protests and uprising around issues of class, income inequality, and the inequitable allocation of resources and social services have taken hold across new and stable democracies. Yet there appears to be something more than struggles for upward economic mobility and financial autonomy at stake: civic exclusion is both a cause and an outcome of waithood. Young people are unable to access their imagined future trajectories because the structures that once facilitated these transitions – or promised to enable them – have weakened or collapsed entirely.

Wait-citizenship offers a lens into the everyday challenges of democracy as experienced by young people whose lives are characterised by the effects of incomplete transitions and radical uncertainty about their prospects for political and economic stability and social belonging. Citizens' experience with 'structural liminality' (Cole 2004, 575) becomes a vantage point from which to critique taken for granted assumptions about what democracy demands of citizens, and how those demands are challenged and interpreted through everyday experiences with insecurity and injustice.

Youth civic engagement and the outcomes of citizenship education are often measured in binaries such as participation and non-participation, or in ways that are quantified so that we can examine which individuals or groups display *more* or *less* agency (Durham 2008, 152), that is, those more or less likely to join political parties, vote, volunteer, and take a stand on political issues. These indicators have been critical in understanding large-scale patterns and systematically analysing group-level effects. But these outcomes tell us little about how young people approach decisions and in what ways they take action on issues of civic and personal significance to them, particularly in contexts with narrow openings for participation. Youth act through, alongside, and at times against the structural forces in their lives, but rarely without some awareness of the openings and closures available to them, and the risks entailed in navigating those spaces.

We cannot transform civic attitudes that have strategic value by simply insisting that young people learn more about the functioning of their democratic systems, or that they find ways to trust in governments displaying high levels of corruption. In order to create more democratic and equitable societies, we need to first understand the ways young people perceive norms and pressures on their expressions of civic agency. The voices of Guatemalan youth demonstrate that there is more at stake than distrust and disillusionment in state institutions. In their withdrawal from public spaces, they question their capacity for meaningful action and the idea that democracy is shaped and reshaped through the everyday actions of ordinary citizens like them. They do not easily see themselves or the demands of civil society in the decisions made by national and local political figures and remain doubtful that their actions can impact the broader social, political, and economic reality they share with morally corrupt others. In detecting significant structural challenges, they recognise the need for structural solutions, yet this critical awareness seems to imply there is little value in individual and collective action. In other words, the need for structural reforms to make democracy more stable, tolerant, and inclusive becomes heard as a call to postpone civic action until these structural reforms are in place.

We might be tempted to conclude that citizenship education in schools has little impact when schools themselves are embedded in, and subject to, undemocratic structures. On the contrary, Guatemalan youth demonstrate that conversations in schools with peers and teachers, though not uniformly empowering, were essential to their civic development and decisions about how and when to employ their agency toward particular ends. In some cases, schools were the only spaces where youth believed adults listened to them and believed in their positive potential, although this was not always the case. If we expect young people to believe that all individuals have the capacity to transform society through thoughtful and deliberate action, then we need to demonstrate to them that 'a citizen is the co-creator of the world to which she or he belongs' (Boyte et al. 2007, 1). Schools thus play an important role in fostering youth conceptions of civic agency, not solely by projecting images and circulating discourses of good citizenship, or by supporting young people in their acquisition of the knowledge and skills required to exercise citizenship rights, but also by making visible the dialectic between structure and agency in young people's lives. More work is needed to understand how schools can better support young people in seeing ordinary citizens as part of structural solutions. Importantly, this work begins with expanding our conceptions of youth agency to encompass deliberation about participation in a not-yet democracy.

Note

1. President Morales, whose campaign promise was 'No more corruption, no more thieves' has allegedly been linked to organised crime networks and is facing potential impeachment for accepting illicit campaign contributions. Shortly after proposing to eradicate the commission investigating his crimes, national courts blocked his ruling. Again praise and critique for Guatemala's democratic progress are featured in global and national media, lamenting corruption in the political sphere and lauding the justice system for holding high-ranking officials accountable. This is, however, an unfortunate validation of the value and utility of young people's 'ethos of pessimism' in this context.

Acknowledgements

Special thanks to Rutgers University Press for allowing me to reprint, with revisions, excerpts from my book (2017), *Youth in Postwar Guatemala: Education and Civic Identity in Transition*. Thank you to Serhiy Kovalchuk, Anatoli Rapoport, and external peer reviewers for their critical feedback on this paper, and to CIES workshop participants for the generative dialogue that led to this special issue.

Disclosure statement

No potential conflict of interest was reported by the author.

Funding

This work was supported by the United States Institute of Peace Jennings Randolph Peace Scholar Dissertation Fellowship and Harvard University's David Rockefeller Center for Latin American Studies.

References

Adams, Tani M. 2011. *Chronic Violence and Its Reproduction: Perverse Trends in Social Relations, Citizenship, and Democracy in Latin America*. Washington, DC: Woodrow Wilson International Center for Scholars.

Appadurai, Arjun. 2002. "Deep Democracy: Urban Governmentality and the Horizon of Politics." *Public Culture* 14 (1): 21–47.

Auyero, Javier. 2012. *Patients of the State: The Politics of Waiting in Argentina*. Durham, NC: Duke University Press.

Bandura, Albert. 2001. "Social Cognitive Theory: An Agentic Perspective." *Annual Review of Psychology* 52: 1–26.

Banks, James A. 2015. "Failed Citizenship, Civic Engagement, and Education." *Kappa Delta Pi Record* 51: 151–154.

Bellino, Michelle J. 2015. "The Risks We Are Willing to Take: Youth Civic Development in "Postwar" Guatemala." *Harvard Educational Review* 85 (4): 537–561.

Bellino, Michelle J. 2016. "So That We Do Not Fall Again: History Education and Citizenship in 'Postwar' Guatemala." *Comparative Education Review* 60 (1): 58–79.

Bellino, Michelle J. 2017. *Youth in Postwar Guatemala: Education and Civic Identity in Transition*. New Brunswick, New Jersey: Rutgers University Press.

Boyte, H., S. Elkin, P. Levine, J. Mansbridge, E. Ostrom, K. Soltan, and R. Smith. 2007. Summer Institute of Civic Studies: Framing Statement.

Burrell, Jennifer L. 2013. *Maya after War: Conflict, Power, and Politics in Guatemala*. Austin, TX: University of Texas Press.

Cesarini, Paola, and Katherine Hite. 2004. "Introducing the Concept of Authoritarian Legacies." In *Authoritarian Legacies and Democracy in Latin America and Southern Europe*, edited by Katherine Hite and Paola Cesarini, 1–24. Notre Dame, IN: University of Notre Dame Press.

Cole, Jennifer. 2004. "Fresh Contact in Tamatave, Madagascar: Sex, Money, and Intergenerational Transformation." *American Ethnologist* 31 (4): 573–588.

Dhillon, Navtej, and Tarik Yousef, eds. 2009. *Generation in Waiting: The Unfulfilled Promise of Young People in the Middle East*. Washington, DC: Brookings Institute.

Dryden-Peterson, Sarah, Michelle J. Bellino, and Vidur Chopra. 2015. "Conflict: Education and Youth." In *International Encyclopedia of the Social & Behavioral Sciences*, edited by James D. Wright, 632–638. Oxford: Elsevier.

Durham, Deborah. 2008. "Apathy and Agency: The Romance of Agency and Youth in Botswana." In *Figuring the Future: Globalization and the Temporalities of Children and Youth*, edited by Jennifer Cole and Deborah Durham, 151–178. Santa Fe, NM: School for Advanced Research Press.

Flanagan, Constance, and Peter Levine. 2010. "Civic Engagement and the Transition to Adulthood." *Future of Children* 20 (1): 159–179.
Flanagan, Constance, Tara Stoppa, Amy K. Syvertsen, and Michael Stout. 2010. "Schools and Social Trust." In *Handbook of Research on Civic Engagement in Youth*, edited by Lonnie R. Sherrod, Judith Torney-Purta and Constance A. Flanagan, 307–329. Hoboken, NJ: John Wiley and Sons.
Grandin, Greg. 2004. *The Last Colonial Massacre: Latin America in the Cold War*. Chicago, IL: University of Chicago Press.
Grandin, Greg, Deborah T. Levenson, and Elizabeth Oglesby. 2011. "Intent to Destroy." In *The Guatemala Reader*, edited by G. Grandin, D. T. Levenson, and E. Oglesby, 361–365. Durham, NC: Duke University Press.
Guatemala Human Rights Commission. 2015-2016. "Jimmy Morales: Guatemala's Next President." *El Quetzal* 20: 7.
Holston, James, and Teresa P. R. Caldeira. 1998. "Democracy, Law, and Violence: Disjunctions of Brazilian Citizenship." In *Fault Lines of Democracy in Post-Transition Latin America*, edited by F. Agüero and J. Stark, 263–296. Miami, FL: North-South Center Press.
Honwana, Alcinda. 2013. *The Time of Youth: Work, Social Change, and Politics in Africa*. Boulder, CO: Kumarian Press.
de Hoyos, Rafael, Halsey Rogers, and Miguel Székely. 2015. *Out of School and out of Work: Risk and Opportunities for Latin America's Ninis*. Washington, DC: The World Bank.
Isaacs, Anita. 2010. "Guatemala on the Brink." *Journal of Democracy* 21 (2): 108–122.
Jackson, Michael D. 2007. *Excursions*. Durham, NC: Duke University Press.
Jeffrey, Craig. 2010. *Timepass: Youth, Class, and the Politics of Waiting in India*. Stanford, CA: Stanford University Press.
Lederach, John Paul. 2005. *The Moral Imagination: The Art and Soul of Building Peace*. Oxford, England: Oxford University Press.
Levenson, Deborah T. 2013. *Adiós Niño: The Gangs of Guatemala City and the Politics of Death*. Durham, NC: Duke University Press.
Levinson, Meira. 2012. *No Citizen Left behind*. Cambridge, MA: Harvard University Press.
Levinson, Bradley A. U., and Juan G. Berumen. 2007. "Democratic Citizenship Education and the State in Latin America: A Critical Overview." *Revista Electrónica Iberoamericana sobre Calidad, Eficacia y Cambio en Educación* 5 (4): 1–15.
Lloyd, Cynthia B., ed. 2005. *Growing up Global: The Changing Transitions to Adulthood in Developing Countries*. Washington, DC: The National Academies Press: National Research Council, The Institute of Medicine.
Mains, Daniel. 2012. *Hope is Cut: Youth, Unemployment, and the Future of Urban Ethiopia*. Philadelphia, PA: Temple University Press.
Moodie, Ellen. 2010. *El Salvador in the Aftermath of Peace: Crime, Uncertainty, and the Transition to Democracy*. Philadelphia, PA: University of Pennsylvania Press.
Oglesby, Elizabeth. 2007. "Educating Citizens in Postwar Guatemala: Historical Memory, Genocide, and the Culture of Peace." *Radical History Review* 97: 77–98.
Rubin, Beth C. 2012. *Making Citizens: Transforming Civic Learning for Diverse Social Studies Classrooms*. New York: Routledge.
Schultz, Wolfram, John Ainley, Tim Friedman, and Petra Lietz. 2011. *ICCS 2009 Latin American Report: Civic Knowledge and Attitudes among Lower-Secondary Students in Six Latin American Countries*. Amsterdam: International Association for the Evaluation of Educational Achievement.
Sommers, Marc. 2012. *Stuck: Rwandan Youth and the Struggle for Adulthood*. Athens: University of Georgia Press.
Swartz, Sharlene, James Hamilton Harding, and Ariane De Lannoy. 2012. "Ikasi Style and the Quiet Violence of Dreams: A Critique of Youth Belonging in Post-Apartheid South Africa." *Comparative Education* 48 (1): 27–40.
Turner, Victor. 1967. *The Forest of Symbols: Aspects of Ndembu Ritual*. Ithaca, NY: Cornell University Press.
UNDP. 2012. "UNDP Warns That Poverty, Exclusion, Violence Are Destroying Guatemalan Youth."

Winton, Ailsa. 2005. "Youth, Gangs and Violence: Analysing the Social and Spatial Mobility of Young People in Guatemala City." *Children's Geographies* 3 (2): 167–184.

Youniss, James, Susan Bales, Verona Christmas-Best, Marcelo Diversi, Milbrey McLaughlin, and Rainer Silbereisen. 2002. "Youth Civic Engagement in the Twenty-First Century." *Journal of Research on Adolescence* 12 (1): 121–148.

Zaalouk, Malak. 2015. "Education in the Twenty First Century in MENA: Can We Reverse the State of Failed Citizens." http://cies2015.org/response-mena.html.

Obstacles and opportunities for global citizenship education under intractable conflict: the case of Israel

Heela Goren and Miri Yemini

ABSTRACT
Global citizenship education (GCE) is a global education trend that, like democratic citizenship education, has been adopted recently by many education systems for the purpose of preparing students to engage in global society. In this study we applied Qualitative Content Analysis to semi-structured interviews with Israeli teachers with the aim of shedding light on some of the barriers and opportunities to GCE in a conflict-ridden state. The main novelty of our study is first and foremost the delineation of factors that would hinder attempts at incorporating GCE in a conflict-ridden state, including a lack of consensus surrounding citizenship, increased nationalism and an ambiguous attitude towards human rights. In addition, we revealed that under these conditions, GCE as a concept may be threatening, and conflict-ridden states may choose to opt-out altogether or at least rephrase it under a less controversial title. Overall, this study suggests that GCE would need to be articulated differently in conflict-ridden states than in other Western contexts. We concluded by addressing the implications of our findings for GCE policy in conflict-ridden states.

Introduction

Global citizenship education (GCE) is a growing educational phenomenon that has been attaining recognition by many Western and non-Western countries; it often consists of contents aimed at preparing students to function in a modern globalised society and economy, while also attempting to encourage empathy and intercultural understanding (Dill 2013). Similarly to democratic citizenship education, GCE stems from an assumption that in this era, citizenship is no longer limited to one's national identification but rather to a wider set of values shared by people in different places (Ahmad and Szpara 2005).

Global citizenship education can be also viewed as a form of curricular internationalisation (Leask 2013) that (like other manifestations of internationalisation) requires an active role on the part of policymakers and curricula developers in designing or adopting appropriate curricular contents to foster integration within the globalised society (Yemini, Ber Nissan, and Yardeni 2014; Yemini and Fulop 2015; Yemini 2014a, 2014b). Global citizenship education is not uniform; different countries emphasise different forms of GCE according to their national contexts and needs. For example, in Canada the adoption of

GCE and its incorporation into the curriculum is usually rationalised in terms of preparing students to function in the increasingly diverse national landscape (Evans et al. 2009; Schweisfurth 2006). Similarly, in Spain the adoption of GCE has been framed as a direct response to increasing immigration (Engel 2014). On the other hand, in the USA, GCE is usually not aimed at creating a common identity construct for the nations' students; rather, it is articulated in terms of maintaining the USA's status as a world leader, which supposedly requires students to have knowledge of different cultures and global issues (Rapoport 2009).

In conflict-ridden or post-conflict societies, which often place greater educational emphasis on imposing the desired national narrative, GCE may be perceived as especially contentious or controversial (Goren and Yemini 2016; Pinson 2007). In Northern Ireland, for example, teachers reported difficulty teaching the GCE curriculum since no consensus exists regarding the issues it covered (Reilly and Niens 2014). In Liberia, GCE was described as secondary to the need for nation-building through the education system and the civics curriculum in particular (Quaynor 2015). Nevertheless, GCE has been widely acknowledged for it potential role (in theory) in peace education and reconciliation (Brown and John Morgan 2008; Davies 2006; Lee and Leung 2006), particularly when referring to humanistic models of GCE, which emphasise human rights, shared valuesand empathy (Gaudelli 2016; Monaghan and Spreen 2016). Although several studies have addressed GCE in post-conflict ridden societies (see Niens and Reilly 2012 [for Northern Ireland]; Philippou 2007 [for the case of Cyprus]), until now limited attention has been given to societies currently experiencing ongoing, intractable conflict that do not have GCE formally incorporated in their curricula. Our study will advance the understanding of the nuances and particularities unique to a conflict-ridden society, and the ways these particularities could advance or hinder attempts at incorporating GCE.

In this study, we analysed 18 interviews performed with Israeli secondary school teachers as part of a larger research project on GCE policies and implementation, to identify context-specific aspects of teachers' perceptions of GCE in a conflict-ridden society. We found a need to articulate GCE in Israel differently than in other Western contexts to enable its local acceptance and incorporation into Israeli classrooms. Moreover, we identified particular obstacles that could hinder attempts at GCE in conflict-ridden states, which require conceptual and practical treatment. This study thus allows a unique perspective due to the current lack of GCE policy in Israel, which enables us to treat the topic theoretically and delineate the teachers' authentic perceptions as to what GCE might entail and how it could be tailored to fit Israeli society and its unique needs.

Theoretical orientation

Global citizenship education

Global citizenship is a broad term with varying definitions, ranging from loose identification with people outside of ones' own country to full embracement of the notion of global society (thereby limiting the importance of nation states, which shaped civic identities in the past) (Oxley and Morris 2013). The lack of consensus regarding the meaning of global citizenship provided a breeding ground for many differing forms of global citizenship education, as well as unique antecedents and expected outcomes in different contexts (Myers 2016).

Definitions and models

Global citizenship education has become a particularly popular global phenomenon in recent years (Buckner and Russell 2013), especially among Western and developed nations, but also elsewhere, mostly through advocacy of supra-national organisations such as UNESCO (Pigozzi 2006) and the International Baccalaureate Organization (Brunold-Conesa 2010). Broadly stated, GCE can be described as curricular contents aimed at preparing students to function in global society through the development of an understanding of global issues, empathy for people of different origins, multicultural appreciation and global skill sets (Davies 2006; Veugelers 2011).

Studies concerning the ways in which GCE is framed in different countries' curricula and education systems revealed the lack of a single, agreed-upon definition for GCE; however, scholars developed several useful typologies. First, Dill (2013) distinguished between the global competencies approach, which involves concrete skills and a more utilitarian view of GCE, and global consciousness, which is focused more on empathy and acceptance of other cultures. Dill's typology is valuable for identifying the goals of GCE in the eyes of policymakers, but its dichotomous approach makes it difficult to note the many intricacies and nuances that GCE can embody simultaneously.

The most comprehensive typology offered to date is that of Oxley and Morris (2013). Oxley and Morris incorporated common typologies of GCE such as those developed by Andreotti (2006), Schattle (2008) and Veugelers (2011) to generate a comprehensive model that enables distinction between what they term 'advocacy' and 'cosmopolitan' modes of global citizenship. Their model addresses the antecedents and outcomes of GCE as described in curricula and policy papers to identify their latent and explicit manifestations. The outcomes reflect a few mutually inclusive modes. While the cosmopolitan mode refers to more traditional aspects of GCE, such as identification with people around the world, global consciousness and understanding of global relations, advocacy-based conceptions concentrate on global problem-solving and agency.

GCE as education for peace

Countries with divided societies and those experiencing inter-state conflicts may be especially concerned about the potential outcomes of global citizenship; they may, for example, forego GCE for fear that it may threaten their sovereignty (Davies 2008; Niens and Reilly 2012). However, GCE has also been suggested as a possible tool for peace education, which could in fact be most useful in divided societies. For example, Davies (2008) and Gill and Niens (2014) placed particular emphasis on the benefits of GCE and multicultural education, especially in complex national landscapes. These scholars claim that GCE could create a common ground of tolerance and understanding that may bridge differences and enable dialogue.

Human rights play a major role in the creation of this common ground, as they do in many global citizenship curricula (Moon and Koo 2011); however, several aspects particular to conflict states must be considered. Global citizenship education in countries experiencing internal or external conflicts must be mindful not to focus solely on human rights, so as to avoid the misguided perceptions that maintaining minorities' basic human rights is sufficient for the normal functioning of society – since human rights should be a minimal requirement rather than the ultimate aim (Appiah 2006; Banks 2008). Banks (2008) argues that for this reason, in conflict-ridden areas and in societies comprised of various ethnicities,

GCE should emphasise issues such as proper representation of minorities in government and the promotion of cultural understanding and tolerance.

The optimistic frameworks for GCE as peace education suggested by Davies (2008) and other scholars do not quite align with the scholarship that investigated GCE implementation in real classrooms, suggesting that teachers in conflict-ridden societies often shy away from discussing controversial issues and that school systems in such areas are often highly conservative regarding the content presented to students in the curriculum (Gill and Niens 2014; Reilly and Niens 2014; Yamashita 2006).

Differing justifications for GCE

Although it constitutes a global phenomenon, GCE has different meanings (Rapoport 2015) and is usually framed in the curriculum in terms of national rather than supranational needs (see Bromley and Cole 2016; Engel 2014; O'Connor and Faas 2012; Rapoport 2009). In general, in countries with high concentrations of immigrants or refugees, GCE is presented as a potential framework for dialogue and creation of a common identity (O'Connor and Faas 2012). Similarly, research conducted in post-conflict Northern Ireland found GCE to be framed as an imperative brought on by the divided nature of Irish society, despite teachers' skepticism regarding its actual contributions (Niens, O'Connor, and Smith 2013). In developing countries, in contrast, GCE is considered a tool for student empowerment and the creation of opportunities; sometimes, however, its meaning is reduced to knowledge of the English language that would enable students to exercise the opportunities for mobility that globalisation offers (see Quaynor 2015). Lastly, in countries that value nationalism highly and are seen as central forces in the globalised world – particularly the USA (see Myers 2006; Rapoport 2009) and China (Law 2007) – GCE is strongly geared towards serving national interests, as opposed to its more cultural and moral foci elsewhere.

It is important to note that in post-conflict Northern Ireland, as mentioned above, the incorporation of GCE was driven, as in other divided societies, by an understanding that a more inclusive model of citizenship is imperative in order to create some common ground. On the other hand, in Israel, there is no such understanding or consensus at policy level regarding the need for a common model of identity and the idea is in fact rejected due to the ongoing nature of the conflict.

Israel and the Israeli education system

Israel is engaged in intractable conflict with the Palestinians and with several countries in the Arab world (Bar-Tal 1998). Moreover, Israeli society is highly divided; many internal struggles have emerged since Israel's establishment in 1948, involving Jews of different religious sectors and origins, the Arab minority and other groups (Agbaria, Mustafa, and Jabareen 2015; Ichilov 2003). Alongside the national conflict, these internal divisions have greatly affected the Israeli education system, which mirrors these conflicts and fluctuations; as different groups gain power, curricular goals and the national narrative promoted through schools change, as do official perceptions of the purpose of education itself (Agbaria 2016; Lemish 2003). Israel, like most countries, is also experiencing the effects of globalisation, causing the education system to be somewhat torn between the nationalism invoked by the ongoing conflict and the expectations posed of a country attempting to participate in the global economy.

Citizenship education and GCE in Israel

Israeli citizenship education is a highly researched topic, due to the delicate balance and perhaps the inherent paradox between the country's self-definition as a Jewish and democratic state (Agbaria 2016; Al-Haj 2005; Pedahzur 2001; Pinson 2007; Smooha 2002). This inherent paradox is highlighted by Smooha (2002), who asserts that Israel does not fall under the category of a Western liberal democracy, as it is often perceived, but rather embodies a model of ethnic democracy, in which the major ethnic or religious group uses state structures and resources in order to maintain its own interests, sometimes at the expense of minority group rights. While in a democratic nation equality and freedom are valorised, in an ethnic democracy or a non-liberal democracy they are hindered by design (Pedahzur 2001). The tension between the Jewish and democratic definition of the state is often raised in the public discourse and comprises a particularly potent issue, while competing notions and conceptions of citizenship have been shown by Cohen (2016) to create some ambivalence in Israeli classrooms.

Although the challenges GCE could face in the Israeli context have been insufficiently explored, several studies dealing with related approaches to citizenship education have highlighted similar obstacles to those noted here. Yonah (2005) maintained that education and the curriculum comprise the main ways through which the Zionist narrative is disseminated in Israeli society. Additionally, as Firer (1998) explained, this narrative and the attempt to harmonise the ideas of the Zionist nation with students' perceptions of themselves as individuals make it nearly impossible to include any progressive forms of civic education or human rights education in the curriculum. Resnik (1999) expressed similar concerns in her historic review of the Israeli curriculum, which showed that over the years the particularistic principles of Jewish nationalism have expanded in the curriculum, pushing universalistic principles to the sidelines – a point echoed by Pedahzur (2001), who claimed that the civics curriculum has been subordinated to the ethnonational principles and decidedly non-liberal nature of the state. Pedahzur (2001) asserts that Israel is a non-liberal democracy, due to the fact that although the state holds democratic elections and allows minorities to participate freely in these elections, it also sacrifices some liberal values in order to maintain its ethno-nationalist nature.

These challenges and obstacles posed by competing national narratives and strong social division are not unique to Israel; as Hanna (2016) showed in her comparative study of the way differences are dealt with in the civics education of divided societies, Israel and Northern Ireland experience similar issues. Nevertheless, almost no research has focused explicitly on GCE in the Israeli context, and due to the expanding nature of GCE as a global phenomenon, more research is necessary.

The present study

In this study, we explored the particular barriers and opportunities embodied in the way Israeli secondary school teachers at secular-Jewish public schools perceive GCE. The study is based on data collected as part of a larger project aimed at identifying how student background might affect the meaning and importance teachers might attribute to GCE. Our focus in this paper is on whether and how teachers consider the particularities of the Israeli context and the Palestinian-Israeli conflict to impede or provide opportunities for GCE. This issue is of particular importance both from theoretical and practical perspectives due

Table 1. Teachers' pseudonyms, subject area and experience.

Pseudonym	Year of experience	Main teaching areas	School socioeconomic status
Shirley	5	Civics	Low
Yoav	3	Civics	Low
Meir	5	History	Low
Daniela	2	English	Low
Omer	22	Civics	Medium
Rotem	35	Literature	Medium
Naama	15	Literature	Medium
Adam	2	History	Medium
Karen	7	History	Medium
Ron	9	Civics	High
Dan	16	Civics	High
Hadas	7	Civics	High
Yael	20	English	High
Shir	15	Literature	High
Anat	11	History	High
Yamit	6	Civics	High
Amit	4	Civics	High
Karin	15	History	High

to the fact that Israel is one of a few Western countries entrenched in ongoing intractable conflict, a context in which GCE has rarely been explored. It is imperative to understand the particular opportunities and obstacles that arise in this context in order to advance our understanding of the way GCE is or could be affected by contextual factors in general, and in order to suggest practical solutions for overcoming the unique barriers GCE policy-makers could face.

Methodology

Data for the study was collected through 18 semi-structured interviews with teachers of civics, history, geography and English from eight schools in the Tel-Aviv area. All of the interviewees taught at schools belonging to the secular-Jewish education stream, with experience ranging from 2 to 35 years. All interviews were conducted by the first author and then recorded and transcribed in full, in Hebrew. Relevant quotes that appear in this paper were translated into English and back into Hebrew to ensure their validity. No schools are identified here, and teachers are referred to by pseudonyms. Teachers' pseudonyms, subject area, school socioeconomic status and years of experience are detailed in Table 1.

We chose to concentrate on teachers in humanistic fields both due to previous research on GCE concentrating on these subject areas and because these are curricular areas in which GCE has been incorporated through educational policy and programmes in other settings (for history and social studies see Myers [2006], for civics see Morris and Cogan [2001] and for English see Cha and Ham [2011]). Literature teachers were also interviewed after literature was pointed out by teachers in our pilot study as one of the curricular fields GCE may be associated with (Goren and Yemini 2016).

The data was analysed jointly and independently by both authors using Qualitative Content Analysis, selected for its flexibility and ability to encompass both inductive and deductive research directions (Schreier 2012). The interviews took place as part of a larger project focusing on perceptions of GCE in relation to student backgrounds; however, in this study we concentrated on the particular parts of the data that addressed the characteristics of the Israeli context. In this sense, the analysis was deductive as the decision to concentrate on the Israeli context was purposeful. Upon examination and initial coding of the relevant data we inductively derived broad categories, which we discussed and fine-tuned through constant comparison of the relevant data.

In this study, we focused solely on public, secular Jewish schools to gain a more comprehensive understanding of teacher perceptions within the largest educational sector in the Israeli education system. As our larger research project progresses, we hope to explore additional sectors of Israeli society and of the Israeli education system, as students from different educational sectors in Israel have been shown to hold very different views of citizenship (as per Sabbagh and Resh 2014). This study is exploratory, aimed at highlighting potential research trajectories for future studies concerning GCE in conflict-ridden states.

The broad categories we initially defined were nationalism, controversy surrounding global norms and the potential benefits of GCE. We recognised that these issues existed in our dataset and were discussed by nearly all of the participants from our previous analyses. We then located and aggregated all instances pertaining to each category within the transcribed interviews and further developed them into their final form, which will be presented in the results and discussion section of this paper: (1) nationalism under siege; (2) demographic challenges and the discourse of betrayal; (3) disputed global norms; and (4) potential benefits of GCE in a conflict-ridden state.

Findings and discussion

As noted above, our qualitative content analysis was deductive and involved a coding frame that focused on four categories we knew to be present in our data: (1) nationalism under siege, (2) demographic challenges and the discourse of betrayal, (3) disputed global norms and (4) the potential benefits of GCE in a conflict-ridden society. In this section, we present examples of the kind of attitudes expressed within each category and a discussion of the way they interact with the literature.

Nationalism under siege

Countries experiencing conflict or those recovering from it often promote nationalism through their education systems (see Philippou [2007] for the case of Cyprus, Smith [2003] for Northern Ireland and Resnik [1999] for Israel). This is particularly true for countries such as Israel with compulsory military service and a militaristic tendency (Kimmerling 1993). Teachers in our study expressed varying views – including fierce criticism – regarding appearances of nationalism in Israeli curricula, but its presence was undisputed. Most of the teachers reported a personal mission to incorporate GCE and its related contents despite its absence in the formal curriculum and contrary to the spirit of nationalism penetrating the education system from the government. Some of our interviewees presented nationalism and GCE as opposing points on a spectrum; others claimed that although they consider GCE to be supplementary rather than contradictory to national citizenship, the Ministry of Education (MOE) is not likely perceive it in this manner, making formal implementation of GCE unlikely.

Teachers felt the Palestinian-Israeli conflict affected the nationalistic tendency of the education system and the country as a whole most prominently by shifting the focus towards national survival, fostering militarism and a victimised narrative that leaves little room for anything else. Yamit (who reported extensive teaching of GCE-related subjects) explained how she perceives the Israeli MOE approach:

> I think Israeli society is by nature a militant one ... and because it's a militant society, it chooses to glorify and emphasize its own values and to look less at what's around it. I also think we're very occupied with survival most of the time. When you're engaged with your own survival, you can't afford to look at the other side.

Several teachers repeated this reasoning, which was sometimes presented as a valid reason for the lack of focus on GCE-related contents but more often as an excuse to continue focusing on the Zionist narrative and to continue fostering the fear that keeps Jewish citizens complacent and closed-off from the world. Anat represented this view:

> I don't think the victimized narrative that's self-focused in Israel is without cause .... It's based on some historic truth and some really unique characteristics. This is the only state of the Jewish people and the Jewish religion ... but I think that in a sense Israel got stuck somewhere in the 1950s in terms of its self-image. Today it's a strong country ... and we can start putting down our guards and understand there's a whole world around us.

Although teachers usually did not dismiss the reality of the threats to Israeli security, many of them noted that these threats should not affect the education system as they undoubtedly have. In fact, as Dan noted:

> ... the MOE doesn't see itself as a system that needs to provide students with tools ... it has a very clear agenda: it needs graduates who will serve in the military and live the Zionist narrative and be loyal to the country. It doesn't aim to allow students to function in the world, but it should.

This statement and similar ones made by teachers in our study may not reflect the MOE's actual goals or agendas, but they certainly reflect the way these agendas are perceived in the field by Israeli teachers.

Nationalism appeared in our interviews as an opposing force to GCE regarding not only teachers' perception of the curricula passed down from the MOE, but also the way students and parents reacted to global curricular contents. Anat recounted that upon deciding to teach the Armenian genocide to her class, she received multiple enraged calls from parents demanding to know why time was being taken away from discussing '*our* holocaust' in order to discuss someone else's. Yoav explained that he needed to be cautious when discussing issues of a global nature or any contents he deemed associated with GCE, due to his students' nationalistic tendencies:

> I have to be very careful here – because sometimes talking about things like global norms or different cultures can be construed as if I'm telling them things that are opposed to their religion or trying to get them to emigrate – they'll say things like, 'wait a minute, are you trying to get me to go live in the Netherlands? This is my country!'

Yoav's struggle is a symptom of the same survivalist discourse presented earlier, the fear of abandoning the Zionist and Jewish ideals the system is supposedly meant to promote in order to create a more global focus. Additionally, it relates to statements made by teachers in Northern Ireland and in the USA – countries also characterised by nationalism – who also expressed concerns that the introduction of GCE-related topics into the classroom could be perceived as unpatriotic (Rapoport 2010) or controversial (Gill and Niens 2014). This seems to be a common apprehension of teachers in nationalist contexts.

Demographic challenges and the discourse of betrayal

Another way in which teachers perceived the conflict to hinder attempts at GCE involved the cultivation of fear of any potential demographic threat, such as emigration or inter-religious marriages. Teachers noted such phenomena – which they consider to be associated with GCE through the blurring of national borders, increased mobility, human rights and universalism – as threatening to Israeli society; if not in their own opinion then in the MOE's attitudes.

One of the more experienced and conservative teachers we interviewed, Rotem, mentioned emigration as something that she was concerned about with regards to GCE. She explained that having been born to parents who were Holocaust survivors, she would never dream of leaving the country; however, she described her students as much more open, in a negative way:

> ... [they] want to live in America, in France, they want to study abroad – I'm very much against that! Some of [the students] have parents who aren't Jewish and they're even more at risk ... kids today are more connected, more multicultural, they have places to go to ...

This narrative of some of the more successful students posing a 'flight risk' was repeated in some of the other interviews as well, usually in a less critical manner. Ron explained that the openness associated with GCE created something of a paradox within the education system:

> There's sort of a dual language – the country promotes excellence and achievements and wants to excel academically ... but the people who excel the most are the ones with the highest chances of leaving. They won't become directors of non-profit organizations and they won't pursue military careers ... the system and the Minister of Education are always talking about how we're a start-up nation, but what does an entrepreneur who founds a start-up do? He moves it to San Francisco, or he sells it and takes the money and buys another company abroad.

In order to deal with these perceived dangers, Ron went on to explain that the MOE fosters the idea of economic globalisation, while socially closing students in:

> ... the power of education lies in the subtext – students go on class trips to Israeli and Jewish landmarks ... they go through seven days of what's called 'Journey through Israel', which is basically emotional blackmail and at the end of the week, they just want to say one thing – 'it's good to die for our country.'

Many teachers mentioned school trips like the one Ron described and the annual youth delegations to Poland as some of the main mechanisms the MOE operates in order to 'balance' whatever ideas of universalism or global citizenship may have inadvertently or purposely penetrated the system. The role these delegations and trips play in maintaining and reinforcing the ideas of Zionism and Israeli nationalism in general have been explored elsewhere with similar conclusions (see Gross 2010; Resnik 2003). Feldman (2002) provides a particularly enticing analysis of the way students' feelings towards Israel are shaped by these trips: 'To the participants ... Israel takes on cosmic proportions and becomes the center of the world, through experiences that are non-Israeli, such as the Holocaust. By experiencing what is not Israeli as mortally dangerous, Israel takes on mythical proportions, as the only place where Jews are secure.' (90)

Ron and other teachers also referred to the collective fear or disapproval of emigration from Israel, a phenomenon previously documented by scholars that is associated with negative stereotypes of Israeli emigrants (also known as Yordim: Gold 1994; Uriely 1995). The negative view of emigration has been nurtured in Israeli society since Israel's formation, as emigration is perceived to be at least somewhat opposed to Zionism (Rebhun and Waxman 2000). Emigration from Israel is not only considered dangerous to Israeli society because of brain drain, which could threaten the country's highly revered status as the 'high-tech nation'; it could also potentially narrow the demographic advantage of the Jewish citizens of the state. We found that this aversion to emigration could pose a potential obstacle to GCE. Ron's statement in which he posits that the most successful students to emerge from the education system are the most likely to leave is in fact supported by research (Gould and Moav 2007).

Disputed global norms: human rights and universalism in a non-liberal state

Human rights play a crucial role in many definitions of GCE (Gaudelli 2016; Gaudelli and Fernekes 2004; Monaghan and Spreen 2017). Israel is a signatory to the UN's 1948 human rights treaty, which is taught to some extent within Israeli curricula (Firer 1998). However, teachers we interviewed stated that delving deeper into issues of human rights through civics education would require critical thinking that their students were not prepared for and that (the teachers felt) the MOE does not formally encourage. Human rights are based on universalistic assumptions that all humans are equal and have equal rights that stem from their humanity (Appiah 2006). Although some scholars have criticised universalism in GCE (Andreotti 2006; Banks 2008), human rights pose a widely agreed-upon starting point for any discussion of global citizenship (Gaudelli and Fernekes 2004).

Ron gave a particularly compelling example while critiquing the way universalistic values are presented to middle school students in the Israeli education system by opening a textbook during his interview and turning to the pages in which universalism and particularism are discussed:

> One of the first chapters is about your identity as a person and as part of a [the Jewish] people – particularistic versus universalistic identity. And then some text excerpts are provided to show the dangers of universalism using some religious text about the tower of Babel with some strange interpretation and then – the text of John Lennon's *Imagine* is presented in a critical way, saying he's trying to make people give up their identities! Now if kids are going to learn this alongside this so-called global citizenship it's very clear which concept is going to have the upper hand. *Imagine* is presented as a huge threat to the Jewish identity of the Israeli people.

The text following the song lyrics asks students to reflect upon whether or not they would be willing to give up their national anthem, flag, holidays and other symbols in order to become part of this delusionary utopia that John Lennon is suggesting. The aversion and demonisation of universalism presented here not only comprises a potent example of a phenomenon that many of our interviewees noted, it also provides a clear understanding of the starting point middle school students enter high school with, having only learned that universalism is a threat to their nationality and its symbols, potentially unaware of any unifying basis for humanity. As Ron went on to somewhat cynically explain:

> We deal with human rights … to some extent; *human* rights, not *Arab* rights, mind you. Who said the Arabs are human? I'm not talking about radical issues here … I'm saying that human rights have no place in the discussion of the Palestinian-Israeli conflict in school …. It's taboo, we have the most moral military in the world. There is a conflict, it is being handled, things happen as part of this conflict, and the students study human rights in school. These are two completely unrelated processes and this is where 'global' serves the MOE – we're part of the Western world … the only democracy in the Middle East, we're democratic and liberal.

Ron not only explains how the curriculum continues to emphasise and create gaps between the way students view themselves and the Palestinian or universally Arab or Muslim 'other', but also shows how the human rights discourse allows teachers and the education system to look past the local conflict, utilising distorted Westernised assumptions, and only study human rights issues in the context of liberal Western democracies. This issue was also explored in the Israeli context by Gordon (2012), who concluded that in order for meaningful human rights education to develop in Israel, a 'desegregated pedagogical model' would need to be implemented throughout the education system. Similarly, Hanna (2016) asserted that in both Israel and Northern Ireland, lack of exposure to other religious groups and segregated school systems created poor conditions for human rights education to be meaningful and relevant.

Another statement made by Ron also sheds light on how disputed universalism and human rights are in the Israeli discourse:

> Anything that undermines the Zionist narrative is considered a threat. If you bring up the fact that [some words] in the anthem should be changed to be more inclusive you're considered a traitor, and if you think that closing the borders to Syrian refugees is like the Nazis closing the borders to Jews then you're considered a traitor ... there's no room for threatening the Zionist narrative in the Israeli discourse, so this whole thing is still very oppressed.

Potential benefits of GCE in a conflict-ridden state

Global citizenship education is often related to peace education in the literature (Brown and John Morgan 2008; Davies 2008); nevertheless, only a minority of teachers in our sample saw its potential benefits in terms of conflict resolution. Some teachers addressed the possibilities GCE holds for enabling students to leave the country and function abroad (which they perceived as a positive or negative phenomenon), while others pointed to GCE's usefulness in preparing students to function convincingly as 'ambassadors' of Israel. In Yael's words:

> If you teach students to be global citizens it can help in promoting the national interests ... and maybe also see a mirror image of yourself ... learn about yourself and make adjustments .... I try to teach my students to be good ambassadors for Israel wherever they go and represent us with honor,

The attempt to appropriate global citizenship to fill national needs is, as we showed in our conceptual background, not uncommon. However, the Israeli context shapes a perception of GCE as a potential tool not for understanding the other, but rather for more effectively presenting one's own position.

Another potential benefit of GCE that our interviewees mentioned repeatedly lies in its ability to bridge gaps within Israeli society, which is divided internally along many lines. Some teachers referred to the ability to create a common ground between Arab-Israeli and Jewish students through GCE, and others pointed to the need to find a similar common ground between Orthodox and non-Orthodox Jews, and those of different ethnic backgrounds.

Shirley, a teacher in the only school with a mixed Arab-Israeli and Jewish population in our sample, recognised GCE as a potential way to bridge the gaps between students and create a common ground for a shared identity. Shirley framed the main question as follows: 'Are we challenging the very conception of Israeli citizenship, or are we saying, "ok, there's Israeli citizenship which is mostly centered around Judaism, and there's this global citizenship which we can all relate to in the same way"?' Teachers at Shirley's school noted that ideally, they would be able to show their students that Israeli citizenship is a suitable identity model for all students, sometimes by stressing the universal aspects of Israeli citizenship rather than the religious ones; however, they conceded the challenges inherent in this approach, which raises questions regarding the Jewish nature of the state's symbols, such as the anthem and flag. This perception of global citizenship as a common ground for dialog aligns teacher perceptions in multicultural countries like Canada (Schweisfurth 2006) and in post-conflict Northern Ireland (Niens and Reilly 2012), but it remains a far cry from peace education to its fullest extent. Additionally, without referring to global citizenship in particular, Lemish (2003) concluded in his study of Israeli civics education that without fundamental changed to Israeli policy and public discourse, it would be difficult if not impossible to incorporate any alternative models of civics education.

Most dominantly, teachers discussed global citizenship education as a neoliberal tool fostering individualism for students (particularly of strong socioeconomic backgrounds) to promote themselves, navigate and compete in a global society, or at least in the globalised national society. Shir explained:

> [GCE] could help students excel in their lives when they finish school, open better career paths for them, help develop their skills so they can make the best of their lives and prosper. I think that there are a lot of benefits [to GCE] because eventually they realize that [any business activities] depend on the ties outside of Israel ... and you realize that if you know the ethical codes, the language, and have the basic ability to communicate with people in other countries ... it'll definitely benefit you. These kids will also be able to study in universities abroad and see things from a different perspective.

This utilitarian, instrumentalist view of GCE demonstrates how the concept is devoid of any content that could undermine nationalism, promote human rights or bridge over social gaps. Scholars criticised utilitarianism and instrumentalism in GCE as a product of neoliberalism and Western assumptions (Andreotti 2006; Pike 2015; Shultz 2007); however, we found that such approaches could also stem from an aversion to the other aspects of the concept. Similarly, Reilly and Niens (2014) showed in their study of teachers and students in post-conflict Northern Ireland that teachers adopted pragmatic and instrumental approaches to GCE so as to avoid sensitive issues, focusing instead on individual benefits and presumably neutral issues, such as sustainable development.

Conclusion

This study offers an exploratory overview of how intractable conflict could influence, shape and overshadow global citizenship education. Due to the lack of policy regarding GCE in Israel, we were able to investigate how teachers perceived the concept itself, the MOE's potential views about it, and the extent to which it could or should be included in the curriculum. We found that interviewees consider the Palestinian-Israeli conflict a barrier to GCE, either directly (by creating a survival urgency that surpasses any desire to socialise students into global society) or indirectly (by encouraging nationalism, stressing the demographic threat minorities pose to the state and complicating the notion of human rights). Additionally, and perhaps consequently, we found that teachers often formed instrumental notions of global citizenship, which have been criticised previously in the literature (Marshall 2015; Shultz 2007). In terms of the models of GCE detailed in the theoretical framework, teachers in this study seemed to favour cosmopolitan modes of citizenship over advocacy-based modes (Oxley and Morris 2013), which may require a higher degree of critical thought and a clearer understanding of human rights.

GCE in Israel: obstacles and opportunities

Like previous studies exploring areas of civic and history education in Israel, our study shows that progressive models of GCE would be quite difficult, if not impossible, to incorporate into the Israeli education system, largely due to the country's conflict-ridden and militaristic nature. The emphasis on particularistic values highlighted by Resnik (1999) and the rejection of any universalistic ideas overshadow GCE, as do the negative public perceptions of emigrants (Gold 1994; Uriely 1995). Furthermore, the partial nature of human rights education within Israeli curricula (Firer 1998; Hanna 2016) fails to create the necessary conditions for GCE. The 'us versus them' narrative that differentiates between Jewish and Arab Israeli citizens cited in much of the literature regarding the Israeli education system seems to further impede the universal ideals associated with GCE, to the extent that Arabs are not necessarily included within students' understanding of human rights. Under the current conditions, GCE seems inconsistent with Israel's ambiguous approach to human rights and contradictory to the ethno-national narrative promoted by its education system (see Agbaria 2016).

This study does not reveal the Israeli MOE's *de facto* stance on GCE but, rather, the way teachers believe the MOE would approach it. Our interviewees all consider GCE important to some extent and said it should be taught, but not one of them believe that it would be wholeheartedly embraced by the system. Some felt that GCE was being introduced into the system through internationalisation processes such as participation in global testing and an expanded focus on English and mathematics. Others posited that the goals of the MOE are to prepare students to function and thrive in Israeli society and to encourage nationalism through the Zionist narrative – which do not coincide with GCE.

GCE in conflict ridden versus post-conflict societies

Although some characteristics of the Palestinian-Israeli conflict are unique, the conditions it creates are similar to those in post-conflict states to a certain extent. The emphasis on nationalism in divided education systems has been documented in several contexts, most notably Cyprus (see Philippou 2007) and Northern Ireland (Hanna 2016; Smith 2003). Neither is the apparent aversion to human rights education or the view of human rights in general as controversial unique to the Israeli context (Hanna 2016). These approaches seem to cause a shallowing of GCE, emptying is of much of its content and leaving teachers with utilitarian notions of it. Studies performed in post-conflict nations (e.g., Reilly and Niens 2014) teach us that although GCE can be appropriated for the purpose of peace education (if the conflict is resolved), the national context could still negatively impact its implementation within schools.

The main difference we found between the Israeli teachers' accounts on GCE and studies from post-conflict societies, and in particular Northern Ireland (Reilly and Niens 2014), is the way teachers view the importance placed on GCE by the state and its institutions, particularly the Ministries of Education and policy-makers in each context. While in Northern

Ireland GCE is seen as an imperative brought on by a need to create a common ground for identity formation and dialogue between the groups that comprise the local society, our study shows that the situation in Israel is completely different. Although teachers in our study were supportive of the ideas of GCE to certain extent, nearly all of them made it quite clear that it would be unlikely for the MOE to embrace it because the MOE does not aim to bridge the gaps between the groups comprising Israeli society.

Closing remarks

Overarching conclusions cannot be drawn from this study due to its relatively small scope and its focus on Jewish Israeli teachers in Tel-Aviv; however, it does highlight some of the potential factors policymakers should note when developing GCE curricula for conflict-ridden states. In particular, our interviews reveal that in order to be incorporated into the Israeli education system, global citizenship would need to be articulated as supplementary to national citizenship rather than clashing with it as an alternative identity model. The GCE terminology in itself may be perceived as threatening and similar constructs such as education for global-mindedness may be preferable in conflict-ridden states. Democratic citizenship education would suffer from similar problems as the particular semantic objection would be to the 'citizenship' aspect of the term. Whichever name it dons, in order to maintain its content and avoid completely utilitarian or instrumental modes the ultimate goals of GCE would need to be carefully considered and properly articulated. As other scholars have asserted, although GCE has transformative potential that could be particularly useful in conflict-ridden states (Davies 2006; Gaudelli 2016), significant structural changes in divided education systems may need to occur before this potential could even be addressed, in part due to the contentious nature of human rights in divided nations (Gordon 2012; Hanna 2016).

Disclosure statement

No potential conflict of interest was reported by the authors.

References

Agbaria, Ayman K. 2016. "The 'Right' Education in Israel: Segregation, Religious Ethnonationalism, and Depoliticized Professionalism." *Critical Studies in Education* (Ahead of print). doi 10.1080/17508487.2016.1185642.

Agbaria, Ayman K., Muhanad Mustafa, and Yousef T. Jabareen. 2015. "'in Your Face' Democracy: Education for Belonging and Its Challenges in Israel." *British Educational Research Journal* 41 (1): 143–175. doi:10.1002/berj.3133.

Ahmad, Iftikhar, and Michelle Y. Szpara. 2005. "Education for Democratic Citizenship and Peace: Proposal for a Cosmopolitan Model." *Educational Studies: Journal of the American Educational Studies Association* 38 (1): 8–23.

Al-Haj, Majid. 2005. "National Ethos, Multicultural Education, and the New History Textbooks in Israel." *Curriculum Inquiry* 35 (1): 47–71. doi:10.1111/j.1467-873X.2005.00315.x.

Andreotti, Vanessa. 2006. "Soft versus Critical Global Citizenship Education." *Development Education Policy and Practice* 3: 83–98. Belfast, UK: Centre for Global Education.

Appiah, Kwame A. 2006. *Cosmopolitanism: Ethics in a World of Strangers*. New York, NY: W. W. Norton.

Banks, James A. 2008. "Diversity, Group Identity, and Citizenship Education in a Global Age." *Educational Researcher* 37 (3): 129–139. doi:10.3102/0013189X08317501.

Bar-Tal, Daniel. 1998. "Societal Beliefs in times of Intractable Conflict: The Israeli Case." *International Journal of Conflict Management* 9 (1): 22–50. doi:10.1108/eb022803.

Bromley, Patricia, and Wade Cole. 2016. "Tale of Two Worlds: The Interstate System and World Society in Social Science Textbooks, 1950-2011." *Globalisation, Societies and Education*. (Ahead of Print). doi 10.1080/14767724.2016.1195730.

Brown, Eleanor J., and W. John Morgan. 2008. "A Culture of Peace via Global Citizenship Education." *Peace Review* 20 (3): 283–291. doi:10.1080/10402650802330089.

Brunold-Conesa, Cynthia. 2010. "International Education: The International Baccalaureate, Montessori and Global Citizenship." *Journal of Research in International Education* 9: 259–272. doi:10.1177/1475240910382992.

Buckner, Elizabeth, and Susan Garnett Russell. 2013. "Portraying the Global: Cross-National Trends in Textbooks' Portrayal of Globalization and Global Citizenship." *International Studies Quarterly* 57: 738–750. doi:10.1111/isqu.12078.

Cha, Yun-Kyung, and Seung-Hwan Ham. 2011. "Educating Supranational Citizens: The Incorporation of English Language Education into Curriculum Policies." *American Journal of Education* 117: 183–209. doi:10.1086/657887.

Cohen, Aviv. 2016. "Navigating Competing Conceptions of Civic Education: Lessons from Three Israeli Civics Classrooms." *Oxford Review of Education* 42 (4): 391–407. doi:10.1080/03054985.2016.1194262.

Davies, Lynn. 2006. "Global Citizenship: Abstraction or Framework for Action?" *Educational Review* 58 (1): 5–25. doi:10.1080/00131910500352523.

Davies, Lynn. 2008. "Interruptive Democracy in Education." In *Comparative and Global Pedagogies: Equity, Access and Democracy in Education*, edited by Joseph Zahjda, Lynn Davies, and Suzanne Majhanovich, 15–33. Dordrecht: Springer.

Dill, Jeffrey S. 2013. *The Longings and Limits of Global Citizenship Education: The Moral Pedagogy of Schooling in a Cosmopolitan Age*. New York: Routledge.

Engel, Laura C. 2014. "Global Citizenship and National (Re) Formations: Analysis of Citizenship Education Reform in Spain." *Education, Citizenship and Social Justice* 9 (3): 239–254. doi:10.1177/1746197914545927.

Evans, Mark, Leigh Anne Ingram, Angela MacDonald, and Nadya Weber. 2009. "Mapping the 'Global Dimension' of Citizenship Education in Canada: The Complex Interplay of Theory, Practice and Context." *Citizenship Teaching and Learning* 5 (2): 17–34.

Feldman, Jackie. 2002. "Marking the Boundaries of the Enclave: Defining the Israeli Collective through the Poland'Experience'." *Israel Studies* 7 (2): 84–114.

Firer, Ruth. 1998. "Human Rights in History and Civics Textbooks: The Case of Israel." *Curriculum Inquiry* 28 (2): 195–208. doi:10.1111/0362-6784.00084.

Gaudelli, William. 2016. *Global Citizenship Education: Everyday Transcendence*. New York: Routledge.

Gaudelli, William, and William R. Fernekes. 2004. "Teaching about Global Human Rights for Global Citizenship." *The Social Studies* 95 (1): 16–26. doi:10.3200/TSSS.95.1.16-26.

Gill, Scherto, and Ulricke Niens. 2014. "Education as Humanisation: A Theoretical Review on the Role of Dialogic Pedagogy in Peacebuilding Education." *Compare: A Journal of Comparative and International Education* 44 (1): 10–31. doi:10.1080/03057925.2013.859879.

Gold, Steve. 1994. "'Israeli Immigrants in the United States: The Question of Community'." *Qualitative Sociology* 17 (4): 325–363. doi:10.1007/BF02393335.

Gordon, Neve. 2012. "The Geography and Political Context of Human Rights Education: Israel as a Case Study." *Journal of Human Rights* 11 (3): 384–404.

Goren, Heela, and Miri Yemini. 2016. "Global Citizenship Education in Context: Teacher Perceptions at an International School and a Local Israeli School." *Compare: A Journal of Comparative and International Education* 46 (5): 832–853. doi:10.1080/03057925.2015.1111752.

Gould, Eric D., and Omer Moav. 2007. "Israel's Brain Drain." *Israel Economic Review* 5 (1): 1–22.

Gross, Zehavit. 2010. "Holocaust Education in Jewish Schools in Israel: Goals, Dilemmas Challenges." *Prospects* 40 (1): 93–113. doi:10.1007/s11125-010-9142-x.

Hanna, Helen. 2016. "Dealing with Difference in the Divided Educational Context: Balancing Freedom of Expression and Non-Discrimination in Northern Ireland and Israel." *Compare: A Journal of Comparative and International Education* (Ahead of Print). doi 10.1080/03057925.2015.1119649.

Ichilov, Orit. 2003. "Teaching Civics in a Divided Society: The Case of Israel." *International Studies in Sociology of Education* 13 (3): 219–242. doi:10.1080/09620210300200111.

Kimmerling, Baruch. 1993. "Patterns of Militarism in Israel." *European Journal of Sociology* 34 (2): 196–223. doi:10.1017/S0003975600006640.

Law, Wing W. 2007. "Globalisation, City Development and Citizenship Education in China's Shanghai." *International Journal of Educational Development* 27 (1): 18–38. doi:10.1016/j.ijedudev.2006.04.017.

Leask, Betty. 2013. "Internationalizing the Curriculum in the Disciplines – Imagining New Possibilities." *Journal of Studies in International Education* 17 (2): 103–118. doi:10.1177/1028315312475090.

Lemish, Peter. 2003. "Civic and Citizenship Education in Israel." *Cambridge Journal of Education* 33 (1): 53–72. doi:10.1080/0305764032000064640.

Marshall, Harriet. 2015. "The Global Education Terminology Debate: Exploring Some of the Issues." In *The SAGE Handbook of Research in International Education*, edited by Mary Hayden, Jack Levy, and Jeff Thompson, 38–50. London: Sage.

Monaghan, Chrissie, and Carol Anne Spreen. 2016. "From Human Rights to Global Citizenship Education: Movement, Migration, Conflict and Capitalism in the Classroom." In *Globalisation, Human Rights Education and Reforms*, edited by Joseph Zajda and Sec Ozdowski, 35–53. Dordrecht: Springer.

Moon, Rennie J., and Jeong-Woo Koo. 2011. "Global Citizenship and Human Rights: A Longitudinal Analysis of Social Studies and Ethics Textbooks in the Republic of Korea." *Comparative Education Review* 55: 574–599. doi:10.1086/660796.

Morris, Paul, and John Cogan. 2001. "A Comparative Overview: Civic Education across Six Societies." *International Journal of Educational Research* 35: 109–123.

Myers, John P. 2006. "Rethinking the Social Studies Curriculum in the Context of Globalization: Education for Global Citizenship in the US." *Theory and Research in Social Education* 34: 370–394. doi:10.1080/00933104.2006.10473313.

Myers, John P. 2016. "Charting a Democratic Course for Global Citizenship Education: Research Directions and Current Challenges." *Education Policy Analysis Archives* 24: 1–16. doi:10.14507/epaa.24.2174.

Niens, Ulrike, and Jacqueline Reilly. 2012. "Education for Global Citizenship in a Divided Society? Young People's Views and Experiences." *Comparative Education* 48: 103–118. doi:10.1080/03050068.2011.637766.

Niens, Ulrike, Una O'Connor, and Alan Smith. 2013. "Citizenship Education in Divided Societies: Teachers' Perspectives in Northern Ireland." *Citizenship Studies* 17: 128–141. doi:10.1080/13621025.2012.716214.

Oxley, Laura, and Paul Morris. 2013. "Global Citizenship: A Typology for Distinguishing Its Multiple Conceptions." *British Journal of Educational Studies* 61: 301–325. doi:10.1080/00071005.2013.798393.

Pedahzur, Ami. 2001. "The Paradox of Civic Education in Non-Liberal Democracies: The Case of Israel." *Journal of Education Policy* 16 (5): 413–430. doi:10.1080/02680930110071020.

Philippou, Stavroula. 2007. "Policy, Curriculum and the Struggle for Change in Cyprus: The Case of the European Dimension in Education." *International Studies in Sociology of Education* 17 (3): 249–274. doi:10.1080/09620210701543916.

Pigozzi, Mary Joy. 2006. "A UNESCO View of Global Citizenship Education." *Educational Review* 58 (1): 1–4. doi:10.1080/00131910500352473.

Pike, Graham. 2015. "Re-Imagining Global Education in the Neoliberal Age." In *Contesting and Constructing International Perspectives in Global Education*, edited by R. Reynolds, D. Bradbery, J. Brown, K. Carroll, D. Donnelly, K. Ferguson-Patrick, and S. Macqueen, 11–25. Rotterdam: Sense Publishers.

Pinson, Halleli. 2007. "Inclusive Curriculum? Challenges to the Role of Civic Education in a Jewish and Democratic State." *Curriculum Inquiry* 37 (4): 351–382. doi:10.1111/j.1467-873X.2007.00391.x.

Quaynor, Laura. 2015. "I Do Not Have the Means to Speak: Educating Youth for Citizenship in Post-Conflict Liberia." *Journal of Peace Education* 12 (1): 15–36. doi:10.1080/17400201.2014.931277.

Rapoport, Anatoli. 2009. "A Forgotten Concept: Global Citizenship Education and State Social Studies Standards." *Journal of Social Studies Research* 33 (1): 91–112.

Rapoport, Anatoli. 2010. "We Cannot Teach What we Don't Know: Indiana Teachers Talk About GCE." *Education, Citizenship and Social Justice* 5 (3): 179–190. doi:10.1177/1746197910382256.

Rapoport, Anatoli. 2015. "Global Aspects of Citizenship Education: Challenges and Perspectives." In *The State of Global Education. Learning with the World and Its People*, edited by Maguth, Brad, and Jeremy Hilburn, 27–40. New York, NY: Routledge.

Rebhun, Uzi, and Chaim Isaac Waxman. 2000. "The Americanization of Israel: A Demographic, Cultural and Political Evaluation." *Israel Studies* 5 (1): 65–91.

Reilly, Jacqueline, and Ulricke Niens. 2014. "Global Citizenship as Education for Peacebuilding in a Divided Society: Structural and Contextual Constraints on the Development of Critical Dialogic Discourse in Schools." *Compare: A Journal of Comparative and International Education* 44 (1): 53–76. doi 10.1080/03057925.2013.859894.

Resnik, Julia. 1999. "Particularistic Vs. Universalistic Content in the Israeli Education System." *Curriculum Inquiry* 29 (4): 485–511. doi:10.1111/0362-6784.00143.

Resnik, Julia. 2003. "'Sites of Memory' of the Holocaust: Shaping National Memory in the Education System in Israel." *Nations and Nationalism* 9 (2): 297–317. doi 10.1111/1469-8219.0008.

Sabbagh, Clara, and Nura Resh. 2014. "Citizenship Orientations in a Divided Society: A Comparison of Three Groups of Israeli Junior-High Students–Secular Jews, Religious Jews, and Israeli Arabs." *Education, Citizenship and Social Justice* 9 (1): 34–54. doi 10.1177/1746197913497662.

Schattle, Hans. 2008. "Education for Global Citizenship: Illustrations of Ideological Pluralism and Adaptation." *Journal of Political Ideologies* 13: 73–94. doi:10.1080/13569310701822263.

Schreier, Margrit. 2012. *Qualitative Content Analysis in Practice*. Thousand Oaks: Sage.

Schweisfurth, Michele. 2006. "Education for Global Citizenship: Teacher Agency and Curricular Structure in Ontario Schools." *Educational Review* 58 (1): 41–50. doi:10.1080/00131910500352648.

Shultz, Lynette. 2007. "Educating for Global Citizenship: Conflicting Agendas and Understandings." *Alberta Journal of Educational Research* 53 (3): 248–258.

Smith, Alan. 2003. "Citizenship Education in Northern Ireland: Beyond National Identity?" *Cambridge Journal of Education* 33 (1): 15–32. doi:10.1080/0305764032000064631.

Smooha, Sammy. 2002. "The Model of Ethnic Democracy: Israel as a Jewish and Democratic State." *Nations and Nationalism* 8 (4): 475–503.

Uriely, Natan. 1995. "Patterns of Identification and Integration with Jewish Americans among Israeli Immigrants in Chicago: Variations across Status and Generation." *Contemporary Jewry* 16 (1): 27–49. doi:10.1007/BF02962386.

Veugelers, Wiel. 2011. "The Moral and the Political in Global Citizenship: Appreciating Differences in Education." *Globalisation, Societies and Education* 9 (3): 473–485. doi:10.1080/14767724.2011.605329.

Yamashita, Hiromi. 2006. "Global Citizenship Education and War: The Needs of Teachers and Learners." *Educational Review* 58: 27–39. doi:10.1080/00131910500352531.

Yemini, Miri. 2014a. "Internationalisation Discourse What Remains to Be Said?." *Perspectives: Policy and Practice in Higher Education* 18 (2): 66–71.

Yemini, Miri. 2014b. "Internationalization of Secondary Education—Lessons From Israeli Palestinian-Arab Schools in Tel Aviv-Jaffa." *Urban Education* 49 (5): 471–498.

Yemini, Miri, Hed Bar-Nissan, and Oriah Yardeni. 2014. "Between "us" and "them": Teachers' Perceptions of the National versus International Composition of the Israeli History Curriculum." *Teaching and Teacher Education* 42: 11–22.

Yemini, Miri, and Alexandra Fulop. 2015. "The International, Global and Intercultural Dimensions in Schools: an Analysis of Four Internationalised Israeli Schools." *Globalisation, Societies and Education* 13 (4): 528–552.

Yonah, Yossi. 2005. "Israel as a Multicultural Democracy: Challenges and Obstacles." *Israel Affairs* 11 (1): 95–116. doi:10.1080/1353712042000324472.

Reframing approaches to narrating young people's conceptualisations of citizenship in education research

Bassel Akar

ABSTRACT
Large-scale quantitative studies on citizenship and citizenship education research have advanced an international and comparative field of democratic citizenship education. Their instruments, however, informed by theoretical variables constructed in Western Europe and North America mostly measure young people's understandings of a predefined construct of democratic citizenship. Recent studies that report on young people's descriptions and interpretations of citizenship issues and concepts show that a new methodology of narrating young people's individual conceptualisations of citizenship is emerging. The author argues that the methods of inquiry into conceptualisations of citizenship require: (1) a social constructionist ontology that views reality as socially constructed; (2) a wide-ranging operational definition of citizenship; and (3) open-ended questions that facilitate the self-reporting, reflection and discussions of experiences regarded as good citizenship. The author draws on evidence from citizenship education research in Lebanon that examines young people's conceptualisations of citizenship and illustrates constructs particular to Lebanon and the wider region.

Introduction

Since the 1990s, the empirical field of citizenship education research has grown remarkably, exploring young people's understandings of citizenship and experiences of learning citizenship in school. Most notably, large-scale international studies measuring young people's competencies for being democratic (e.g. Schulz et al. 2010; Torney-Purta et al. 2001) or active (e.g. Hoskins et al. 2008) citizens have pioneered comparative and quantitative approaches to citizenship education research. These measurements have developed over a relatively long-standing history. In 1971, the International Association for the Evaluation of Educational Achievement (IEA) launched a comparative civic education study on 14-year-olds in 10 countries (Torney, Oppenheim, and Farnen 1975). Over two decades later, the IEA carried out the Civic Education study (CivEd) that surveyed 90,000 14-year-olds across 28 countries in 1999 (Torney-Purta et al. 2001) and, later in 2000, 50,000 16- to 19-year-olds in 16 countries (Amadeo et al. 2002). The subsequent 2008/9 International Civic and

Citizenship Education Study (ICCS) spanned further to 38 countries collecting data from 140,000 grade 8 students, 62,000 teachers and 5300 school principals. The ICCS surveys further developed the CivEd questionnaire by incorporating indicators on education to distinguish civic education from citizenship education and measure competencies necessary to meet growing challenges in the twenty-first century. The IEA most recently launched the 2016 ICCS study, which is still in progress. The 1999 CivEd study also informed the development of a composite indicator to measure the civic competence (CCE) of 14-year-old students in European countries needed to address issues related to globalisation and make changes in their community (Hoskins et al. 2008). The Government of Lebanon and United Nations Development Programme (UNDP) also found the 1999 CivEd instrument valuable in measuring the intersectionality of civic education, national identity, sectarianism and the political system in Lebanon to produce the Lebanon National Human Development Report (UNDP 2008) and a test of 3111 ninth-grade students' civic knowledge, attitudes and values (UNDP 2009; UNDP, Mehe, and CDR 2008).

These giant international and comparative studies on citizenship and education aim to measure how ready or competent young people are to take action as citizens informed by knowledge of their local civic institutions and wider democratic and human rights principles. The quantitative close-ended design of questions facilitates the gathering and management of data from tens of thousands of students and teachers from around the world. As the IEA holds the largest bank of data on citizenship education in the world, researchers are able to carry out multivariate and longitudinal analyses. Hoskins et al. (2012), for example, drew on data from the 1999 CivEd and 2009 ICCS results to graph changes in civic values, attitudes and practices in selected countries over time (see pp. 23–32). The exceptional growth of quantitative international research on democratic citizenship and citizenship education, however, does not address the paucity of learning people's own understandings of citizenship. Below, I introduce two shortcomings in the large-scale quantitative approaches to learning about young people's conceptualisations of citizenship.

One shortcoming stems from the ontological assumption that a particular concept of citizenship can be normative across all cultures around the world. The IEA studies have developed their instruments based on a political dimension of citizenship, namely a national democratic one that is reflected in the first two of three 'core international domains': (1) democracy; (2) national identity, regional and international relationships; and (3) social cohesion and diversity (Husfeldt and Torney-Purta 2004). Questions in the technical report (Schulz and Sibberns 2004) under the 'democracy' domain test students on knowledge of features of democratic and non-democratic governments with one correct answer per question (173) and survey attitudes towards 'anti-democratic groups' without correct answers (e.g. should anti-democratic groups be prohibited from organising peaceful demonstrations) (109). Furthermore, when writing the indicators of democratic citizenship and their questions, the researchers consulted theoretical variables developed in Western Europe and North America. For instance, the CivEd study technical report instruments (Schulz and Sibberns 2004; Torney-Purta et al. 2001) drew from models of ecological development (Bronfenbrenner 1988), situated cognition (Wenger 1998), political socialisation (e.g. Diamond 1999; Inglehart 1997; Norris 1999) and political science literature that aimed to define democratic citizenship (e.g. Beetham 1993; Held 1996; Janoski 1998). For example, research from Inglehart (1997) inspired questions to measure attitudes towards government institutions, like how much they trust the government in doing what is right (Torney-Purta et al. 2001). According to the same report (ibid 2001), questions on national pride and trust in government institutions that covered the first two domains were also influenced by Norris (1999). Similar assumptions based analyses of large-scale quantitative studies in European countries on civic competence (Hoskins et al. 2008), active citizenship (Hoskins and Mascherini 2009) and participatory citizenship (Hoskins et al. 2012). Inquiry questions based on selected theoretical constructs of citizenship (e.g. democratic, active, participatory) may overlook people's individual conceptions of citizenship. Such instruments make it more difficult to identify unique and shared humanistic principles and practices found across cultures. Thus, we return to the validity threats posed by researching the social realities and phenomena of a particular culture using the lenses of another culture (Said 1978).

Another shortcoming lies in the epistemological approaches used to learn about individual conceptualisations of citizenship. According to the CivEd technical report (Husfeldt and Torney-Purta 2004), students were administered (1) a test comprising multiple choice questions with one correct answer testing knowledge of content and the ability to interpret civic or political literature and (2) a close-ended survey on understandings of democracy and citizenship and related attitudes and practices but without correct answers. Some test questions ask students to interpret a 'main message of cartoon about' democracy, political leader or history textbooks. Their responses indicate their abilities to interpret images or texts; however, without justifications, we learn very little about the understandings and experiences of citizenship young people hold. In other words, citizenship studies continue to overlook individual experiences when 'constructing cultural meanings and practices' (Miller-Idriss 2006, 543). Furthermore, the empirical field of citizenship and citizenship education mostly neglects students' and teachers' understandings of citizenship-related concepts across cultures (Hahn 2010). Indeed, current civic education research has disregarded young people's understandings and experiences of citizenship beyond the scope of researchers' constructed definitions of citizenship (Ruben 2007). Consequently, Kennedy (2007) found the CivEd data limited in the extent to which it drew out students' conceptualisations of active citizenship and participation. Therefore, to a great extent, established quantitative-based citizenship education studies have essentially measured students' understandings of **others'** understandings of citizenship. These shortcomings prompt a re-examination of the ontological and epistemological assumptions that underpin investigations of individual conceptualisations of citizenship when researching citizenship education.

In this paper, I argue that citizenship and citizenship education research requires: (1) a view of citizenship as a socio-cultural construct; (2) a wide-ranging operational definition; and (3) qualitative methods to explore individual conceptualisations of citizenship. I demonstrate through a citizenship education research study in Lebanon that such a methodological framework enhances the content validity of accounts of how young people learn citizenship, yields culture-specific indicators of 'good citizenship', and empowers young people to express their understandings of and attempts to practise 'good citizenship'. I first present an emerging empirical field of citizenship education research that investigates the learning and teaching of citizenship by qualitatively examining students' and teachers' individual conceptualisations of citizenship. I then frame these innovative studies within an ontology that assumes reality and knowledge are socially constructed, and present a wide-ranging operational definition of citizenship that allows research participants to narrate their conceptualisations of citizenship. I also explain how this methodological framework facilitates an inside-out approach to investigating citizenship education. Finally, I draw on the methodology, findings and outcomes of a qualitative-based exploration into young people's conceptualisations of citizenship and experiences of learning citizenship in Lebanon to demonstrate the validity and ethical strengths of this methodology.

Citizenship and citizenship education according to young people

Students' and teachers' conceptualisations of citizenship provide a critical perspective for understanding and interpreting their experiences of learning and teaching citizenship. This is because our understandings of citizenship influence our approaches to learning and teaching citizenship (Cogan, Morris, and Print 2002). Only in the past two decades have research studies begun to facilitate opportunities for young people to reflect on their understandings of citizenship and on how their notions have been constructed.

In my search for such studies, I found two that took place in West Asia and North Africa, the geopolitical region in which Lebanon is located. In Kuwait, Al-Nakib (2012) facilitated student research workshops in several phases to examine the influence of a 'Constitution and Human Rights (CHR)' module for a total of 60 students in grades 10, 11 and 12. During these workshops, students were asked to reflect on their learning about citizenship, human rights and democracy by responding on a poster, discussing their responses with group members and then adding to the responses in a different ink colour. Findings suggested that students who completed the three-year CHR programme articulated their positions, challenged teachers, illustrated agency and demonstrated confidence in a far more advanced manner than those who studied CHR for one year only.

A study in South Lebanon explored the constructions of the Palestinian identity as a people in exile. Fincham (2012) interviewed and facilitated focus groups to a total of 76 Palestinians ($n = 50$ 15–24-year-olds; $n = 26$ over 30 years old) across three refugee camps in the port city of Tyre. Their testimonies and reflections suggested that the school was least effective because they follow the highly nationalistic Lebanese national curriculum, which excludes any mention of Palestine and its culture. At school, however, they sustain their heritage, 'Palestinianness' and sense of belonging through symbolic activities like singing the national anthem every morning, graffiti of national symbols on the school walls and replacing 'Israel' with 'Occupied Palestine'. Family emerged as the most effective space for building and sustaining the Palestinian identity through narratives of being Palestinian, constructed gender roles declared as particular to Palestinian culture and cultural practices like the Arabic dialect, folk dance and food. They also attributed the construction of the Palestinian identity to the political organisations and their respective visions of Palestine, symbols, celebrated historical events and figures and even garments like the checked headscarf. Some believe that the survival of the Palestinian nation relied mostly on the reproduction of its children. In the religious sphere, the Palestinian Sunnis, Shi'as and Christians each have a discourse with distinct religious symbols and struggles within the construct of being Palestinian. The dominant discourse, however, constructs the Palestinian as Sunni, which creates feelings of exclusion for Shi'a and Christian Palestinians.

In the UK, O'Toole (2003) conducted a series of group and individual interviews, along with images presented for interpretation, with a sample of 16–24-year-olds from seven areas in Birmingham. The participants engaged in a free association exercise when describing the images, prompting group discussions on politics, which were later probed in depth during one-to-one interviews. Through the interviews, the participants spoke about topical political issues and described how they had been marginalised from political participation. This study challenged previous research that identified young people in the UK as politically apathetic.

Exploring teenagers' attitudes towards and experiences of citizenship on the Isle of Wight in Britain, Weller (2007) adopted a geographical perspective to understanding their 'space and place', two key elements in young people's practices of citizenship. Data was collected from web forum discussions and a community radio phone-in, from student surveys in Years 9, 10 and 11 (ages 13–16), and via 20 teenagers from Year 9 who wrote diaries, took photographs, took part in interviews and focus groups, and exchanged emails and chats with the researcher. While these teenagers described ways in which they were marginalised and neglected in their community, they also explained how they had established specific spaces for hanging out and built skate-park facilities.

Over a three-year (1999–2001) qualitative longitudinal study in Leicester, UK, Lister et al. (2003) conducted three waves of interviews with 64 young people, examining changes in their understandings of citizenship and self-perceptions as citizens. Participants spoke about where they thought they stood in society and issues that meant most to them. The conversations resulted in findings that suggested five models of citizenship: (1) universal status based on membership in a nation or the world; (2) respectable economic independence, demonstrating financial independence; (3) constructive social participation, entailing action that helps build the community; (4) a social-contractual relationship of rights and responsibilities; and (5) right to a voice that protects the freedom of expression. Lister et al. found that participants spoke mostly about 'universal status' during the first phase but, with time, spent more time articulating 'respectable economic independence' and 'constructive social participation'. Participants also described levels of citizenship, such as first- and second-class and 'good' and 'bad', and showed mixed feelings about national identity and volunteerism.

Another study in two schools in Leicester aimed to examine young people's learning and living experiences of citizenship in and out of school (Osler and Starkey 2003). In addition to the 600 questionnaires, the researchers facilitated a workshop in each school for a sample of students who were asked to define themselves through writing and present photographs of their community in the form of an exhibition with captions for each. Based on the findings, Osler and Starkey (2003) found that these students valued their multiple levels of identities but were unlikely to have opportunities to express these multiple identities and experiences in an educational setting for national citizenship. In a slightly similar study across three schools in the US Midwest, 36 fifth graders were interviewed in pairs about their understandings of core democratic values (CDVs) and good citizenship (O'Mahony 2009). Students quoted family, social studies class, posters in school and television programmes as sources for learning about justice and other CDVs.

Tereshchenko (2013) explored conceptualisations of citizenship of young people from conflicting East and West borders of Ukraine. They wrote descriptive words on a map of Ukraine and were then asked to describe Ukraine to someone who is unfamiliar with the state. The descriptions were further explored through group discussions revealing a rather poetic patriotic discourse also found in Ukrainian state education. The group discussions also 'became increasingly politicised and emotional' when explaining differences across the regions based on language and political positions. The media and schooling appeared to largely shape their individual feelings of identity and sense of pride. History education, for example, credits Galicia as the first region to fight for the state's independence and, so, those from Galicia claimed they held stronger feelings of Ukrainian national identity.

In the Canadian city of Vancouver, Kennelly and Dillabough (2008) examined how low-income young people conceptualise their notions and practices of citizenship and their experiences of being marginalised in their schools and everyday living. The team of researchers designed an ethnographic study that engaged 24 young people in classroom activities. In addition to classroom and community observations, 16 of the 24 participated in open-ended interviews that probed their perceptions of school and themselves, as well as of their relationships with others and the surrounding cultures. Among the findings, young people described economic self-sufficiency as crucial to gaining respect and living in Canada, indicating little or no reliance on the state. Also, being a 'good citizen' was related to helping others and, yet, seen as a serious risk to one's safety unless the activities were aimed at charity. Some also suggested that 'bad citizens' are those not conforming to the Canadian ethnic identity.

The findings of the aforementioned studies highlight two significant outcomes from employing qualitative-based methodologies when exploring young people's conceptualisations of citizenship. First, young people's open-ended responses challenge suggestions made by large-scale quantitative national surveys, as in the case of the UK. For instance, the youth in O'Toole et al.'s (2003) study emerged as politically marginalised rather than politically apathetic, as had been suggested by previous quantitative studies (cf. Parry, Moyser, and Day 1992; Seyd, Whiteley, and Pattie 2001). O'Toole et al. (2003) maintained that closed-ended surveys 'impose a conception of politics and political participation' that limits opportunities for young people to explain their understandings of political participation and perceived roles in the political sphere (47). Second, many of the findings illustrated context-specific variables that shape the kind of citizenship that students learn. For example, experiences from school and home can provide sources for democratic values (O'Mahony 2009). Narratives of injustice and cultural symbols presented through home, media, religious groups and political parties can generate a strong sense of belonging to a country despite having been born and raised in exile (Fincham 2012). Besides this, the emphasis of nationalism in school can, on the one hand, cause distress to students who want to express other levels of identity (Osler and Starkey 2003) and, on the other hand, view non-allegiance to national identity as a concept of 'bad citizenship' (Kennelly and Dillabough 2008). Conceptualisations of citizenship explored in these studies may have been more difficult to discover and engage with using closed-ended questions constructed with reference to specifically defined concepts of citizenship.

A methodological framework for examining citizenship education from the inside out

Measuring students' understandings of democratic citizenship and experiences of learning democratic citizenship requires us to first set defining indicators of democratic citizenship. This **outside-in** approach to citizenship education research yields responses towards a pre-defined citizenship. When trying to learn about people's own conceptualisations of citizenship, then an **inside-out** approach allows people from distinct cultural contexts to present their own understandings and experiences. An inside-out approach to researching citizenship education utilises a wide-ranging operational definition of citizenship to narrate other people's conceptualisations of citizenship. Conceptualisations, in this sense, include participants' understandings of citizenship and how they have constructed them. Starting from the 'inside' also means learning about the cultural discourse of citizenship, which includes narratives and literature on values, principles and practices of trying to live in dignity and diversity. This view is similar to Hobsbawm's (1990) call for 'analysing nations and their associated phenomena' like national identity 'from below' (9), a view to discover everyday people's thoughts, experiences, intentions and visions and a task that is 'exceedingly difficult' (10). Drawing on Hobsbawm (1990), Fox and Miller-Idriss (2008) attempt to examine everyday nationalism from below by exploring how people have spoken about their national identities and feelings of belonging and how such conversations and interactions with national symbols and commodities have influenced their everyday choices. Starting from the inside and moving out means that we adopt an ontology that allows participants to openly express their experiences and reflections, which can later inform us about their conceptualisations and learning of citizenship.

Socially constructing knowledge as a view of the world

Social scientists have explored social phenomena through the view that knowledge and reality are socially constructed. Stemming from this ontology, research paradigms like naturalistic inquiry (Lincoln and Guba 1985), the interpretivist approach (Wellington 2000), social constructionism (Berger and Luckmann 1966; Searle 1995), social constructivism (Bruner 1990), hermeneutics (Ricœur 1991) and phenomenology (Moustakas 1994) aim to objectify (inter)subjective understandings and interpretations into knowledge and reality. Social constructionist approaches, for example, examine the processes of how bodies of knowledge become reality, including the repetition of rhetoric and action and establishment of these actions within society's institutions (Berger and Luckmann 1966). Integral to the collective macro-level processes of social constructionism is social constructivism, a micro-level activity of individual conceptualisations. Social constructivists' research methods investigate how individuals interpret, reflect upon and present their observations and experiences (Hartas 2010). They also underscore the significance of individuals' experiences and perspectives and the context in which the meanings were personally constructed (Creswell 2005). Moreover, in this understanding, knowledge of social phenomena is constructed through the researcher's interaction with people as they communicate their perceptions and understandings of the world or reality around them. The reality constructed by peoples' understandings and, to a certain degree, the researchers' values are, indeed, real (Lynch 2006). (Inter)subjectivity is inherent in social constructivist approaches to research. Hence, the significance of the findings lies mainly in the reflections and discussions of emerging themes (Seale 2004). Notwithstanding concerns about impartiality and potential bias (Hammersley 1995), personalised reports and reflections strengthen the internal validity of open-ended citizenship studies.

Exploring socially constructed understandings and experiences falls directly within the nature of citizenship, a social construction. Concepts of citizenship are organically moulded by the beliefs, rhetoric and actions of individuals and groups (Bank, Delamont, and Marshall 2007) and, thus, diverse across cultures (Arnot and Dillabough 2000). The state of cultural diversities – whether at a global, national or microcosmic scale – requires us to hypothesise for diverse constructs of citizenship. A social constructivist research paradigm can explore people's individual conceptualisations of citizenship by facilitating spaces in which they can better communicate their understandings. The researcher would show sensitivity to the power dynamics in developing parts of the world by trying various methods to enable children, mothers, refugees and other vulnerable groups to express their perceptions and experiences (Laws, Harper, and Marcus 2003). By capturing and communicating stakeholder voices, Lincoln (2001) maintains, constructivist research methods uphold principles of social justice typically undermined by research agendas that centre on generalisability. Young people communicating their experiences and reflections practise their right to be heard as set out in Article 12 of the United Nations Convention on the Rights of the Child (United Nations 1989). When young people reflect on their understandings, observations and experiences of social and political issues around them, they participate in pedagogical research which can empower them as citizens (Starkey et al. 2014).

Operationalising citizenship

An inside-out approach to citizenship education research does not suggest entering a research site free of any conceptual or analytical framework for citizenship. It acknowledges, though, that applying pre-set indicators of an ideal type of citizenship would merely measure young peoples' conceptualisations of that particular type. Examining the social phenomena of learning and teaching citizenship within a constructivist paradigm requires a set of defining indicators of 'citizenship'. Indicators of a broad definition of citizenship facilitate the open space for research participants to express **their** conceptualisations of citizenship. Conceptualisations comprise one's notion of an ideal citizenship and one's experiences in constructing it. I operationalise 'citizenship' based on the widely accepted premise that citizenship is the relationship between the individual and her/his surrounding communities. Below, I present a conceptual framework of citizenship that has allowed for an open inquiry into individual conceptualisations of these relationships.

Dimensions of citizenship

Amongst the scores of evidence-informed literature on citizenship, finding a definition of citizenship for an instrument that would allow individuals to express their meditations on citizenship is a challenge, especially in scholarly literature from West Asia and North Africa. Traditionally, citizenship is viewed as a relationship between the individual and the state. In Arabic, two words can be translated into 'citizenship'. *Jinsiyyah* is nationality as a legal status. *Muwātanah* is derived from the root word that gives us *watan*, or nation, and *muwātin*, a citizen; it lexically denotes feelings and practices towards the nation-state (like patriotism). In an edited book that examines citizenship in the Middle East [sic] (Butenschøn, Davis, and Hassassian 2000), authors of the contributing chapters refer to citizenship as a relationship between the individual and the nation-state that includes dynamics of participation, access to rights, feelings of belonging and the legal/contractual relationship with the governing authority. Citizenship in West Asia and North Africa is also defined by kin and religion.

Kinship and religion are far more deeply engrained and rooted in cultural (social, institutional, legal) constructions of citizenship than is the modern, politically constructed nation-state (Parolin 2009). Prior to and during the rise of Islam, survival in the tribal world depended on the social organisation, solidarity and forms of democratic living that evolved through kinship. Ibn Khaldūn ([1370] 2005), the prominent fourteenth-century historian and anthropologist, observed that group feeling or *'asabiyyah* that was critical for collaboration, consensus and protection during tribal wars was strongest among family relations, and then with allies, neighbours and protected minority groups (Christian and Jewish groups). Religion, too, influenced the social constructions of citizenship in West Asia and North Africa. In this region, Islam, for example, is the dominant religion with 93% of the population being Muslim (Pew Research Center 2017); the faith is described as *dīn wa dawlah,* or religion and State (Khalidi 1992). The Holy Qur'ān is the highest authority in Islam and, thus, the basis for social doctrine and legislation for all Muslims (Rahman [1987] 2005); examples of such regulations based upon it include the Sunnah and the Sharī'ah. Interpretations of the Holy Qur'ān by Al-Ghazālī (1980), an eleventh-century theologian and Imam, constructed a more conservative and exclusive notion of citizenship within the Islamic community by prohibiting non-Muslims to access any rights and privileges, despite his advocacy for justice, politeness, humility and worship. The elements of kinship and religion continue to underpin social constructions of citizenship – and all contentions within them – in modern currents of nationalism (cf. Hourani 1991), movements of pan-nationalism (cf. Tibi 1997), and the international championing of human rights instruments (cf. Hamzawy 2006).

The second idea is that each relationship is shaped by the individual's status (i.e. social, legal, religious, occupational and so on), feelings of belonging and behaviours. Osler and Starkey (2005) define citizenship as status, feelings and practice – three interrelated dimensions. One's (legal) status is typically determined by a higher governing authority, such as nationality. Feelings inform us about senses of belonging and feelings of identity. Citizenship as a practice includes the behaviours that individuals carry out, like voting, paying taxes, recycling, debating and advocacy. In West Asia and North Africa, correlations between status, feelings and practice inform us about social constructions of citizenship and its complexities, as illustrated in the following examples. Expatriates in the Gulf States can neither be naturalised as citizens nor access all civil rights, a restriction intended to protect and preserve cultural heritage. Among the largest population of forcibly displaced people in the region, Palestinians have extremely limited access to protection and other human rights from host governments (UNRWA 2015). Hence, they are either dependent on services by UNRWA or join militia groups for safety and security (Danish Immigration Service 2014). Also, children whose mothers from either Lebanon, Egypt, Syria, Morocco, Tunisia or Jordan marry fathers of a different nationality are not entitled to their mother's legal citizenship status and thus cannot access basic social securities and civil rights (Abou-Habib 2003), resulting in numerous children's human rights violations. The same injustice is also found among stateless people in Kuwait, Iraq and the United Arab Emirates, who are referred to as *bidūn* (short for *bidūn jinsiyyah,* or without nationality). Whether the community is a neighbouring tribe, the nation-state or the Arab region, various cultural elements (religious status and doctrines, familial relationships, legislature, conflicts and so on) define the relationship between people and that community.

Applying a wide-ranging framework of citizenship for inquiry

Investigating individual conceptualisations from the inside out necessitates a wide-ranging framework of citizenship to provide the conceptual space for people to communicate and reflect on their experiences of citizenship. The proposed dimensions – status, feelings and practice – provide a set of apolitical and universal indicators that define citizenship. In many cases, the term 'citizenship' may either be too abstract to use in an inquiry with young people, or may bias responses based on traditional understandings of citizenship as corresponding to citizens with national legal status and strong feelings of nationalism. Instead, researchers can ask young people to reflect on personal experiences of what they would consider to be of 'good citizens' or 'good people in the community'. Young people's reflections on their practices and views of what they consider to be 'good citizenship' can reveal a great deal about the communities they feel connected with, principles they value the most and the dynamics of their interactions. So, when we gather accounts and reflections from the 'inside', we can step 'out' and use evidence-informed conceptual frameworks of citizenship to interpret and critically analyse their personalised constructs.

Qualitative instruments informed by indicators of a wide-ranging operational definition of citizenship provide the space necessary for young people to describe their understandings of citizenship and experiences in constructing these understandings. In the following study, I outline the methodology, findings and outcomes when capturing young people's self-reported conceptualisations of citizenship. This study demonstrates the significance of a social constructivist approach to: (1) learning more about how young people conceptualise citizenship; (2) yielding culture-specific indicators of 'good citizenship'; and (3) empowering young people to reflect on and co-construct meanings of citizenship.

Researching conceptualisations of citizenship in Lebanon

Between 2006 and 2007, I explored the classroom learning and teaching of citizenship in the civics national curriculum programme for grades 10 and 11 in schools across four of the six governorates in Lebanon. The qualitative study examined 19 civics teachers' understandings of citizenship and classroom teaching experiences (Akar 2012) and 435 students' conceptualisations of citizenship and classroom learning experiences (Akar 2016a). I administered all the students' survey packs. The school principals granted me access to their civics hour after recognising the pedagogical benefits that the students could potentially gain from participation (Starkey et al. 2014).

The survey pack was made up of four parts. Part A asked students to write down three things they had already done that they considered to have made them 'feel an important or good person in society or the community'. In Part B, I asked students to write three things they would like to 'know or do later on that would make you feel like a better person in society or the community'. The third part was a one-page diamond ranking exercise. Students were provided with nine citizenship-related themes and asked to individually glue what they considered to be most important on top and work their way down to least important at the bottom. The nine themes, generated from a pilot study (Akar 2007), represented degrees of participation (e.g. maximal/minimal and active/passive). Students were also asked to write a short sentence next to the top and bottom themes explaining why they had placed them there. A tenth space was provided for them to write a practice or theme of citizenship they considered important that could be added to the nine provided. In the final part of the survey pack, students were asked to reflect on classroom learning activities they found most challenging and successful. During the final 10 minutes of the class hour, I facilitated a whole-class discussion so they could further explain their responses.

Main findings

The evidence gathered from the students' self-reported conceptualisations of citizenship suggests three key findings: (1) students apply a maximal-based notion and communitarian approach to citizenship; (2) school trips and activities in civil society have a significant influence on students' conceptualisations of citizenship; and (3) knowledge of communities, universal values and active participation suggest a basic model of citizenship education.

A maximal and communitarian construct of citizenship

The students' responses illustrated their relationships with numerous communities, including national (reducing youth emigration to build Lebanon); social (improving women's rights, medical care, access to education); environmental (protecting nature); political (avoiding or participating in politics); and, to a much lesser extent, global levels (improving Lebanon's international reputation, welfare of children in Africa). Most frequently, the students described active levels of participation, or practices beyond what is expected from the law. Such practices included cleaning beaches, 'build[ing] houses for poor people', 'open[ing] a free school' and hospital that provide free services for the poor, providing recreational services like youth centres and libraries for young people, volunteering, 'establish[ing] an organisation … to protect the environment', making new laws, participating in demonstrations and even parenting. Students who wrote 'helping war victims' and refugees and caring for orphans came from areas in Lebanon most affected by armed conflict. Fewer students wrote about behaviours either expected by the legal system, like paying taxes and 'avoid throwing things on the ground', or of minimal agency for change, such as visiting nursing homes and, arguably, donating money. Over 80% of the students in *Have done* and 75% in *Would like to* wrote about supporting individuals in need and benefiting the community before the self. In the open-ended tenth space of the diamond ranking activity, the majority of responses included collaborating with others, learning about religion, paying taxes, respecting others and defending the country.

These findings suggest a strong sense of collective identity at national and social levels that supersedes individual interests. Their sense of collectiveness illustrates a communitarian tradition for the provisions of basic needs, social securities and environmental sustainability. Moreover, the students' constructs of communitarianism illustrate a social capital grounded in virtues of **sacrifice** (giving time, money or life), **benevolence** (caring, collaboration and altruism), **solidarity** (unifying group feelings) and **kinship** (benefits for family). Some of these virtues appear synonymous with defined indicators of democratic citizenship in the IEA and CCE studies. For example, these large-scale studies inquire about volunteerism, which requires a degree of sacrifice when time is dedicated for work without remuneration. The studies also inquire about perceived effectiveness of acting together, which displays a degree of solidarity. However, the questions in large-scale quantitative surveys on democratic citizenship are not really designed to reproduce young people's socially constructed notions of citizenship. For example, solidarity in this study extended to the 'Arabic community' in order to ensure 'equality between a man and a woman'. Also, the close-ended questions on family (or kinship) are in the contexts of corruption (when government gives positions to relatives) and discourse (if they talk politics with family members) while students in this open-ended study described the family as a community where good parenting and helping parents at home are forms of good citizenship. Indeed, the purposes of open-ended and close-ended inquiry differ from each other. However, these students' responses suggest constructs of citizenship (e.g. familial support, using faith-based spaces to help others, helping vulnerable people affected by armed conflict) that may only be revealed when narrating responses to open-ended inquiry.

Influences on conceptualising citizenship

Students frequently noted their notions of good citizenship by reflecting on activities in which they had participated within contexts of school, home, non-governmental organisations (NGOs) and their local community. Incidentally, no one mentioned the classroom. Schools in Lebanon typically organise excursions to nursing homes, orphanages and nature reserves. Students in a school that had started a community service programme all mentioned volunteering. The vast majority of their aspirations toward good citizenship, though, were related to participation in civil society. Indeed, there even appeared to be something of a Red Cross phenomenon, with frequent mentions of either volunteering or wanting to 'volunteer in the Red Cross'.

Incidents within the region also appeared to have contributed to the experiences and aspirations that construct these students' notions of good citizenship. Students from North and Mount Lebanon noted an interest in housing and supporting internally displaced people like 'people who left South Lebanon during the [2006] war'; students in Beirut participated most frequently in demonstrations; students in South Lebanon supported NGOs for human rights and 'the people who come to Lebanon to dismantle the landmines' and wanted to participate with the Civil Defence. Also, greater numbers of students in the South focused on defending the country, while students in other regions focused on development. In the diamond ranking's blank space, only two wrote about the resistance; both were from the South. The South Lebanon governorate shares a border with Israel and was mostly targeted during the Israeli artillery attack on Lebanese territory in 2006. These findings suggest that organisations that promote activities and events in the local community significantly influence how we conceptualise understandings of good citizenship.

Many statements claimed a willingness to participate for change as a response to social, environmental and political issues like protecting the environment, providing free medical care and education for all, and changing a corrupt government. Moreover, their descriptions of active political engagement under *Concern for rights and responsibilities across communities,* such as interrogating government leaders, were consistent with attributing politics to conflict and corruption in the justifications of 61% who ranked *voting in elections* as a low priority. One possible explanation for having high participatory attitudes could be that young people in countries with less stable democracies have more purpose and drive to actively improve the state of their social security and their liberal freedoms (Hoskins et al. 2008). The state of political instability, social insecurity, reconstruction and poor sustainability appear to motivate an active notion of citizenship among young people in Lebanon.

Universalities, knowledge and participation: the students' model

Findings from the diamond ranking exercise suggest a three-part model of learning citizenship: (1) universal values; (2) knowledge of communities; and (3) active participation.

As a top priority, or initial stage, the students emphasised the importance of humanistic and democratic values that underpin the feelings and practices of democratic and active citizenship. Nearly 66% of the students placed *knowing good manners* in the top region, with justifications similar to those for the secondary code: *respect and communicate*. Students emphasised politeness, respect, benevolence, kinship, sacrifice, solidarity and civility. The majority of these students explained in writing that 'knowing good manners are the key to peace' and among 'the only values that lead to progress' and, therefore, a prerequisite for practising active citizenship. The notion of behaviours underpinned by principles like respect is clearly articulated in literature that institutionalises concepts of citizenship in West Asia and North Africa, like religious scriptures and human rights instruments. A similar position is made in literature from Western Europe and North America for humanistic and democratic principles as presuppositions for democratic citizenship (Crick 2000; Kymlicka 2001; Parekh 2000). When justifying their rankings, students also wrote that a knowledge of human rights and civil laws is imperative for active participation. Knowing rights and laws, the majority of students argued, provides the individual with the security of having freedoms and rights and a sense of commitment to rules, and means that people will know what they can and cannot do.

The presupposition of universal values combined with substantive knowledge about how communities function could enhance how students conceptualise citizenship when participating in activities. This model resonates with literature from West Asia and North Africa on learning to engage in dialogues. Prior to discussions and debates, Al-Jirari (2000) argues for the importance of establishing a base of principles for dialogue and cites verse 29:46 from the Holy Qur'ān, which calls for respect and mutual care when in dialogue with people from different religions. Khātami (2000), too, maintains that an open-minded attitude towards rationality will facilitate appreciation of different cultures, one that builds a common ground where those engaging in dialogue feel safe and respected. Such principles and practices of dialogic engagement overlap and vary to differing degrees from those developed through scholarly literature in Western Europe and North America (Akar 2016b).

Conclusions

The findings from examining young people's self-reported conceptualisations of citizenship in Lebanon and the cited empirical studies contribute to the development of an inside-out qualitative methodology for international and comparative research on citizenship and citizenship education. Starting from the inside means capturing people's experiences with and reflections on the practices they consider beneficial or desirable, without assuming pre-set variables that define a type of citizenship (e.g. democratic, active) to measure. By narrating young people's conceptualisations of citizenship, we then have a more culturally accurate construction of the concepts involved, one that can be juxtaposed against evidence-informed concepts of citizenship from other parts of the world. This approach requires an ontological assumption that people's realities are socially constructed. Following this, the epistemological framework will need to incorporate a wide-ranging definition of citizenship and qualitative methods of inquiry to facilitate the necessary space for participants to reflect on their understandings and experiences of citizenship. In reframing a methodology to enhance the validity and ethics of citizenship and citizenship education research, I underline two main outcomes for further critical exploration.

First, findings from research into conceptualisations of citizenship and citizenship education suggest that we enhance the ethicality and validity of inquiry when we use a wide-ranging definition of citizenship with a view that individuals socially construct their reality. Through a pedagogical research methodology (Starkey et al. 2014), the research instruments facilitate activities that engage young people in communicating their personal experiences and reflections. Not only can they reconstruct and discuss ideas together (cf. Al-Nakib 2011), but the experience of expressing personal views in an open space is an empowering one for vulnerable groups like young people. Furthermore, we can identify a positive degree of content and construct validity in the close alignment between, on the one hand, the students' conceptualisations of citizenship and the suggested model of citizenship education, and on the other, the localised and international citizenship and citizenship education discourse. The students' references to sacrifice, kinship, solidarity and benevolence emerged as key themes that frame their constructions of citizenship. In the discussion, I demonstrated the significance of kinship in social constructions of citizenship in West Asia and North Africa and the extent to which it can be problematic in local and international cultures.

Second, an inside-out approach to inquiry about citizenship and citizenship education challenges the external validity of a normative construction of citizenship, especially when focusing on democratic citizenship. Democratic citizenship is a dominant form of citizenship that educational programmes in Western Europe and North America aim to foster (cf. Banks 2004; Osler and Starkey 2006; Stevick and Levinson 2007). In diverse communities, however, principles of democratic citizenship may not be as sensitive to cultural sovereignties as universal principles of equality (i.e. human rights). The principles and institutions of equal rights and political freedoms for democratic citizenship in Western Europe and North America construct a form of solidarity that is based more on ethnic nationality than among pluralistic or diverse communities (Habermas 2005). Furthermore, the secular political liberties embedded in the constructions of democracy in Western Europe and North America differ and even conflict with the Arab and Islamic philosophies of democracy that incorporate social, political and religious traditions (Ali 2002; Sadiki 2004).

Qualitative explorations that narrate people's individual conceptualisations of citizenship builds a unique and valuable empirical field in international and comparative research. Evidence drawn from narratives, discussions and reflections, allow education researchers and practitioners to advance informed debates on ideal notions of citizenship that educational programmes aim to promote. The collection of individual constructs of citizenship from cultures around the world can enrich the social constructions of democratic citizenship and even challenge the extent to which democratic citizenship is indeed an ideal form of citizenship. Perhaps other forms of citizenship (e.g. cosmopolitan citizenship) champion the freedoms and principles necessary for learning to live together in contexts of diversity and social reconstruction around the world. Finally, an internationally rich empirical field of young people's conceptualised notions of citizenship can even (re)construct universal or normative elements of an ideal notion of citizenship. Also, the methodological assumption that reality is socially constructed and supporting epistemological approaches can together facilitate opportunities for young people to critically examine the extent to which schools foster, ignore or counter the development of an ideal citizenship through education.

Disclosure statement

No potential conflict of interest was reported by the author.

ORCID

Bassel Akar http://orcid.org/0000-0002-5300-6348

References

Abou-Habib, Lina. 2003. "Gender, Citizenship, and Nationality in the Arab Region." *Gender & Development* 11 (3): 66–75.
Akar, Bassel. 2007. "Citizenship Education in Lebanon: An Introduction into Students' Concepts and Learning Experiences." *Educate* 7 (2): 2–18. doi: http://www.educatejournal.org/index.php?journal=educate&page=article&op=viewFile&path[]=119&path[]=142.
Akar, Bassel. 2012. "Teaching for Citizenship in Lebanon: Teachers Talk about the Civics Classroom." *Teaching and Teacher Education* 28: 470–480. doi:10.1016/j.tate.2011.12.002.
Akar, Bassel. 2016a. "Learning Active Citizenship: Conflicts between Students' Conceptualisations of Citizenship and Classroom Learning Experiences in Lebanon." *British Journal of Sociology of Education* 37 (2): 288–312. doi: 10.1080/01425692.2014.916603.
Akar, Bassel. 2016b. "Dialogic Pedagogies in Educational Settings for Active Citizenship, Social Cohesion and Peacebuilding in Lebanon." *Education, Citizenship and Social Justice* 11 (1): 44–62. doi:10.1177/1746197915626081.
Al-Ghazālī. 1980. *Freedom and Fulfillment: An Annotated Translation of Al-Ghazālī's al-Munqidh min al-ḍalāl and Other Relevant Works of al-Ghazālī*. IV vols. Translated by R. McCarthy. Boston, MA: Twayne Pulishers.
Ali, Zeenat. 2002. "Democracy at the Heart of Islam." In *Religions in Dialogue: From Theocracy to Democracy*, edited by Alan Race and Ingrid Shafer, 99–109. Aldershot: Ashgate.
Al-Jirari, Abbas. 2000. *Dialogue from the Islamic Point of View*. Translated by Jilali Saïb. Salè: ISESCO.
Al-Nakib, Rania. 2012. "Human rights, education for democratic citizenship and international organisations: findings from a Kuwaiti UNESCO ASPnet school." *Cambridge Journal of Education* 42 (1): 97–112. doi: 10.1080/0305764X.2011.652072.
Al-Nakib, Rania. 2011. "Citizenship, Nationalism, Human Rights and Democracy: A Tangling of Terms in the Kuwaiti Curriculum." *Educational Research* 53 (2): 165–178.
Amadeo, J., J. Torney-Purta, R. Lehmann, V. Husfeldt, and R. Nikolova. 2002. *Civic Knowledge and Engagement: An IEA Study of Upper Secondary Students in Sixteen Countries*. Amsterdam, the Netherlands: International Association for the Evaluation of Educational Achievement (IEA).
Arnot, Madeleine, and Jo-Anne Dillabough. 2000. *Challenging Democracy: International Perspectives on Gender, Education and Citizenship*. London: Routledge Falmer.
Bank, Barbara, Sara Delamont, and Catherine Marshall. 2007. *Gender and Education: Gendered Theories of Education*. Westport, Connecticut: Praeger Publishers.
Banks, James A. 2004. "Introduction: Democratic Citizenship Education in Multicultural Societies." In *Diversity and Citizenship Education: Global Perspectives*, edited by James A. Banks, 3–15. San Fransisco: Jossey-Bass.
Beetham, D. 1993. "Key Principles and Indices for a Democratic Audit." In *Defining and Measuring Democracy*, edited by D. Beetham, 25–43. Bakersfield, CA: SAGE Publications.
Berger, Peter, and Thomas Luckmann. 1966. *The Social Construction of Reality: A Treatise in the Sociology of Knowledge*. New York: Doubleday & Co.
Bronfenbrenner, U. 1988. "Interacting Systems in Human Development." In *Persons in Context: Developmental Processes*, edited by N. Bolger, C. Caspi, G. Downey and M. Moorehouse, 25–50. Cambridge: Cambridge University Press.
Bruner, Jerome S. 1990. *Acts of Meaning, the Jerusalem-Harvard Lectures*. Cambridge, Mass.: Harvard University Press.

Butenschøn, Nils, Uri Davis, and Manuel Hassassian. 2000. *Citizenship and the State in the Middle East: Approaches and Applications*. Syracuse, NY: Syracuse University Press.

Cogan, John, Paul Morris, and Murray Print. 2002. "Civic Education in the Asia-Pacific Region: An Introduction." In *Civic Education in the Asia-Pacific Region: Case Studies across Six Societies*, edited by John Cogan, Paul Morris and Murray Print, 1–22. New York: RoutledegeFalmer.

Creswell, John. 2005. *Educational Research: Planning, Conducting, and Evaluating Quantitative and Qualitative Research*. 2nd ed. New Jersey: Pearson Education.

Crick, Bernard. 2000. *Essays on Citizenship*. London: Continuum.

Danish Immigration Service. 2014. *Stateless Palestinian Refugees in Lebanon: Report from Danish Immigration Service's Fact Finding Mission to Beirut, Lebanon*. Copenhagen: Danish Immigration Service. https://www.nyidanmark.dk/nr/rdonlyres/091d8946-cc06-4659-a864-773fa0d69ffc/0/rapportlibanon8102014pdf.pdf.

Diamond, J. 1999. *Developing Democracy: Toward Consolidation*. Balitmore: Johns Hopkins University Press.

Fincham, Kathleen. 2012. "Learning the Nation in Exile: Constructing Youth Identities, Belonging and 'Citizenship' in Palestinian Refugee Camps in South Lebanon." *Comparative Education* 48 (1): 119–133. doi:10.1080/03050068.2011.637767.

Fox, Jon E., and Cynthia Miller-Idriss. 2008. "Everyday Nationhood." *Ethnicities* 8 (4): 536–563. doi:10.1177/1468796808088925.

Habermas, Jürgen. 2005. "Equal Treatment of Cultures and the Limits of Postmodern Liberalism." *Journal of Political Philosophy* 13 (1): 1–28. doi:10.1111/j.1467-9760.2005.00211.x.

Hahn, C. 2010. "Comparative Civic Education Research: What We Know and What We Need to Know." *Citizenship Teaching and Learning* 6 (1): 5–23.

Hammersley, Martyn. 1995. *The Politics of Social Research*. London: SAGE.

Hamzawy, A. 2006. "Globalization and Human Rights: On a Current Debate among Arab Intellectuals." In *Human Rights in the Arab World: Independent Voices*, edited by A. Chase and A. Hamzawy, 51–63. Philadelphia, PA: University of Pennsylvania Press.

Hartas, Dimitra. 2010. "The Epistemological Context of Quantitative and Qualitative Research." In *Educational Research and Inquiry: Qualitative and Quantitative Approaches*, edited by Dimitra Hartas, 33–53. London: Bloomsbury.

Held, D. 1996. *Models of Democracy*. Stanford, CA: Stanford University Press.

Hobsbawm, E. J. 1990. *Nations and Nationalism since 1780: Programme, Myth, Reality*. Cambridge: Cambridge University Press.

Hoskins, Bryony L., and Massimiliano Mascherini. 2009. "Measuring Active Citizenship through the Development of a Composite Indicator." *Social Indicators Research* 90 (3): 459–488. doi:10.1007/s11205-008-9271-2.

Hoskins, Bryony, Ernesto Villalba, Daniel Van Nijlen, and Carolyn Barber. 2008. *Measuring Civic Competence in Europe: A Composite Indicator Based on IEA Civic Education Study 1999 for 14 Years Old in School*. Luxembourg: European Communities.

Hoskins, Bryony, David Kerr, Hermann Abs, Germ Janmaat, Jo Morrison, Rebecca Ridley, and Juliet Sizmur. 2012. *Analytic Report: Participatory Citizenship in the European Union*. Brussels: European Commission.

Hourani, Albert. 1991. *A History of the Arab Peoples*. London: Faber and Faber.

Husfeldt, Vera, and Judith Torney-Purta. 2004. "Development of the CivEd Instruments." In *IEA Civic Education Study Technical Report*, edited by Wolfram Schulz and Heiko Sibberns, 17–26. Amsterdam: IEA.

Inglehart, R. 1997. *Modernization and Postmodernization: Cultural, Economic and Political Change in 43 Societies*. Princeton: Princeton University Press.

Janoski, Thomas. 1998. *Citizenship and Civil Society: A Framework of Rights and Obligations in Liberal, Traditional and Social Democratic Regimes*. Cambridge: Cambridge University Press.

Kennedy, K. 2007. "Student Constructions of 'Active Citizenship': What Does Participation Mean to Students?" *British Journal of Educational Studies* 55 (3): 304–324.

Kennelly, Jacqueline, and Jo-Anne Dillabough. 2008. "Young People Mobilizing the Language of Citizenship: Struggles for Classification and New Meaning in an Uncertain World." *British Journal of Sociology of Education* 29 (5): 493–508.

Khaldūn Ibn. (1370) 2005. *The Muqaddimah: An Introduction to History*. Translated by Franz Rosenthal. Princeton: Princeton University Press.

Khalidi, T. 1992. "Religion and Citizenship in Islam." In *Religion and Citizenship in Europe and the Arab World*, edited by J. Nielsen, 25–30. London: Grey Seal.

Khātami, Mohammad. 2000. *Islam, Dialogue and Civil Society*. Canberra: Australian National University.

Kymlicka, Will. 2001. *Politics in the Vernacular: Nationalism, Multiculturalism and Citizenship*. Oxford: Oxford University Press.

Laws, Sophie, C. Harper, and R. Marcus. 2003. *Research for Development: A Practical Guide*. London: SAGE.

Lincoln, Yvonna. 2001. "Engaging Sympathies: Relationships between Action Research and Social Constructivism." In *Handbook of Action Research: Participative Inquiry and Practice*, edited by Peter Reason and Hilary Bradburdy, 124–132. London: SAGE.

Lincoln, Yvonna, and E. Guba. 1985. *Naturalistic Inquiry*. Newbury Park, California: SAGE.

Lister, Ruth, Noel Smith, Sue Middleton, and Lynne Cox. 2003. "Young People Talk about Citizenship: Empirical Perspectives on Theoretical and Political Debates." *Citizenship Studies* 7 (2): 235–253. doi:10.1080/1362102032000065991.

Lynch, M. 2006. "Social Constructionism." In *The Philosophy of Science: An Encyclopedia*, edited by S. Sarkar and J. Pfeifer, 774–779. New York: Routledge.

Miller-Idriss, Cynthia. 2006. "Everyday Understandings of Citizenship in Germany." *Citizenship Studies* 10 (5): 541–570.

Moustakas, Clark E. 1994. *Phenomenological Research Methods*. Thousand Oaks, Calif: SAGE.

Norris, P. 1999. *Critical Citizens: Global Support for Democratic Government*. Oxford: Oxford University Press.

O'Mahony, Carolyn. 2009. "Understanding Core Democratic Values and Citizenship in the Fifth Grade." *Social Studies Research and Practice* 4 (3): 1–16.

O'Toole, Therese, Michael Lister, Dave Marsh, Su Jones, and Alex McDonagh. 2003. "Tuning out or Left out? Participation and Non-Participation among Young People." *Contemporary Politics* 9 (1): 45–61. doi:10.1080/1356977032000072477.

Osler, Audrey, and Hugh Starkey. 2003. "Learning for Cosmopolitan Citizenship: Theoretical Debates and Young People's Experiences." *Educational Review* 55 (3): 243–254. doi:10.1080/0013191032 000118901.

Osler, Audrey, and Hugh Starkey. 2005. *Changing Citizenship: Democracy and Inclusion in Education*. Maidenhead: Open University Press.

Osler, Audrey, and Hugh Starkey. 2006. "Education for Democratic Citizenship: A Review of Research, Policy and Practice 1995-2005." *Research Papers in Education* 21: 433–466.

O'Toole, Therese. 2003. "Engaging with Young People's Conceptions of the Political." *Children's Geographies* 1 (1): 71–90. doi:10.1080/1473328022000041670.

Parekh, Bhikhu. 2000. *The Future of Multi-Ethnic Britain: Report of the Commission on the Future of Multi-Ethnic Britain*. London: Runnymede Trust.

Parolin, Gianluca. 2009. *Citizenship in the Arab World : Kin, Religion and Nation-State*. Amsterdam: Amsterdam University Press.

Parry, Geraint, George Moyser, and Neil Day. 1992. *Political Participation and Democracy in Britain*. Cambridge: Cambridge University Press.

Pew Research Center. April 5, 2017. "The Changing Global Religious Landscape." http://assets.pewresearch.org/wp-content/uploads/sites/11/2017/04/07092755/FULL-REPORT-WITH-APPENDIXES-A-AND-B-APRIL-3.pdf

Rahman, Fazlur. (1987) 2005. "Islam: An Overview." In *Encyclopedia of Religion*. (1st ed), edited by Lindsay Jones, 4560–4577. Detroit, MI: Thomson Gale.

Ricœur, Paul. 1991. *From Text to Action, Essays in Hermeneutics*. Evanston, Ill.: Northwestern University Press.

Ruben, Beth. 2007. "'There's Still Not Justice': Youth Civic Identity Development amid Distinct School and Community Contexts." *Teachers College Record* 109 (2): 449–481.

Sadiki, Larbi. 2004. *The Search for Arab Democracy: Discourses and Counter-Discourses*. London: Hurst & Company.

Said, Edward. 1978. *Orientalism*. Vol. reprinted in 2003. London: Penguin Books.

Schulz, Wolfram, and Heiko Sibberns. 2004. *IEA Civic Education Study Technical Report*. Amsterdam: IEA.

Schulz, Wolfram, John Ainley, Julian Fraillon, David Kerr, and Bruno Losito. 2010. *Initial Findings from the IEA International Civic and Citizenship Education Study*. Amsterdam: International Association for the Evaluation of Educational Achievement (IEA).

Seale, Clive. 2004. "Validity, Reliability and the Quality of Research." In *Researching Society and Culture*, edited by Clive Seale, 71–83. London: SAGE Publications.

Searle, J. 1995. *The Construction of Social Reality*. London: Allen Lane and The Penguin Press.

Seyd, Patrick, Paul Whiteley, and Charles Pattie. 2001. "Citizenship in Britain: Attitudes and Behaviour." *The Political Quarterly* 72: 141–148. doi:10.1111/1467-923X.72.s1.17.

Starkey, Hugh, Bassel Akar, Lee Jerome, and Audrey Osler. 2014. "Power, Pedagogy and Participation: Ethics and Pragmatics in Research with Young People." *Research in Comparative and International Education* 9 (4): 426–440.

Stevick, E., and B. Levinson. 2007. "Introduction: Cultural Context and Diversity in the Study of Democratic Citizenship Education." In *Reimagining Civic Education: How Diverse Societies Form Democratic Citizens*, edited by E. Stevick and B. Levinson, 1–14. Plymouth: Rowman & Littlefield Publishers.

Tereshchenko, Antonina. 2013. "Regional Diversity and Education for 'National' Citizenship in Ukraine: The Construction of Citizenship Identities by Borderland Youth." In *Naturalization Policies, Education and Citizenship: Multicultural and Multination Societies in International Perspective*, edited by Dina Kiwan, 123–149. London: Palgrave Macmillan UK.

Tibi, Bassam. 1997. *Arab Nationalism: Between Islam and the Nation-State*. 3rd ed. London: MacMillan Press.

Torney, Judith, A. N. Oppenheim, and Russell Francis Farnen. 1975. *Civic Education in Ten Countries: An Empirical Study*. New York: Wiley.

Torney-Purta, Judith, Rainer Lehmann, H. Oswald, and W. Schulz. 2001. *Citizenship and Education in Twenty-Eight Countries: Civic Knowledge and Engagement at Age Fourteen*. Amsterdam: The International Association for the Evaluation of Educational Achievement.

UNDP. 2008. *Lebanon National Human Development Report: Toward a Citizen's State*. Beirut: UNDP.

UNDP. 2009. *Lebanon National Human Development Report: Toward a Citizen's State*. Beirut: UNDP.

UNDP, Mehe, and CDR. 2008. *Education and Citizenship: Concepts, Attitudes, Skills and Actions: Analysis of Survey Results of 9th Grade Students in Lebanon*. Beirut: UNDP.

United Nations. 1989. *Convention on the Rights of the Child*. Geneva: United Nations.

UNRWA. 2015. *Protecting Palestine Refugees*. East Jerusalem: UNRWA. http://www.unrwa.org/sites/default/files/content/resources/resource_26476_23321_1456388534.pdf.

Weller, Susie. 2007. *Teenagers' Citizenship*. Oxon: Routledge.

Wellington, Jerry. 2000. *Educational Research: Contemporary Issues and Practices*. London: Continuum.

Wenger, E. 1998. *Communities of Practice: Learning, Meaning and Identity*. Cambridge: Cambridge University Press.

Citizenship education discourses in Latin America: multilateral institutions and the decolonial challenge

Diego Nieto

ABSTRACT
Understanding multilateral institutions' role in the construction of desirable goals for educational reform is a key element to grasp the weight globalisation has on local practices of education. Comparative studies of civics and moral education point to the idea of 'citizenship' as a site revealing not only the political economy but also the cultural politics involved in the globalisation of education. Through political discourse analysis, this paper analyses key multilateral agencies' discourses on citizenship education for Latin America. It traces the concerns, diagnoses, definitions and proposals of what citizenship education is (or should be) in agenda-setting documents and policy reports promoted by these organisations. Drawing on Latin American decolonial theories, it challenges concerns with civic disengagement and *convivencia* underpinning multilateral citizenship education discourses. As a counterpoint, it presents research from scholars highlighting alternative – often overlooked – participatory and decolonial pedagogical experiences present in Latin America that open new standpoints for citizenship education comparative research in the region.

Hegemonic discourses of citizenship shape the meanings and imaginaries with which we build our own identities as (global) citizens, and the relationships and daily interactions among peoples and communities in different locales around the world. In particular, in the context of Latin America, multilateral institutions have been important actors disseminating hegemonic conceptualisations of citizenship education. I propose to examine these multilateral discourses and pedagogical alternatives available that defy dominant views on civics and citizenship education present in the region.

To do this, I first present conceptual debates on citizenship education and propose to analyse the globalisation of these citizenship education conceptions from the lenses of Latin American decolonial theorists. I advocate for the use of political discourse analysis and vertical comparisons as a method to disclose the connections between global discourses of citizenship education and their dissemination in relevant policy documents by key multilateral institutions in Latin America. Challenging some of the basic underpinnings of these hegemonic discourses from a decolonial perspective, I draw on other scholars' research to present alternative experiences available in the region of what citizenship education entails, suggesting them as a way to overcome the limited view of the globalisation of citizenship education present in multilateral agencies' discourses.

Citizenship conceptualizations and citizenship education, from the world to Latin America

With the fall of the Berlin Wall, Francis Fukuyama (1992) infamously declared the *end of history*, the triumph of the formula of capitalism and liberal democracy and, in the absence of Communism, the beginning of an era devoid of ideological confrontations. Samuel Huntington (1993) countered Fukuyama – his former student – by arguing that, instead of the end of history, the world would face a *clash of civilizations*, conflicts whose source would not be ideological or economic, but cultural.

Discourses of a clash of civilizations and the end of history represent two ways in which citizenship education became a *global* issue (Haste 2010). Fukuyama and Huntington outlined the setting in which questions of citizenship education were to be addressed, in the absence of the bipolar system that hitherto had divided the world. They represented two sides of the same conceptual coin for citizenship and education: on the one hand, an individualistic-neoliberal version of *cosmopolitan citizenship,* which implicitly presents Western liberal-democratic principles as the only version of citizenship valuable for disseminating around the world. On the other hand, a *reactionary-conservative* concern with citizenship as social cohesion, civilization and order, reflecting cultural fears of Other(s) (Apple 2011).

Neoliberal and neoconservative are only two, albeit very prevalent, conceptions of the role of citizenship education in relation to the challenges of globalisation. Three other democratic theories have made their way into pedagogical proposals as attempts to counter neoliberal and neoconservative narratives of citizenship and education: deliberative approaches, critical or social justice approaches and poststructuralist (democracy as a mode of living) approaches (Carretero, Haste, and Bermudez 2015).

Deliberative theories consider viewpoint exchanges and intersubjective communicative action to be at the root of democratic legitimacy. Accordingly, they formulate reasonable, inclusive, reciprocal public deliberations as a way to deal with disagreements and difference. Here, the main task of citizenship education is to develop capacities of critical inquiry, communication, and moral argumentation that foster active participation in democratic discussions of public issues and controversies (Bai 2001; Gutmann and Ben-Porath 2015).

Critical pedagogy and social justice education theories provide a framework to understand and transform power relations towards creating more just and democratic societies in and beyond the school (Giroux 2003). Critical pedagogy emphasises the development of students' capacity to critically understand multiple forms of systemic oppression and social (in)justice structured along racial, economic and gender lines. Social justice education stresses students' empowerment to challenge dominant forms of knowledge that reproduce structures of inequity and marginalisation (Freire 1970; Kincheloe 1999).

Rejecting the rationalist and Enlightenment ideals of moralism and emancipation implied in deliberative and critical pedagogy proposals, poststructural theories emphasise the role of emotions, identity-formation, contestation and imagination in understanding democratic education as a way of living. Here, disagreement and plurality are positive and necessary features of democratic politics, the engines of the contingent expansion of ourselves and the world in the encounter of self and other. They argue that education can contribute to dealing with difference through the promotion of a democratic *ethos* of hospitality and be-coming. Thus, democratic education would entail public encounters in which subaltern and marginalised voices – whose identity and presence are contingent, not structurally pre-established – have opportunities for agonistic – meaning constructive and passionate – contestation to interrupt the hegemonic inclusions and exclusions of citizenship (Biesta 2009; Ermarth 2007; Ruitenberg 2010; Todd 2010).

As Westheimer and Kahne (2004) have argued, these different emphases and understandings of citizenship and democracy each have a bearing upon curricular and youth civic engagement expectations and outcomes. In their study of democratic education programmes in the USA, they distinguished among programmes aimed at personally responsible, participatory or justice-oriented ideals of the 'good citizen'. Using these categories, it could be argued that neoliberal-neoconservative views privilege a *personally responsible* citizen, compliant with the law, embracing moral values of the dominant community and participating as needed through formal institutions and procedures. Deliberative approaches, in partial contrast, promote a citizen capable of engaging with others in public debates and ready to *participate actively* in public issues, community organisations and government processes. Critical pedagogy, in turn, aims to provide citizens with tools to analyse deep causes of *social (in)justices* and to develop strategies for social mobilisation and systemic change. In their study, however, the authors did not address or found relevant data concerning poststructural theories of citizenship education.

In a different study, Kahne, Crow and Lee (2013) compared the pedagogical use of 'social issues discussion' and 'service learning initiatives' to show how diverse civic learning opportunities promote different types of political engagement. The authors argue that, while the first promotes interest in deliberative 'big P' politics – public debates on governmental issues – the second orients youth towards volunteering, community-based and expressive civic engagement, what they call 'little p' politics. It would be possible to draw a parallel between each the 'big P' politics and deliberative views and 'little p' with some ideas expressed in the poststructuralist or 'way of living' approach to democratic citizenship education.

Thus, different approaches to citizenship education create opportunities for youth to engage in distinct dimensions of civic and political life. Examining the prevalent emphases in the Latin American context and the consequences of diverse curricular approaches is a necessary feature of any comparative research. Underlining what these conceptions consider relevant to include in educational policy agendas and what they overlook or dismiss is a fundamental part of any critical curricular analysis in global times.

Decolonial theory from Latin America and the globalisation/localisation of citizenship education

Postcolonial theories highlight the fact that understanding the dissemination, implementation, appropriations and counter-expressions of education in non-Western contexts must attend to the co-constitution between Western and non-Western images (Tikly 1999). As pointed out by these approaches to civics and moral education, global citizenship education proposals reveal not only the political economy but also the cultural politics involved in the globalisation of education. These include forces shaping the definitions of a *global citizen* and the educational processes to achieve or produce such a citizen (Abdi, Shultz, and Pillay 2015; Andreotti and de Souza 2012).

Certainly, the globalisation of a desirable image of a good citizen is not culturally neutral. On the contrary, as Sousa Santos (2001) argues, globalisation is a process whereby a given local condition succeeds in presenting itself as a universal (hegemonic) expression, detached from any cultural location. In the process, it develops the capacity to designate a rival social condition or entity as (merely) local. Thus, localisation represents the globalisation of those whose local expressions do not become universalised. Decolonial theorists argue that when Eurocentric knowledge is granted this superiority, it has meant – since the Enlightenment – that other knowledges and histories are subalternised, excluded or ignored as inferior, irrelevant or mythical lived experiences (Castro-Gómez and Grosfoguel 2007).

Often, (global) democratic citizenship education discourses, by disavowing their own cultural embeddedness, speak precisely from what Castro-Gómez (2005) calls the epistemological *zero point* of the universalised Western white man, as if devoid of any geo-historical or gendered location. As a result, by presenting democratic citizenship as a universal ideal, these discourses create and exclude an opposed uncivilised *Other*, marked as *different* from the cosmopolitan (Western Eurocentric) human (Man), already conceived as *The* proper subject of democracy, the 'good' global citizen (Wynter 2004).

Decolonial theory invites us to challenge the false universalism of global discourses in democratic citizenship education by tracing how the 'Others' of the (global) world – the displaced and dispossessed, immigrants and refugees, indigenous and diasporic populations, the 'under-developed', 'Third world' and 'rogue' regions – are products of imperial capitalist development tied to long historical trajectories of colonial mentalities of governance, including those fostered by educational discourses of development and democratisation.

Neoliberal, neoconservative, deliberative and even poststructural and critical approaches to citizenship and democratic education, often conceive diversity and plurality *as a given fact* of postmodern societies. A decolonial approach, in turn, is concerned with uncovering how Western Eurocentric knowledge constantly produces these *Others* in localised spatialities of global relations, establishing the (unequal) positions they come to occupy in global structures of power (Ahmed 2000).

As Andreotti (2006, 2015) argues, citizenship education may become an instrument of a civilizing mission by promoting an uncritical, depoliticised, ahistorical version of liberal-democratic, capitalist, Western values and worldviews. In this way, it contributes to the reproduction of global inequities, insofar as it sustains the historical privilege of Western values and worldviews across global structures of power, while confining other expressions of democratic politics to the realms of 'local knowledge'.

As a counterpoint, decolonial theories from Latin America aim at revealing expressions of contradiction and resistance from those experiencing the weight of colonial power in various spheres of life. Efforts by communities to 'rescue' their historical ways of knowing and resistance in order to de-link their knowledges and beings from such long and global scales of colonial ruling (Mignolo 2011). Hence, these theories challenge most of the aforementioned conceptualisations of citizenship education and democracy in global times yet from a different standpoint. They question the abstract and universalistic character of such conceptions by interrogating the *positionality* – geographical and epistemological – from where they are formulated.

These dominant frameworks of democratic citizenship education have led to omit an exploration of the movement of dominant curricular discourses of citizenship and democracy through the global geographies of power and knowledge. Decolonial theories contribute to explore the significance of studying the top-down dynamics and the bottom-up contestations by providing a point of entry that sheds light on this blind spots of mainstream conceptualisations of democratic citizenship.

Analysing multilateral institutions' discourses as vertical comparisons

As already stated, a decolonial study of the scope and implications of citizenship education conceptualisations requires inquiring about the ways in which particular conceptions of democracy and citizenship are constructed to shape curricular inputs and outcomes in different locations of the global world. I contend that an ideal way to study citizenship education dissemination in local practices is to analyse discourses of multilateral institutions as part of what Bartlett and Vavrus (2009) call 'vertical comparisons'. They suggest tracing vertical relationships across local, national and international levels and looking at the flows of influence, ideas and actions through these levels, taking into consideration the growing interconnections between national educational systems and global organisations that fund and evaluate their operations.

As institutional forms that coordinate relations among three or more states on the basis of generalised principles of conduct (Mundy 1998), multilateral agencies and organisations are crucial sites to trace these contested vertical flows of conceptions of citizenship education, for instance, by looking at the ways they are presented in policy and agenda documents and programmes. To carry out this analysis, I have brought together policy documents, reports and agenda-setting documents from influential multilateral institutions and agencies related to citizenship, democracy and education in Latin America.[1] Together, these documents give us a context of the educational agendas and policy prescriptions within which citizenship education plays a role. However, I have focused on two of them – one from the IDB and one from the OEI – in more detail, because they speak more explicitly about citizenship education and epitomise the most common threads present in the other documents.

To trace these vertical flows of ideas and discourses, I rely on political discourse analysis as a strategy to analyse hegemonic discourses (Howarth 2000) of citizenship education. In this body of literature, *hegemonic* discourses are not conceived as rational interpretations of the world that come to dominate the production of subjects and actions. They are understood as the product of social antagonisms – heterogeneous, contingent and politically constituted constructs – fields of dispute over the meanings and desired courses of action regarding political decisions (Torfing 1999). Under these premises, these documents are not considered simply 'technocratic and objective' reports, but political arguments in their own right, filled with ideas and beliefs that seek to persuade governments towards certain normative principles, policy propositions and political decisions (Bacchi 2000).

Following the suggestions from policy discourse analysis, I trace in these documents their diagnoses of needs and problems, definitions and principles of democratic citizenship and pedagogical proposals, as they seek to become the dominant views on democratic citizenship education currently prevalent in Latin American citizenship education policy. In addition, I uncover limits and contradictions present in some of their premises by relying on research done in Latin America about youth and citizenship education, which help us challenge some of their main tenets and highlight alternative voices and trajectories to widen our views on citizenship education in this part of the world.

Multilateral agencies discourses of citizenship education in Latin America

In 2013, revisiting his (in)famous 1993 thesis on *The Clash of Civilizations*, Huntington argued:

> Osama bin Laden has given back to the West its common identity ... we need to continue the expansion of the European Union and NATO ... [and] *The United States also needs to encourage the 'Westernization' of Latin America*. (53,emphasis added)

By the early-1990s, many Latin American countries were experiencing the initial years of democratic regimes after transition from authoritarian rule. In resonance with Fukuyama's theory that world 'history' held no further viable political options, political regimes turned into liberal democracies, implementing neoliberal policies of economic liberalisation and privatisation. Perhaps as a consequence, by the late-1990s, many Latin American populations became disenchanted with these governments. Their great expectations for democratic change were minimally fulfilled, or blatantly denied, by the combination of neoliberalism and the minimalist version of democracy as electoral rule (Martí i Puig 2009; Nieto and Milanese 2016).

The first influential studies that outlined the setting in which discussions on democratic citizenship education (DCE) later took place were produced by the UNDP and OAS. In these reports, it was argued that Latin American democracies had to shift attention from consolidating formal electoral institutions towards building *quality democracies*. They prescribed state reform and policy alternatives to help create these *democracies of citizens*: protect a robust set of civic, social and economic rights to reduce the high levels of inequality; address the crisis of representation and accountability through the improvement of institutional controls; and solve problems of insecurity by strengthening and modernising state institutions (PNUD and OEA 2010; UNDP 2004).

Accordingly, in response to the declining popular support and loss of credibility for democracy, at the end of twentieth century influential multilateral institutions in education and citizenship policies began to support a network of intellectuals, regional policy dialogues and some curricular reforms in Latin America focusing specifically on DCE (Reimers 2007). Citizenship education secured a preponderant position through the consideration that *quality democracies* need *quality education* that nurtures active and tolerant citizens. They shared the idea that democratic education should understand citizenship as more than voting. However, as I will argue, the concern with equality, institutions and rights has been expanded to include concerns with adaptation to the global world and with social cohesion and individual responsibility.

Youth (dis)engagement and active (responsible) citizenship competences

In 2005, the IDB sponsored the preparation of strategy papers making the case for explicit attention to DCE in the region, outlining policy recommendations for the Fourth Summit of the Americas (Cox, Jaramillo, and Reimers 2005; Espínola et al. 2005; see also Tibbitts and Torney-Purta 1999). It also provided support for the creation of a Regional Observatory on Citizen Competences, stemming from an earlier Regional System for the Evaluation and Development of Citizenship Competences.

These IDB-sponsored documents address what they identify as *disengagement* of youth from democratic participation. In their view, DCE curricular reform should replace narrow civics with active citizenship education and promotion of deeper identification with democratic values. Narrow civics education informs passive citizens about the nation, state institutions and laws. In contrast, their proposal for democratic citizenship education promotes an *active citizen* through curriculum incorporating deliberative practices tackling contemporary political debates, moral dilemmas, human rights and developing conflict resolution competencies. Active citizenship competences are expected to address challenges brought about by *postmodernity* and *globalisation* such as individualisation, civic distrust, and the use of information and communication technologies (Cox, Jaramillo, and Reimers 2005; see also Levinson, Schugurensky, and González 2009). The report states:

> *Trust* in others (the foundation of all civic participation) needs to be raised to a higher level. *Respect for the law*, a necessary condition for all democratic regimes, must be matched by criteria for justice and the knowledge and skills needed to *change laws through peaceful and responsible means*. The principles of transparency and accountability must steer relations between citizens, their representatives, and government authorities. Citizens must be *politically informed and educated* and believe they have a say in community issues and government affairs at every level. (Cox, Jaramillo, and Reimers 2005, 6, emphasis added)

Underpinning these conceptions we find the moral development and deliberative democracy theories of Kohlberg, Habermas and Cortina, complemented with the 'caring approach' of Noddings. These proposals argue that schools must cultivate a deliberative ethics, sustained within a *minimum morality* of human rights. These principles are then transformed into three citizenship competences: *cognitive*, including critical inquiry and the autonomous analysis of moral dilemmas; *socio-emotional*, practicing emotional management and interpersonal conflict resolution skills; and *communicative*, fostering cooperative learning, community service, and deliberation and debate about historical and contemporary conflictual issues (Cox, Jaramillo, and Reimers 2005; see also Jaramillo and Murillo 2013).

I argue that by labelling youth as disengaged, incapable or unprepared to deal with globalisation (the basic diagnosis presented), discourses of active citizenship competences attribute the problems of democracy to the deficits of *irresponsible citizens*. The individual citizen is deemed responsible to gain the competences and skills for his/her qualified participation in the opportunities offered by the global knowledge economy and 'liberal' democracies: the role of (citizenship) education is to promote, above all, the development of this *neoliberal cosmopolitan subject*. Using a Freirian argument, this classic governing mechanism demands that students adapt to the dominant institutions of society, deploying individualistic developmental discourses of welfare and 'banking education' practices, instead of promoting the transformation and flourishing of their own collective selves (Freire 1998).[2]

That is so because the imagined citizen, here, is rooted in cosmopolitan ethics tied to deliberative democracy approaches to human rights and moral education. Deliberative and cosmopolitan views of democracy are, in turn, attached to a Eurocentric normative understanding of the citizen subject: the rational body of the public sphere, derived from liberal and republican Western traditions of political thought. This makes the Western cosmopolitan man – situated at the heart of the histories of coloniality – *the* standard subject of democracy, disregarding any other alternative expression of democratic politics.

Remarkably, the above discourses of youth disengagement also contrast with recent events and research on youth civic engagement and participation in Latin America (Bermudez 2012; Oliart and Feixa 2012). These studies show us that multilateral institutions' diagnoses of civic deficits and disengagement miss recognising youth's own lived experiences, understandings and diverse forms of political engagement as citizenship action. Such misrecognition is a consequence of their narrow view of civic engagement as solely affirmation of prevailing political and cultural structures and institutions to which these forms of political engagement do not necessarily conform.

Students' strikes, for example, which have played a very significant role in an unprecedented spread of youth mobilisations in countries such as Brazil, Chile, Colombia, Venezuela, México and Puerto Rico (Cubides 2015; Fleet 2011; García-Guadilla and Mallén 2010; Olivier Téllez and Tamayo 2015), showed that participation in electoral politics was not a primary channel of expression for youth. Yet, this does not mean they are only interested in community-based forms of engagement either. Many claims in these mobilisations were system-challenging, targeting political elites and usually questioning structural neoliberal policies of austerity and privatisation affecting not only education but responsible for widening inequality gaps in these countries. They were not limited to local issues and scales; it was not uncommon for them to involve nationwide activist organisation, and in some instances even transnational solidarity.

Furthermore, these mobilisations pushed the boundaries of 'reasonable deliberation', given the great role played by symbolism and metaphors in their activism. Youth engaged in creative forms of political participation, such as artistic demonstrations, use of pop culture symbolism and extensive social media interactions in order to convey their messages and endow their endeavours with a sense of effectiveness and collective identity. As Rosario (2015) puts it, through these actions, mobilised students sought to interrupt the hegemonic logic of the status quo in educational discourses of human capital, activating broad solidarity beyond the student body.

These features challenge conceptions of youth as passive, disengaged or apathetic, prevalent in citizenship education discourses in Latin America. Instead of framing youth in developing countries as the problem (threat) and/or most vulnerable (at risk) – as if lacking voice or agency – they reveal the importance of working from the 'ground up', acknowledging youth' lived experiences and their actual forms of participation as creative forces of cultural production (Gaztambide-Fernández and Arráiz Matute 2015).

In contrast, the systemic, expressive and passionate features of recent student mobilisations in Latin America show the importance for DCE curricula and research to overcome hegemonic conceptions reluctance to embrace activism and expressive politics as valuable forms of political participation (Young 2001). While such political engagement practices do not always correspond to the 'reasonable' standards of moral argumentation typical of democratic citizenship education discourses, they are closer to contemporary youth grammars of world making and political participation. Understanding youths' (counter and sub)cultural expressions – alternative lifestyles, and promotion of new values and social relations – as forms of participation in their own right, we can recreate a better picture of the diversity of political expressions, as well as the limits, scope and pedagogical implications of what youth understand as enacting citizenship.

Promoting more active and engaged citizens is certainly important. Yet we can see that Latin America is not alien to what researchers in other parts of the world have found about the link between active citizenship discourses and neoliberal ethics (Aldenmyr, Wigg, and Olson 2012; Janmaat and Piattoeva 2007; Kennelly and Llewellyn 2011). Alignment with international standards that respond to the 'forces' of globalisation, privileging an ethics of tolerance, civic rights and freedom not only may invite complex tensions with nation-building, indigenous cultural traditions and social cohesion agendas. When these programmes become entangled with neoliberal demands for individual development in discourses of education quality and student achievement, active citizenship competencies may become subordinated to human capital goals of academic and work performance. Skills such as effective communication, capacity for conflict resolution and teamwork are mostly valued for their contribution to global economic competitiveness rather for what they can do to foster diverse youth democratic expressions.

Citizenship as *convivencia* and the slippery slope to securitisation

Promoting peaceful coexistence or *convivencia* in schools represents the other major discourse underlying the development of citizenship education, considered in this case a fundamental element to improve the quality of education in Latin America.[3] Discourses of citizenship education as *convivencia* can be traced to efforts from OAS, alongside other organisations such as UNESCO and the OEI, to promote programmes of democratic values and practices since the Second Summit of the Americas in 1998 and the signature of the Inter-American Democratic Charter in 2001 (Levinson and Berumen 2007).

Framed within the United Nations' *Education for All* goals, the OEI (2010)[4] publication *Educational Goals 2021: The Education We Want for the Bicentennial Generation*, has become an important referent in educational policy debates in the region. One of the general goals established – 'improving the quality of education and school curricula' – includes the specific goal of 'promoting education in values for a democratic active citizenship, both in the curriculum and in the organisation and management of the schools' (OEI 2010, 52–53). About the role of schools in citizenship and values education it states that:

> [S]chool has an important role in *the development of the moral autonomy* of its students, in the *care of their emotions* and the opening of possibilities for exercise of a *consistent moral behavior*. The *social integration* of all students, strengthening bonds of friendship, *respect for differences* and weak students, *caring for emotional literacy*, participation of learners in school activities, learning through forms of cooperation among equals, support of the more capable to those who have difficulties learning, *the defense of peace, the environment and equality of people*, whatever their culture, their origin and gender, as well as certain activities of community work, are necessary elements to build *school communities based on responsibility and solidarity behaviors*. (OEI 2010, 39 my emphasis and own translation from Spanish)

Under this premise, the document considers that, in unequal societies – like those in Ibero-America – formation of free, fair, responsible and solidary citizens capable of living together in plural and multicultural societies with great inequalities, represents a major strategy to overcome poverty, marginalisation and inequality (OEI 2010). These *convivencia* approaches epitomised by the OEI programme emphasise moral values education and social integration. Closely related to UNESCO's discourses, these views resonate with the fostering of cosmopolitan minimum ethics (Cortina 2010), such as the recognition of diversity, the search for inclusion and a concern with social cohesion. Democratic values education present in school curricula and building school environments that foster the 'transversal' implementation of *convivencia* – understood as a culture of peace and the reduction of violence and discrimination, become a central strategy of citizenship education in Latin America (see also Inter-American Institute of Human Rights, and UNESCO 2011; Toro and Tallone 2010).

The moral character of *convivencia* education as the key to social cohesion and integration is, in many respects, reminiscent of centuries-old conservative sociological theories of civilization underlying ideologies of modernity/coloniality (Gaztambide-Fernández 2012). Even within the more integral policies of *sustainable human development* endorsed by the UNDP and UNESCO, welfare is defined as the development of individual capabilities in conformity to a global social system more worried about controlling the explosion of difference than with addressing power differentials and transnational inequities (Walsh 2010).

Moreover, while these aims may be valuable for many Latin American societies, Novelli (2010) has warned against the conflation often taking place, in the age of terror, between educational concerns with social cohesion and neoconservative securitisation agendas. Some scholars in Latin America have criticized *convivencia* programmes because their good intentions have ended up promoting narrow agendas emphasising 'soft control' measures such as government surveillance and targeting of certain social groups – the impoverished, unemployed, 'criminal and violent', sexually 'abnormal', racialised and ethnically different – labelled as deviant, at risk, or threats to safety and social wellbeing. Such narrow approaches to *convivencia* education encourage compliance, and privilege behavioral control programmes of values transmission and socioemotional anger management (Carbajal Padilla 2013; Nieto and Bickmore 2016; Zurita Rivera 2013). They also legitimise the use of punitive measures to control bullying and violence, with disregard for human rights and the structural conditions of inequality within and outside the educational system causing violence (Bickmore 2011; Magendzo, Toledo, and Gutiérrez 2012).

In sum, conceptualisations of DCE promoted by multilateral institutions have shifted questions of equity, collective participation and rights to include concerns for adaptation to the global world, social cohesion and individual responsibility, downplaying youth's own forms of participation and the unequal structures of power affecting the implementation of *convivencia*-oriented curricular reforms.

Alternatives to the Western citizen in Latin American experiences

As I have argued so far, DCE curricula in Latin America, strongly shaped by discourses transmitted by multilateral organisations, seek to engender a young person who practices rational individualistic values and deliberation in ahistorical (and sometimes ostensibly apolitical) ways, who complies with the law, and who (fruitlessly) is encouraged to look like the normative young individual from an idealised western democracy.

Deliberation and cosmopolitan ethics, as well as endeavours in democratic *convivencia*, do have a place in democratic education, but not alone. As I will illustrate below by drawing on research on alternative experiences of citizenship education present in Latin America, multilateral discourses disregard longer traditions of popular education, political participation and political struggle that remind us that democratic practices, reactions towards the law and citizenship models are diverse and can be otherwise.

Critical pedagogy, community engagement and pedagogies of citizen participation

Popular education and pedagogies of activism have been an important tradition in social movement non-formal education in Latin America. Yet, some scholars have also shown their potential translation into citizenship classroom curricula and public schooling. I bring up two examples from Brazil that provide us with a counterpoint to multilateral discourses' downplaying of the significance that critical pedagogy, and particularly Freire, has had in political education in Latin America.

Gandin and Apple (2002) present the case of the *Citizen School* in Porto Alegre. They show how the (then) ruling Worker's Party recognised that its participatory democracy initiatives in local governance, involving the poorest and most marginalised citizens, required a strong programme for the development of collective participatory capacities from early-childhood and elementary education. The Citizen School project, they argue, emerged from a participatory process committed to three principles: (1) democratisation of school management based on participatory school councils, financial autonomy and elected principals; (2) democratisation of access to schooling, reducing dropout rates by changing the structure of the school to cycles of formation; and (3) the democratisation of knowledge, with teachers building curricula informed by the cultural backgrounds and concerns of the communities through participatory action research.

Tarlau (2015) draws attention to the example of the *Landless Workers' Movement* (MST) pedagogies for rural schooling in Brazil. She argues that the MST movement realised the strategic significance of fighting the devaluation of their knowledge, history and struggles in the public schools attended by their children. Their efforts made the point that rural communities had a right to participate in defining not only classroom pedagogy, but also the goals of their schools. Developing school curricula and pedagogies that would support their socioterritorial worldviews – collectivity, manual labour and sustainable farming – became crucial endeavours of the social movement. Attention to formal schooling also allowed for experimentation in teacher training programmes involving critical pedagogies that attended to the necessities and aims of the social movement. In one of its most important 'movement schools', the MST developed a participatory governance structure where students are involved in every aspect of the school decision-making process, where issues are socialised and debated 'upward' and 'downwards' in representative bodies and class and school-wide collectives.

The exceptional character of these initiatives are a consequence of their counter-hegemonic impulse. They demonstrate, I argue, an alternative approach in which, instead of a pre-established set of citizenship competencies or minimum moral values, people engage through participation in the definition of valuable knowledge, drawing from their own everyday experiences and needs, to debate what kind of education and citizenship they consider worth fostering. These participatory processes, and the administrative and institutional structures that support them, become pedagogical spaces of democracy in their own right. They demand that teachers, students, school administrators and staff, parents and community organisations learn about the technical demands of governing education, maintain processes of accountability on implemented decisions, and oversee the use of resources while attending to practices of reciprocity, solidarity and collective deliberation.

These scholars recognise that these programmes are not without their own internal tensions and contradictions. However, they represent what Schugurensky (2009) understands, based on Freire, as forms of experiential pedagogies of citizen participation: hands-on ways of learning the potentialities and difficulties of democratic collective endeavours – showing the potential to achieve ambitious democratising goals when they are part of larger political projects transcending spaces within and beyond schools.

Citizenship education otherwise: decolonial pedagogies, interculturality and buen vivir

Indigenous communities and Afrodescendant diasporic populations in Latin America have long recognised education as a space of struggle, intervention and creation. Education has been one of the main instruments of their assimilation and annihilation but also of their resistance. In Latin America, a prime example of this is the engagement of many indigenous and Afrodescendant peoples in what I will call, following Walsh (2013), *decolonial pedagogies*: epistemic and political (educational) projects in which, literally, their communities' thought and their everyday ways of life is at stake.

Certain political conditions have opened up the space – in Colombia, Ecuador, Bolivia and Mexico – for experimentation with projects of alternative globalisation and *educación propia* [own education] (cf. Aman 2017; Bajaj 2015; Baronnet, Stahler-Sholk, and Mora Bayo 2011; Botero-Gómez 2015; Smith 2013). School curricula where ethno-educational pedagogical principles embrace and sustain indigenous and Afrodescendant traditions of political engagement and organisation.

In her work, Walsh (2007) has highlighted three aspects that would make these experiences decolonial. Firstly, decolonial pedagogies from indigenous and Afrodescendant communities seek to craft and build (new) social orders based on *pensamiento propio* [own-thought] drawn from collective memory, ancients, nature and *cotidianidad* [everyday life]. They are decolonial insofar as they rediscover and unearth centuries-old lived practices and methodologies of struggle, insurgency, organisation and action employed by indigenous and Black populations to guarantee autonomy in their relations to land and subverting slavery and colonial power (Walsh 2014).

Secondly, they advocate for a conception of interculturality which, unlike cosmopolitan and multicultural principles avoidance of any challenge to the privileged place of the dominant *white* [blanca] and *mestizo* [miscengenated] culture in Latin America, starts from acknowledging the inherent conflictual relations and the power asymmetries among communities' *ways of being* in these countries. Intercultural education demands complex interactions, negotiations and exchanges based on equitable interrelations between peoples, knowledges and practices. It is not simply and effort to guarantee bilingual education, nor to privilege social justice claims that may subordinate the weight that race, ethnicity and *mestizaje* (miscegenation) has had in Latin American societies (Walsh 2005).

Finally, they rely on the idea of *buen vivir* [living well, good life or collective wellbeing] as a challenge to human capital theories' narrow concern with economic growth and the commodification of life and nature, as well as against human development discourses' emphasis on individual capabilities and wellbeing. In its place, practices of *buen vivir* imagine systems of knowledge and living based on the communion of humans and nature, that is, they appeal to the necessary constitutive interrelations – sociocultural, territorial, spiritual, ancestral, ethical, epistemic and esthetic – between beings, knowledge and nature (Walsh 2010).

As with any other political struggles, the implementation of these initiatives has not been exempted of contradictions, difficulties and tensions. However, the significant aspect of these experiences is that they aim to de-link and un-mark themselves from Eurocentric legacies, neoliberal globalisation and discourses of development. In addition, by questioning the very central place of the modern *White-mestizo* Western Man, intercultural decolonial pedagogies challenge a central node in DCE conceptualisations (Walsh 2014). These experiences are not only about resistance, interruption or participation but first and foremost about creating and living actual *world-Others*. Here the problem is not of addition or inclusion, recognition or redistribution, of learning how to deliberate in the public sphere, or the values of good citizens. The issue is that these communities refuse to enter the public sphere under the standards of rationality and expression that hegemonic views of DCE connote.

Conclusion: re-creating pedagogical imaginaries of DCE in comparative perspective

According to curricular research in Latin America, little is known about the real impact on classroom and teaching practices of the proposed reforms and reconceptualisation in citizenship education from multilateral institutions. Available evidence seems to show that, for the most part, citizenship education practices still rely primarily on narrow civic education views concerned with moral values and conformity to the state and authority (Bascopé et al. 2015; Cox et al. 2014). However, the existence of a diversity of discourses and contrasting experiences in citizenship education in Latin America – sometimes in opposition to each other, other times simply as alternatives – speak of a rich field for comparative research. In the last decade, there has been growing research on Colombia, Chile and Mexico, whose governments have more closely followed multilateral frameworks, participating in the IEA Civic Education tests and promulgating *convivencia* laws (cf. García-Cabrero 2017). We know less about the comparative characteristics of DCE curricular proposals and practices from Ecuador, Bolivia and Brazil, for instance, because they do not participate in these tests and have not followed these trajectories (OEI 2014).

This critical and decolonial analysis of the main tenets of multilateral discourses on citizenship education has aimed to question the insistence by governments and global discourses of education with limiting democratic education to a pre-established set of skills or moral discourses. A starting point is to avoid pre-definitions of 'what kind of a citizen' we fail to achieve based on 'global standards'. A fruitful avenue recommended is to acknowledge the plurality of citizenship enactments that grow as relevant, desirable and pertinent from a given context and for a particular generation of peoples and struggles. In short, we need to avoid speaking of democratic citizenship in the singular and commit to teach and research on democratic *citizenships*.

A critical decolonial approach contributes to this pending task in citizenship and democratic education research by emphasising the collective memories, epistemological pluralism, historical injustices and structural-global power configurations that democratic citizenship education research cannot neglect without failing to its own principles. Bringing up examples that illustrate experiences of what citizenship and democracy may otherwise mean in Latin America is a way to challenge the foreclosure of what democratic education entails. Instead of trying to find a new inventive solution from scratch for citizenship education, this kind of comparative research open avenues to find alternatives, study longer trajectories and assess their achievements and shortcomings within the realms of what is already happening in the margins of Latin America.

Notes

1. Included in this exercise are the following documents: *Democracy in Latin America: Towards a Democracy of Citizens* (United Nations Development Program 2004), *The State of Education in Latin America and the Caribbean: Towards a Quality Education for All – 2015* (UNESCO 2013), *Our Democracy* published together by the UNDP and the Organization of American States (OAS) (PNUD and OEA 2010), two policy documents on democratic citizenship education supported by the Inter-American Development Bank (IDB) (Cox, Jaramillo, and Reimers 2005; Espínola et al. 2005), reports on the *Educational Goals 2021* produced by the Organization of Iberoamerican States (OEI 2010, 2014, 2016a) and relevant reports by the World Bank (Aedo and Walker 2012) and the Organization for Economic Co-operation and Development (OECD, CAF, and ECLAC 2014).
2. It is significant that in recent years even the IDB's concern with citizenship education has given way to the World Bank (Aedo and Walker 2012; Cunningham et al. 2008; de Hoyos, Rogers, and Székely 2015) and the OECD's (OECD, CAF, and ECLAC 2014) promotion of educational goals concerned with human capital skills over democratic citizenship education.
3. Although *convivencia* could be translated as 'peaceful coexistence' or 'living together', due to the wide debates on its actual meaning and interpretations in the context of Latin America, I prefer to maintain the term in Spanish.
4. The OEI is an inter-governmental body for cooperation among Ibero-American countries in the fields of education, science, technology and culture in the context of development, democracy and regional integration (OEI 2016b). While the IDB is influenced by the USA, the OEI does not include the USA or Canada, but instead Spain and Portugal, in addition to most Latin American countries.

Disclosure statement

No potential conflict of interest was reported by the author.

ORCID

Diego Nieto http://orcid.org/0000-0002-6163-1573

References

Abdi, Ali A., Lynette Shultz, and Thashika Pillay, eds. 2015. *Decolonizing Global Citizenship Education*. Rotterdam: Sense Publishers.
Aedo, Cristian, and Ian Walker. 2012. *Skills for the 21st Century in Latin America and the Caribbean*. Washington, DC: The World Bank.
Ahmed, Sara. 2000. *Strange Encounters: Embodied Others in Post-Coloniality*. London: Routledge.
Aldenmyr, Sara, Ulrika Wigg, and Maria Olson. 2012. "Worries and Possibilities in Active Citizenship: Three Swedish Educational Contexts." *Education, Citizenship and Social Justice* 7 (3): 255–270.
Aman, Robert. 2017. "Colonial Differences in Intercultural Education: On Interculturality in the Andes and the Decolonization of Intercultural Dialogue." *Comparative Education Review* 61 (S1): S103–S120.

Andreotti, Vanessa. 2006. "Soft versus Critical Global Citizenship Education." *Policy & Practice-a Development Education Review* 3: 21-31.

Andreotti, Vanessa. 2015. "Global Citizenship Education Otherwise: Pedagogical and Theoretical Insights." In *Decolonizing Global Citizenship Education*, edited by Ali A. Abdi, Lynette Shultz, and Thashika Pillay, 221–230. Rotterdam: SensePublishers.

Andreotti, Vanessa, and Lynn Mario T. M. de Souza. 2012. *Postcolonial Perspectives on Global Citizenship Education*. New York: Routledge.

Apple, Michael W. 2011. "Democratic Education in Neoliberal and Neoconservative Times." *International Studies in Sociology of Education* 21 (1): 21–31.

Bacchi, Carol. 2000. "Policy as Discourse: What Does It Mean? Where Does It Get Us?" *Discourse: Studies in the Cultural Politics of Education* 21 (1): 45–57.

Bai, Heesoon. 2001. "Cultivating Democratic Citizenship: Towards Intersubjectivity." In *Philosophy of Education : Introductory Readings*. 3rd ed, edited by William Hare and John P. Portelli, 307–319. Calgary, Alta: Detselig Enterprises.

Bajaj, Monisha. 2015. "'Pedagogies of Resistance' and Critical Peace Education Praxis." *Journal of Peace Education* 12 (2): 154–166.

Baronnet, Bruno, Richard Stahler-Sholk, and Mariana Mora Bayo, eds. 2011. *Luchas "Muy Otras": Zapatismo Y Autonomía En Las Comunidades Indígenas de Chiapas* ["Very Other" Struggles: Zapatismo and Autonomy in the Indigenous Communities of Chiapas]. Chiapas: CIESAS; Universidad Autónoma Metropolitana UAM-Xochimilco; Universidad Autónoma de Chiapas.

Bartlett, Lesley, and Frances Vavrus. 2009. *Critical Approaches to Comparative Education: Vertical Case Studies from Africa, Europe, the Middle East, and the Americas*. New York: Palgrave Macmillan.

Bascopé, Martín, Macarena Bonhomme, Cristián Cox, Juan Carlos Castillo, and Daniel Miranda. 2015. "Curricular Guidelines and Citizenship Attitudes in Latin American Students: A Comparative Analysis." *Revista Latino Americana de Ciencias Sociales, Niñez y Juventud* 13 (2): 1169–1190.

Bermudez, Angela. 2012. "Youth Civic Engagement: Decline or Transformation? A Critical Review." *Journal of Moral Education* 41 (4): 529–542.

Bickmore, Kathy. 2011. "Policies and Programming for Safer Schools: Are 'Anti-Bullying' Approaches Impeding Education for Peacebuilding?" *Educational Policy* 25 (4): 648–687.

Biesta, Gert. 2009. "Sporadic Democracy: Education, Democracy, and the Question of Inclusion." In *Education, Democracy, and the Moral Life*, edited by Michael S. Katz, Susan Verducci, and Gert Biesta, 101–112. Dordrecht: Springer Netherlands.

Botero-Gómez, Patricia. 2015. "Pedagogía de los movimientos sociales como prácticas de paz en contextos de guerra." [Pedagogy of Social Movements as Peace Practices in Contexts of War.] *Revista Latino Americana de Ciencias Sociales, Niñez y Juventud* 13 (2): 1191–1206.

Carbajal Padilla, Patricia. 2013. "Convivencia Democrática En Las Escuelas. Apuntes Para Una Reconceptualización." [Democratic Peaceful Coexistence at Schools. Notes for a Reconceptualization.] *Revista Iberoamericana de Evaluación Educativa* 6 (2): 13–35.

Carretero, Mario, Helen Haste, and Angela Bermudez. 2015. "Civic Education." In *Handbook of Educational Psychology*, edited by L. Corno and E. M. Anderman, 295–308. London: Routledge Publishers.

Castro-Gómez, Santiago. 2005. *La hybris del punto cero: ciencia, raza e ilustración en la Nueva Granada (1750–1816)* [The Hybris of Zero Point: Science, Race and Illustration in New Granada (1750–1816)]. Colombia: Pontificia Universidad Javeriana.

Castro-Gómez, Santiago, and Ramón Grosfoguel. 2007. "Giro Decolonial, Teoría Crítica y Pensamiento Heterárquico." [Decolonial Turn, Critical Theory and Heterachic Thought.] In *El Giro Decolonial. Reflexiones Para Una Diversidad Epistémica Más Allá Del Capitalismo Global* [The Decolonial Turn. Reflections for an Epistemic Diversity Beyond Global Capitalism], edited by S. Castro-Gómez and R. Grosfoguel, 9–23. Bogotá, DC: Siglo del Hombre Editores S.A.

Cortina, Adela. 2010. "Los Valores de Una Ciudadanía Activa." [The Values of an Active Citizenship.] In *Educación, Valores y Ciudadanía* [Education, Values and Citizenship], edited by Bernardo Toro and Alicia Tallone, 95–107. Madrid: Organización de Estados Iberoamericanos para la Educación, la Ciencia y la Cultura (OEI).

Cox, Cristián, Martín Bascopé, Juan Carlos Castillo, Daniel Miranda, and Macarena Bonhomme. 2014. *Citizenship Education in Latin America: Priorities of School Curricula*. No. 14. IBE Working Papers on Curriculum Issues.

Cox, Cristián, Rosario Jaramillo, and Fernando Reimers. 2005. *Educar Para La Ciudadanía y La Democracia En Las Américas: Una Agenda Para La Acción* [Education for Democratic Citizenship in the Americas: An Agenda for Action]. Washington, DC: Banco Interamericano de Desarrollo.

Cubides, Juliana. 2015. "Lo Instituido y Lo Instituyente En Los Procesos de Subjetivación Política Juvenil En Colombia, Chile y México." [The Instituted and the Instituent in the Processes of Youth Political Subjectivation in Colombia, Chile and Mexico.]In *Jóvenes, Juventudes, Participación y Políticas. Asociados, Organizados y En Movimiento* [Youth, Participation and Policies. Associated, Organized and Mobilized], edited by Fabián Acosta, 135–183. Bogotá, DC: OBJUN-Secretaria Distrital de Integración Social.

Cunningham, Wendy, Linda McGinnis, Rodrigo Garcia Verdu, Cornelia Tesliuc, and Dorte Verner. 2008. *Youth at Risk in Latin America and the Caribbean: Understanding the Causes, Realizing the Potential*. Washington, DC: The World Bank.

Ermarth, Elizabeth Deeds. 2007. "Democracy and Postmodernity: The Problem." In *Rewriting Democracy: Cultural Politics in Postmodernity*, edited by Elizabeth Deeds Ermarth, 1–21. Aldershot, England: Ashgate.

Espínola, Viola, Audrey Osler, Hugh Starkey, Fernando Reimers, Eleonora Villegas Reimers, Cristián Cox, Rosario Jaramillo, and Lorenzo Gómez-Morín. 2005. *Educación para la ciudadanía y la democracia para un mundo globalizado: Una perspectiva comparativa* [Education for Citizenship and Democracy in a Globalized World: A Comparative Perspective]. Washington, DC: Inter-American Development Bank.

Fleet, Nicolás. 2011. "Movimiento Estudiantil y Transformaciones Sociales En Chile: Una Perspectiva Sociológica." [Student Movement and Social Transformations In Chile: A Sociological Perspective.] *Polis (Santiago)* 10 (30): 99–116.

Freire, Paulo. 1970. *Pedagogy of the Oppressed*. New York: Continuum.

Freire, Paulo. 1998. *Pedagogy of Freedom: Ethics, Democracy, and Civic Courage*. New York: Rowman & Littlefield.

Fukuyama, Francis. 1992. *The End of History and the Last Man*. New York: Maxwell Macmillan International.

Gandin, Luis A., and Michael W. Apple. 2002. "Can Education Challenge Neoliberalism? The Citizen School and the Struggle for Democracy in Porto Alegre, Brazil." *Social Justice* 29 (4): 26–40.

García-Cabrero, Benilde, ed. 2017. *Civics and Citizenship: Theoretical Models and Experiences in Latin America*. Rotterdam, The Netherlands; Boston, [Massachusetts]; Taipei, [Taiwan]: Sense Publishers.

García-Guadilla, María Pilar, and Ana L. Mallén. 2010. "El Movimiento Estudiantil Venezolano: Narrativas, Polarización Social y Públicos Antagónicos." [The Venezuelan Student Movement: Narratives, Social Polarization and Antagonistic Audiences.] *Cuadernos Del CENDES* 73: 71–95.

Gaztambide-Fernández, Rubén A. 2012. "Decolonization and the Pedagogy of Solidarity." *Decolonization: Indigeneity, Education & Society* 1 (1): 41–67.

Gaztambide-Fernández, Rubén A., and Alexandra Arráiz Matute. 2015. "Creation as Participation/Participation as Creation: Cultural Production, Participatory Politics, and the Intersecting Lines of Identification and Activism." *Curriculum Inquiry* 45 (1): 1–9.

Giroux, Henry A. 2003. "Public Pedagogy and the Politics of Resistance: Notes on a Critical Theory of Educational Struggle." *Educational Philosophy and Theory* 35 (1): 5–16.

Gutmann, Amy, and Sigal Ben-Porath. 2015. "Democratic Education." In *The Encyclopedia of Political Thought*, edited by Michael T. Gibbons, 863–875. Malden, MA: Wiley-Blackwell.

Haste, Helen. 2010. "Citizenship Education: A Critical Look at a Contested Field." In *Handbook of Research on Civic Engagement in Youth*, edited by Lonnie R. Sherrod, Judith Torney-Purta, and Constance A. Flanagan, 161–188. Hoboken, NJ: Wiley.

Howarth, David. 2000. *Discourse*. Philadelphia: Open University Press.

de Hoyos, Rafael, Halsey Rogers, and Miguel Székely. 2015. *Out of School and out of Work. Risk and Opportunities for Latin America's Ninis*. Washington, DC: The World Bank.

Huntington, Samuel P. 1993. "The Clash of Civilizations?" *Foreign Affairs* 72: 22–49.

Huntington, Samuel P. 2013. "The Clash of Civilizations Revisited." *New Perspectives Quarterly* 30 (4): 46–54.

Inter-American Institute of Human Rights, and UNESCO. 2011. *IV Jornadas de cooperación iberoamericana sobre educación para la paz, la convivencia democrática y los derechos humanos: Montevideo, Uruguay, marzo 2010* [IV Conference of Iberoamerican Cooperation on Education for Peace, Democratic Peaceful Coexistence and Human Rights: Montevideo, Uruguay, March 2010]. Santiago de Chile: UNESCO.

Janmaat, Jan Germen, and Nelli Piattoeva. 2007. "Citizenship Education in Ukraine and Russia: Reconciling Nation-building and Active Citizenship." *Comparative Education* 43 (4): 527–552.

Jaramillo, Rosario, and Gabriel Murillo. 2013. "Education and Critical Thinking for the Construction of Citizenship: An Investment toward Strengthening Democracy in the Americas." *Policy Brief Series: Education and Democracy*, Policy Brief Series, 4 (September): 1–20.

Kahne, Joseph, David Crow, and Nam-Jin Lee. 2013. "Different Pedagogy, Different Politics: High School Learning Opportunities and Youth Political Engagement." *Political Psychology* 34 (3): 419–441.

Kennelly, Jacqueline, and Kristina R. Llewellyn. 2011. "Educating for Active Compliance: Discursive Constructions in Citizenship Education." *Citizenship Studies* 15 (6-7): 897–914.

Kincheloe, Joe L. 1999. "Critical Democracy and Education." In *Understanding Democratic Curriculum Leadership*, edited by J. Henderson and K. Kesson, 70–83. New York: Teachers College Press.

Levinson, Bradley AU, and Juan G. Berumen. 2007. "Educación Para Una Ciudadanía Democrática En Los Países de América Latina: Una Mirada Crítica." [Education for a Democratic Citizenship In Latin American Countries: A Critical Look.] *REICE. Revista Iberoamericana Sobre Calidad, Eficacia y Cambio En Educación* 5 (4): 16–31.

Levinson, Bradley A. U., Daniel Schugurensky, and Roberto González. 2009. "Democratic Citizenship Education: A New Imperative for the Americas." *Inter-American Journal of Education for Democracy* 1 (1): 1–8.

Magendzo, Abraham, María Isabel Toledo, and Virna Gutiérrez. 2012. "Descripción y Análisis de La Ley Sobre Violencia Escolar (No 20.536): Dos Paradigmas Antagónicos." [Description and Analysis of The Law on School Violence (No 20,536): Two Antagonistic Paradigms.] *Estudios Pedagógicos (Valdivia)* 39 (1): 377–391.

Martí i Puig, Salvador. 2009. "Los Múltiples Debates (y Realidades) de La Democracia En América Latina." [The Multiple Debates (and Realities) of Democracy in Latin America.] *Revista CIDOB D'Afers Internacionals* 85–86: 53–74.

Mignolo, Walter. 2011. "Epistemic Disobedience and the Decolonial Option: A Manifesto." *TRANSMODERNITY: Journal of Peripheral Cultural Production of the Luso-Hispanic World* 1 (2): 44–66.

Mundy, Karen. 1998. "Educational Multilateralism and World (Dis)Order." *Comparative Education Review* 42 (4): 448–478.

Nieto, Diego, and Kathy Bickmore. 2016. "Educación Ciudadana y Convivencia En Contextos de Violencia: Desafíos Transnacionales a La Construcción de Paz En Escuelas de México." [Citizenship and Convivencia Education in Contexts of Violence: Transnational Challenges to Peacebuilding Education in Mexican Schools.] *Revista Española de Educación Comparada* 28: 109–134.

Nieto, Diego, and Juan Pablo Milanese. 2016. "De Las Transiciones Al Estancamiento. Revisitando La Democratización En La Obra de Guillermo O'Donnell." [From Transitions to Stagnation. Revisiting The Democratization in the Work of Guillermo O'Donnell.] *Revista Co-Herencia* 13 (24): 145–177.

Novelli, Mario. 2010. "The New Geopolitics of Educational Aid: From Cold Wars to Holy Wars?" *International Journal of Educational Development* 30 (5): 453–459.

OECD, CAF, and ECLAC. 2014. *Latin American Economic Outlook 2015. Education, Skills and Innovation for Development*. Paris: Organisation for Economic -operation and Development.

OEI. 2010. *Metas educativas 2021 la educación que queremos para la generación de los bicentenarios: documento final* [Educational Goals 2021 the Education We Want for the Bicentennial Generation: Final Document]. Madrid: OEI.

OEI. 2014. *Miradas sobre la educación en iberoamérica 2014. Avances en las Metas Educativas 2021* [Views on Education in Ibero-America 2014. Progress on the Educational Goals 2021]. Madrid: OEI.

OEI. 2016a. *Miradas Sobre La Educación En Iberoamerica 2016. Avance En Las Metas Educativas 2021* [Views on education in Ibero-America 2016. Progress on the Educational Goals 2021]. Madrid: Organización de Estados Iberoamericanos para la Educación, la Ciencia y la Cultura (OEI).

OEI. 2016b. "Acerca de La OEI." [About the OEI.] Accessed April 18. http://www.oei.es/acercadelaoei.php

Oliart, Patricia, and Carles Feixa. 2012. "Introduction: Youth Studies in Latin America–On Social Actors, Public Policies and New Citizenships." *Young* 20 (4): 329–344.

Olivier Téllez, Guadalupe, and Sergio Tamayo. 2015. "Tensiones Políticas En El Proceso de Movilización-Desmovilización: El Movimiento #YoSoy132." [Political tensions in the process Mobilization-Demobilization: The Movement # YoSoy132.] *Iztapalapa. Revista de Ciencias Sociales y Humanidades* 79 (36): 131–170.

PNUD, and OEA, eds. 2010. *Nuestra Democracia* [Our Democracy]. 1a ed. Sección de Obras de Sociología. México, D.F: Fondo de Cultura Económica : Programa de las Naciones Unidas para el Desarrollo : Secretaría General de la Organización de los Estados Americanos.

Reimers, Fernando. 2007. "Civic Education When Democracy is in Flux: The Impact of Empirical Research on Policy and Practice in Latin America." *Citizenship Teaching and Learning* 3 (2): 5–22.

Rosario, Melissa. 2015. "Public Pedagogy in the Creative Strike: Destabilizing Boundaries and Re-imagining Resistance in the University of Puerto Rico." *Curriculum Inquiry* 45 (1): 52–68.

Ruitenberg, Claudia. 2010. "Conflict, Affect and the Political: On Disagreement as Democratic Capacity." *Factis Pax* 4 (1): 40–55.

Schugurensky, Daniel. 2009. "Citizenship Learning for and through Participatory Democracy." In *Learning Citizenship by Practicing Democracy: International Initiatives and Perspectives*, edited by E. Pinnington and D. Schugurensky, 1–17. Newcastle Upon Tyne: Cambridge Scholars Publishing.

Smith, Andrea. 2013. "The Problem with 'Privilege'." *Andrea Smith's Blog*. https://andrea366.wordpress.com/2013/08/14/the-problem-with-privilege-by-andrea-smith/.

Santos, Boaventura de Sousa. 2001. "Nuestra América." [Our America.] *Theory, Culture & Society* 18 (2-3): 185–217.

Tarlau, Rebecca. 2015. "How Do New Critical Pedagogies Develop? Educational Innovation, Social Change, and Landless Workers in Brazil." *Teachers College Record* 117 (11): 1–36.

Tibbitts, Felisa, and Judith Torney-Purta. 1999. *Citizenship Education in Latin America: Preparing for the Future*. Argentina: Education Unit of the Inter-American Development Bank. Human Rights Education Associates (HREA).

Tikly, Leon. 1999. "Postcolonialism and Comparative Education." *International Review of Education/ Internationale Zeitschrift Fr Erziehungswissenschaft/ Revue Inter* 45 (5–6): 603–621.

Todd, Sharon. 2010. "Living in a Dissonant World: Toward an Agonistic Cosmopolitics for Education." *Studies in Philosophy and Education* 29 (2): 213–228. doi:10.1007/s11217-009-9171-1.

Torfing, Jacob. 1999. *New Theories of Discourse : Laclau, Mouffe, and Zizek*. Malden, Mass.: Blackwell Publishers.

Toro, Bernardo, and Alicia Tallone, eds. 2010. *Educación, Valores y Ciudadanía* [Education, Values and Citizenship]. Madrid: OEI.

UNDP. 2004. *La Democracia en América Latina: hacia una democracia de ciudadanas y ciudadanos* [Democracy in Latin America. Towards a democracy of citizens].Buenos Aires, Argentina; New York: Aguilar, Altea, Taurus, Alfaguara S.A. ; Programa de las Naciones Unidas para el Desarrollo.

UNESCO. 2013. *Situación Educativa de América Latina y El Caribe: Hacia La Educación de Calidad Para Todos Al 2015* [The State of Education in Latin America and the Caribbean: Towards Quality of Education for All - 2015]. Santiago de Chile: OREALC/UNESCO.

Walsh, Catherine. 2005. "Interculturalidad, conocimientos y decolonialidad." [Interculturality, Knowledges and Decoloniality.] *Signo Y Pensamiento* XXIV (46): 39–50.

Walsh, Catherine. 2007. "Interculturalidad, Colonialidad y Educación." [Interculturality, Coloniality and Education.] *Revista Educación y Pedagogía* XIX (48): 25–35.

Walsh, Catherine. 2010. "Development as Buen Vivir: Institutional Arrangements and (De)Colonial Entanglements." *Development* 53 (1): 15–21.
Walsh, Catherine. 2013. "Introducción. Lo Pedagógico y Lo Decolonial. Entretejiendo Caminos." [Introduction. The Pedagogical and the Decolonial. Interweaving Paths.] In *Pedagogías Decoloniales: Prácticas Insurgentes De Resistir, (Re)Existir y (Re)Vivir. Tomo I* [Decolonial Pedagogies: Insurgent Practices of Resisting, (Re) Existing and (Re) Living. Volume I], edited by Catherine Walsh, 23-68. Quito, Ecuador: Ediciones Abya-Yala.
Walsh, Catherine. 2014. "Pedagogías decoloniales caminando y preguntando. Notas a Paulo Freire desde Abya Yala." *Revista Entramados: Educación y Sociedad* 1 (1): 17–31.
Westheimer, Joel, and Joseph Kahne. 2004. "What Kind of Citizen? The Politics of Educating for Democracy." *American Educational Research Journal* 41 (2): 237–269.
Wynter, Sylvia. 2004. "Unsettling the Coloniality of Being/Power/Truth/Freedom: Towards the Human, after Man, Its Overrepresentation–An Argument." *CR: The New Centennial Review* 3 (3): 257–337.
Young, Iris Marion. 2001. "Activist Challenges to Deliberative Democracy." *Political Theory* 29 (5): 670–690.
Zurita Rivera, Úrsula. 2013. "Las Escuelas Mexicanas y La Legislación Sobre Convivencia, Seguridad y La Violencia Escolar." [Mexican Schools and the Legislation on Coexistence, Security and School Violence.] *Educación y Territorio* 2 (1): 19–36.

Rendering technical the responsible citizen: implementing citizenship education reform in Kosovo

Jennifer Otting

ABSTRACT
In the last 20 years, there has been a growing preoccupation with fragile contexts. International development and diplomatic communities have focused on implementing Western-oriented education policies centered on democratisation efforts to transform fragile contexts. In order to understand what happens when education reform policies are enmeshed with the world they are designed to change, this project focuses on the educational actors who create and take up citizenship education in Kosovo. Using ethnographic methods, the research examines how educational actors are making sense of the citizenship education competency within the economic, political and social conditions framing Kosovo as a fragile state. This article highlights how the curriculum was rendered technical in the implementation process producing the unintended consequence of perpetuating conditions that have justified Kosovo's categorisation as a fragile state. This research raises important questions about the implementation of education reform policies used as a panacea to address state fragility.

Introduction

Education for democracy-building purposes has consistently been incorporated into development agendas to promote state building. Starting in the late-1800s to early-1900s, education was believed to move societies along a development continuum by creating globally competitive economies and democratic societies (Fagerlind and Saha 1983; Turrent and Oketch 2009). At the end of World War II, as development and democracy became increasingly linked, education policies were used to strengthen Western notions of liberal democracy (Fagerlind and Saha 1983; Mundy1998; Tikly 2004), and schools were seen as key sites for preparing students to be active citizens (Counts 1969; Dewey 1916; Parker 2003, 2005). Education's role in shaping the desired citizen for the state building project has only intensified in fragile contexts as development agendas view the restoration and reform of education as a key component for building social cohesion (Shah and Cardozo 2015; Tawil and Harley 2004).

International governing bodies consider fragile contexts, categorised as ineffective, illegitimate and/or weak, to be one of the most serious security threats facing the world. Fragile states, such as Pakistan, Sudan and Kosovo, have become central intervention sites for international development organisations and foreign governments (Brinkerhoff 2007; François and Sud 2006; Grimm, Lemay-Hébert, and Nay 2014). Generally, international governing bodies categorise a state as 'fragile' when the state has a breakdown in law and order; cannot provide basic public services to its citizens; and is unable to represent the state beyond its border (Brinkerhoff 2007). A country is measured using these characteristics and placed along a continuum between failed and fragile. The label 'failed state' is used to describe extreme collapse of a state, such as Somalia and Sudan, and at the opposite end is the less extreme 'fragile state' teetering on the brink of collapse due to growing violence, poverty and lack of governance (Brinkerhoff 2007; Carment, Samy, and Landry 2013). Over the last three decades, humanitarian assistance to fragile states has increased by over 600% (Novelli 2010). This has resulted in the 2015 Sustainable Development Goals heightened interest in states of fragility, which call for greater resource allocation for peacebuilding and state-building efforts (OECD 2015). These efforts have been brought together by the international development sector and diplomatic communities in the education arena.

Conflict areas and fragile contexts create particular challenges for educational initiatives. On one hand, international development and diplomatic sectors rationalise educational initiatives as a means of re-establishing social contracts between the individual and the state (International Institute for Educational Planning 2011; Shah 2012). Development agendas outline improvement in school governance, curricula reform and capacity development for teachers and students. Language policies and the teaching of history and citizenship education are particular key subject areas seen to address national identity and diversity issues plaguing fragility contexts (Tawil and Harley 2004). On the other hand, these educational policies and practices are never value free. In translating policy into pre-existing schooling structures composed of individuals with competing interests, reform efforts have the potential to be implicated in conflict and/or exacerbate social divisions (Ball 1994; Davies and European Training Foundation [Italy] 2009; Smith 2005; Tawil and Harley 2004).

To examine the implementation of education policy in fragile contexts, this study focuses on the example of citizenship education reform in Kosovo. The purpose of this article is not to condemn or commend Kosovo's current education reform. Rather, it seeks to examine what happens when education reform policies in fragile contexts enmesh with the world they are designed to transform. In this article, I demonstrate that while the design of Kosovo's citizenship competency is integral to the country's peacebuilding and state building agendas, the implementation of the policy produces outcomes that actually counter these intentions. As part of the state building process, Kosovo is currently implementing a new national curriculum that aligns with European goals of fostering 'knowledge, skills, positions and values suitable to a democratic society' (Ministry of Education Science and Technology 2011a, 15). The new curriculum outlines six competencies to be taught across all subjects. My research focuses on the 'Responsible Citizen Competency' as it directly relates to citizenship education. The aim of this competency is to help prepare students to be 'national and global citizens by understanding their immediate and wider social context;' and this includes learning to value diversity and demonstrate tolerance; exercising rights and responsibilities while respecting others' rights; participating in democratic decision-making processes; and opposing poverty and discrimination (Ministry of Education Science and Technology 2011a, 21).

Yet my research indicates that the actual content of what should constitute the citizenship education has been sidelined in the implementation process. Instead, through the import of the European competency model and under the guidance of outside expertise, the reform has focused on technocratic issues, standards and accountability measurements. The Kosovo curriculum has been 'rendered technical' (Li 2007), a process that takes difficult-to-solve problems and frames them in technocratic terms that make intervention practices offered by experts possible (Ferguson 1994; Li 2007; Mitchell 2002). Expert knowledge takes what is essentially a political, economic or social problem and recasts it in neutral language (Dreyfus and Rabinow 1983), simultaneously rendering it non-political (Ferguson 1994; Li 2007). The 'rendering technical' of Kosovo's citizenship competency has averted focus away from discussions of content outlined in the competency. Without serious conversations around implementing citizenship *content*, Kosovo remains firmly embedded in the conditions that have justified its categorisation as a fragile state.

The contribution of this article is to provide awareness into how the actual outcomes of planned policies end up producing unintended results that shape societal trajectories. Understanding how education policies are appropriated and practiced can provide important insights into how policy dynamics influence socioeconomic and political relationships. This research illustrates the strengths and limitations of universal citizenship education approaches, particularly European and peacebuilding models, being implemented to address sociopolitical issues causing fragility. While this study focuses on the events and conditions of Kosovo, there are numerous other states encountering policy measures associated with fragility. This study aims to provide a foundational base for understanding the complexities of education policy reform in fragile contexts and raise important questions about current development discourse and policies aimed at constructing democratic teaching.

Policy as technology of governing

Power relationships embedded in policy processes and relationships are often obscured. Policy is presented as an instrument for efficiency and effectiveness giving the illusion that it is politically and ideologically neutral and objective (Shore and Wright 1997). Yet behind policy's neutral, technical facade lies a governing system by which subjectivities are formed and individual identities are constructed (Ball 1990; Popkewitz 1991). Drawing on Foucault's (1991) notion of power and discourse reveals the way in which language and ideas in policy organises and disciplines 'how the world is to be seen, acted on, felt and talked about' and this both changes, and in some instances limits, the possibilities for thinking about what is possible (Popkewitz 1991, 14). In the field of education, Ball's (1990) study of education policy in Britain deconstructs the discourses in policy to show how a new rationality and ideology were introduced into the education system. His findings show how 'political, ideologically-loaded decisions are choked by bureaucratic-administrative systems and [how] attempts are made to displace issues of moral and cultural identity with the imperatives of administrative efficiency' (Ball 1990, 154). By offering efficiency-based solutions, policy-makers discount problems and limit effective change solutions to issues that are connected to moral and cultural values.

The discursive effects of policy articulate a mode of personal existence. The individual is categorised and given such status and roles as 'subject', 'citizen', 'professional', 'national', 'criminal' and 'deviant' (Shore and Wright 1997, 4). However, this existence is not shaped because policy bears down to control and/or coerce the individual. Rather, policy shapes the identity and subjectivity of the individual through the assemblage of technologies – programmes, calculations, techniques, apparatuses, documents and procedures – that authorities seek to employ (Rose 2005; Rose and Miller 1992). These policy technologies govern through the minute art of self-scrutiny, self-evaluation and self-regulation using powers of expertise (Ball 1990; Rose 2005). Mitchell (2002) argues that twentieth century politics has become deeply connected to the role of expertise. According to Mitchell (2002), 'politics of national development and economic growth is a techno-science which claims to bring the expertise of modern engineering, technology, and social science to improve the defects of nature, to transform peasant agriculture, to repair the ills of society, and to fix the economy' (47). Mitchell illustrates how the politics of expertise in development discourse creates a dichotomous relationship between the West and non-West whereby the West is seen as possessing the expertise, technology and management skills that the non-West is lacking. The policies of the non-West become intrinsically linked to the activities of expertise whose role it is administer the conduct choices and values of the individuals for the purpose of aligning them with the West (Rose and Miller 1992).

Expertise is solidified in the discourse of development through rational planning and policy approaches and techniques. Development identifies deficiencies and these problems are framed in terms that are amendable to technical solutions usually offered by so-called experts in the development field (Ferguson 1994; Li 2007; Mitchell 2002). Li (2007) calls the process of linking a solution to a trained expert 'rendering technical' (7). Technical problems are 'exaggerated or invented' to take the place of things that are illusory or difficult to solve and this makes policy interventions from the development sector possible (Ferguson 1994, 88). As questions and problems are rendered technical, they are simultaneously rendered non-political and anti-political. Problems are rendered non-political when experts exclude the structure of political-economic relations from their diagnoses and prescriptions (Ferguson 1994; Li 2007). Yet not only do development agendas continuously render issues technical, but they do so in ways that detach themselves from the problems they seek to eradicate. By presenting policy as detached from the problems they wished to change, the policies and practices offered by development are unable to be diagnosed integral to the problem (Mitchell 2002, 260). Therefore, the policies themselves act as an anti-political mechanism that maintains the status quo (Ferguson 1994).

Education policy as a solution to fragility

In recent decades there has been increased attention on identifying, diagnosing and managing fragile contexts for the purpose of preventing state collapse. The events of September 11, 2001, led to a growing urgency to understand the links between development, human security, state effectiveness and peacebuilding. International Development's commitment to peacebuilding and state building sparked the New Deal for Engagement in Fragile State (G7+'New Deal for Engagement n.d.). Development agencies like the World Bank, USAID and the Department for International Development (DfID) renewed efforts to improve overall political, social, economic and security conditions, believing that policy interventions can reverse and/or alleviate fragile conditions (Carment, Samy, and Landry 2013; Shah and Cardozo 2015). Each international development organisation has its own working definition of the fragile state, which drives policy practices. For example, DfID generally describes fragile states as lacking core state functions and recognises that education needs to be provided through non-governmental channels, whereas USAID makes a distinction between fragile states, categorising them as vulnerable states and crisis states, and places greater importance on securitisation policies (Kirk, Mundy, and Dryden-Peterson 2011). Despite the various working definitions of and policy practices within fragile states, there is a consensus among development organisations that education plays a vital role in restoring stability.

Education policy initiatives in fragile contexts are not a recent phenomenon. Grassroots refugee education and the rebuilding of school infrastructures date back to post-World War II development agendas (Winthrop and Matsui 2013). In the mid-1990s, educational policies in conflict areas focused on human capital and human rights initiatives implemented through the Education for All and the Millennium Development Goals agendas, but currently these agendas have expanded to include the complex processes of state building and peacebuilding (McCowan, Unterhalter, and Bloomsbury Publishing 2016; Winthrop and Matsui 2013).

Recently there is growing scrutiny of the development-fragility relationship. As indicated by Shah and Cardozo (2014), 'there has been a shift away from "grand narratives" towards more contingent, specific and contextually driven understandings of how educational processes, decisions and actions unfold in fragile settings' (3). Scholars have begun to interrogate how conflict dimensions and educational aspects (access to schooling and quality education) converge to produce outcomes impeding transformative qualities in education. Since Bush and Saltarelli's (2001) seminal study highlighting the 'two-faces' of education in conflict settings, growing research has shown how education systems not only negate but also perpetuate conditions of fragility (Davies 2011; Novelli and Cardozo 2008; Rose and Greeley 2006; Smith 2005).

Research has shown that education policies can often times counter state building goals and exacerbate conflict. Corruption, limited transparency and unaccountable delivery of education can reduce trust in the government and limit the capacity to serve the population (Davies 2011; Rose and Greeley 2006). Moreover, the unequal allocation of educational resources and outcomes can reproduce historical patterns of inequality and unjust power systems leading to attitudes of passivity and lack of agency among the citizenry (International Institute for Educational Planning 2011). Finally, while curriculum development is crucial to the state building process, curriculum that manipulates history, silences or erases minority voices or reinforces stereotypes produces negative effects on state cohesion (Rose and Greeley 2006). A 2004 UNESCO study of seven post-conflict countries indicated that to build national identity, there needed to be multiple voices in designing the curriculum so that numerous views about the conflict are understood (Tawil and Harley 2004). The study also emphasised that in developing curriculum, policy planners needed to examine national conceptions and explore the teaching of history that influence the cohesion of the society in which the school system is embedded (Tawil and Harley 2004; Weinstein, Freedman, and Hughson 2007).

Similarly, a 2007 curriculum study of post-conflict countries by Weinstein et al. (2007) showed that without collaboration from teachers and local school officials around sensitive subject areas such as history and literature, social reconstruction and cohesion could not be achieved. The study also found that the legacies of war were preserved through the use of top-down, rote-based teaching practices that did not promote democratic participation, critical thinking and independent action. Conversely, Jana Bacevic's (2014) study of curriculum in former- and post-Yugoslav states cautioned against a critique that artificially dichotomises the communist past and the European future. Bacevic (2014) argued that curriculum development and the assessment of curriculum policies in post-Yugoslav states are primarily understood as part of the modernisation process where the sole purpose of curriculum is centred around the acceptance into the European 'family of nations' (17). Curriculum policies in post-Yugoslav states can be seen to exacerbate fragility conditions because people are caught between choosing to position themselves with the Europeanisation project or the communist past, a choice that represents a fully developed modern citizen versus an underdeveloped, past-looking individual.

Kosovo as a fragile context

Kosovo embodies the complexities associated with fragile states. It has been defined as a 'poor performer, a weak state, a shadow state, a neo-patrimonial state or quasi-state' (Montanaro 2009, 6). Kosovo has not been recognised by all nation states as an independent, sovereign nation. As a result of its precarious position, it has been interpreted as both a story of success and of failure. The success of Kosovo is linked to the implementation of democratic values and best European practices (Musliu 2015). At the end of the 1998–1999 war, Kosovo became one of the largest nation-building development projects in recent history receiving more international money, staff and effort per local person than any mission before or since (King and Mason 2006). Yet the high concentration of development aid also correlates to Kosovo's story of failure, as the country struggles with 35% percent unemployment for adults and 60% unemployment for youth (UNDP 2015), a 30% poverty rate (UNDP 2015) and chronic corruption (Open Data Kosovo 2016) despite social and economic development support.

While Kosovo has followed neoliberal economic trends of liberalisation and privatisation as part of their strategy to accession into the EU, the weak rule of law, a large informal economy and an underdeveloped policy framework continue to stymie the economy and to fuel corruption (Stambolieva 2015). Economic challenges have been further exacerbated by issues of nationalism and ethnic polarisation in the region. Yugoslavia's collapse created divisions along ethnic and national lines and also created clientelistic relations among political, economic elites and the dependent populations. As the former Yugoslav welfare state dissolved, dysfunctional state structures emerged in its place serving mainly elite interests, which created exclusionary and ethnicised models of citizenship (Cerami and Stubbs 2011). According to Stambolieva (2015), nowhere in former Yugoslavia have democratisation efforts been more defective than in Kosovo: ethnic conflicts, elite-dominated political and economic structures and neutralised labour forces, as well as top-down development agendas, have all contributed to exclusionary policies and the minimisation of public voices.

To address the economic stagnation and ethnic divisions challenging democratisation efforts, Kosovo sought to reform its education system. The inadequate or decreasing levels of citizenship involvement and lack of social cohesion have called for a revitalisation of citizenship education (Council of Europe 2005; Putnam 2004). In the EU, the recognition of citizens' rights and duties is a central tenant to democratic education. As signatories to European and international instruments, all post-Yugoslav countries have incorporated provisions of protecting individual rights as well as group rights, such as cultural and linguistic minority rights into their curriculums.

Curriculum reform process in Kosovo

Since the war, the education system in Kosovo has undergone several reforms, including new contracts for teachers, a restructuring of the educational system from an 8-year compulsory model to a 9-year one and the creation of a new curriculum framework (OECD 2003). The new curriculum, which is widely accepted as an ambitious and well-planned framework bolstering the democratic values of pupils, has been a long and tumultuous process in the making.

In 2002, the United Nations Mission in Kosovo believed that a new curriculum was needed to heal post-war ethnic divisions. Under UNICEF's guidance, a small group of 10 local specialists attended an intensive training program run through UNESCO-International Bureau of Education in Geneva for the purpose of outlining a new curriculum. Experts from UNICEF and the local specialist drafted a curriculum that aligned with the European Union's curriculum framework model rather than the traditional syllabus content model (Sommers and Buckland 2005). A major focus of the new curriculum framework sought to develop students' knowledge, attitudes and skills that would 'enable them to engage competently in public affairs and to be active and responsible citizens in a pluralistic and democratic society' (UNICEF Kosovo 2001, 18).

According to one of the curriculum developers, even though the curriculum was widely praised by international education experts and ministry officials, it was never officially adopted due to a turbulent political situation (Interview, June 11, 2015). It was not until 2008 that a new education minister re-initiated the curriculum development process as a first step in reforming pre-university education (Ministry of Education Science and Technology 2011a). With support from the European Commission and financial assistance from the Instrument for Pre-accession Assistance (IPA), Kosovo drafted and implemented the sector-wide Education Strategic Plan 2011–2016 to address the lack of adequate facilities and education quality (Ministry of Education Science and Technology 2011b). To specifically deal with citizenship issues, numerous stakeholders, including the Democracy for Development and the Council for a Community of Democracies, approved the National Democracy Education Action Plan to align Kosovo's democratisation efforts with Western nations (National Democracy Education Action Plan 2014, 6).

The initial plan for implementing the curriculum was broken into three phases: the preparatory phase (2010–2011), the trial phase (2011–2013) and the national implementation phase (2013–2014). Two local experts who worked on the 2001 draft of the curriculum were invited back by the minister of education to lead the project. The 2-year drafting phase involved international and local experts and educational ministers, as well as input from the teachers state council and some parent groups. According to one of the local curriculum development experts, the goal of Kosovo's new curriculum was to follow 'trends that were happening in modern, developed countries' by shifting from a content-based to a competency-based mode of instruction and assessment (Interview June 11, 2015). The local expert explained that while the EU promotes eight competencies in their curriculum, the developers of Kosovo's curriculum decided to integrate some of the competencies together in order to have six competencies. The six competencies (effective communicator; creative thinker; successful learner; productive contributor; healthy individual; responsible citizen), each addressing specific learning outcomes, were to be taught and assessed in all content areas (Ministry of Education Science and Technology 2011a).

In 2011, the Ministry of Education, Science and Technology approved the new curriculum and in the 2013–2014 school year, teachers in 90 pilot schools were trained in the new curriculum. Supported by the USAID 'Basic Education Project' and the Teacher Training component of EU IPA 2009, as well as by the German Technical Cooperation Agency and the World Bank, the teacher training programme aimed to develop the core skills of teachers needed to teach the new curriculum (Boshtrakaj et al. 2010). To implement the curriculum, the ministry of education used a cascading training system whereby in each of the 90 pilot schools one teacher from each subject area received training in the new curriculum and went back to their schools to train the other teachers. After a year of training, it was determined that more training was needed and the trial phase was extended into the 2014–2015 school year.

Methodology

This research stems from my work in Kosovo with a large international organisation from 2010–2014. The privileges and opportunities I experienced during this 4-year development project were an important part of this research as it provided an avenue to unravel and challenge the knowledge and power dynamics in the education reform process. This position allowed me access to high-level NGO workers and ministry officials as well as the means to meet civic education teachers throughout the entire country.

The research for this article was conducted in the summer of 2015 after the new curriculum had been implemented in 90 schools during the trial phase of the project. The data was collected using ethnographic methods of participant observations and interviews. I did daily participant observations within the country's largest national education NGO, a leader of teacher training and educational research. A total of 22 semi-structured interviews, each lasting 45–60 minutes, were conducted with the help of a research assistant. Interviews were conducted in either English or Albanian, depending on the interviewee's choice. My research assistant and I met with three current ministers from education and culture and two individuals who were involved with designing the curriculum framework. We also interviewed seven educational staff members from large international organizations based in the capital and smaller community-based organisations located in the other major cities of Prizren and Mitrovica. Since the curriculum framework was being piloted in 90 schools throughout Kosovo, we met with primary and secondary teachers who were teaching in the pilot schools as well as with teachers who were not part of the pilot phase in order to have a point of comparison. In addition to these ethnographic tools, I analysed all of the curriculum framework documents starting with the Discussion White papers from 2001 to the final draft of the 2011 Curriculum Framework. While I recognise that more time in the field and a second round of interviews could have provided richer information on the reform process, my continued communication with the on-site research assistant has provided me with consistent and up-to-date research on the project.

All field notes, interview transcripts and policy documents were uploaded into the MAXQDA program. For the initial coding, I employed verbatim and descriptive coding to search for categories (Saldaña 2013). After, I re-categorised and consolidated categories to progress towards what Saldaña (2013) calls a thematic and conceptual understanding of the data. First, I examined the themes that emerged from discussions with educators about the behaviours, values, knowledge and skills outlined in the responsible citizen competency. Then I analysed how these ideas of Kosovo's citizenship education competency intersected with policy and development documents centred on peacebuilding and state building initiatives. Based on my analysis, there was a schism between the intentional design of the educational policy and its actual implementation. Citizenship learning embodied a technical processes, which was replacing substantive content material that was crucial for mediating issues of fragility.

Rendering the responsible citizen technical

Kosovo's numerous education policy documents support the creation of an inclusive education system that provides people with life-long skills and knowledge of active citizenship integral to European society. In particular, the Kosovo Curriculum Framework reinforces the goals of education for democratic citizenship and education for human rights, as defined in the 2010 Council of Europe Charter on Education for Democratic Citizenship and Education for Human Rights. These ideals are reinforced by the citizenship competency, which aims to develop 'the knowledge, skills, attitudes and values required by a democratic society' for the purpose of enabling young people to be 'active and responsible citizens, constructively cope with differences and challenges and respect their own rights and the rights of others' (Ministry of Education Science and Technology 2011a, 16). My research sought to understand the competency's goal by asking 'what knowledge, skills, attitudes and values are reportedly being taught?'

When asked to explain the responsible citizen, the majority of NGO workers, education ministers, administrators and teachers found it difficult to bring this citizen into focus. One educational officer from a large multilateral organisation responded that it was challenging to describe the responsible citizen and believed that 'what teachers here teach about the responsible citizen is a cliché thing, a stereotypical thing– you should pay taxes and vote.' When a top ministry official was asked to explain the behavior of the responsible citizen he responded with:

> In grade 12th, I think when we look at the curriculum documents the expectation is that they become, umm, if I use some political words uh, you know, responsible citizen, they become critical thinkers, they become democratic citizens and blah, you name it.

Part of the difficulty in explaining the responsible citizen is that ideals of human rights and democracy embedded in the competency are not only lofty and contested (Castles and Davidson 2000; Parker 2005), but the new curriculum framework itself does not provide in-depth details or discussions of these ideas. The citizenship competency includes bullet points like 'value diversity and demonstrate tolerance, manage and solve conflicts, demonstrate human rights values and principles' (Ministry of Education Science and Technology 2011a, 21). In interviews with educators, while they talked about the importance of multiculturalism and diversity, they did not discuss the bulleted content (diversity and tolerance) itself. The content subject in the curriculum appeared detached from the implementation of the curriculum

It is not that educators did not care about citizenship education – they did. Even though educators found it difficult to articulate the responsible citizen, they all believed in the *idea of* a 'responsible citizen'. For the majority of the interviewees, the responsible citizen competency represented a solution to the social ills of corruption, clientelism and ethnic divisions plaguing Kosovo. Yet, educators also recognised that education itself was part of the problem. A high-level minister talked openly about the pervasiveness of cheating in the school system. He lamented on how 'parents teach their kids how to cheat so that their children get better marks in the hope of securing a better job.' While some educators contributed the cheating scandal to new economic policies creating high youth unemployment, others spoke about a moral shift that had taken place during the transition from pre-war Yugoslavia to post-war Kosovo. One primary school teacher explained how society had become more individualised than in the past and that now people have 'turned to their personal interests, like, group interest, including politics', creating what she described as a negative atmosphere. Another teacher noted a growing interest in material things, explaining that as development was being linked to money, more young people now are more concerned with money than with education.

Problems plaguing society at large, and education specifically, became the justification for the teaching of the responsible citizen. While all of the participants in my study believed that the responsible citizenship competency should be part of the solution to current problems, educators were unable to specifically articulate how the citizenship competency would achieve these aims. When I pressed ministry officials, administrators and teachers to tell me how they were using or should use the competency in their classrooms, their answers focused on the terminology and structure of the curriculum that they learned about during the training sessions. When I asked one high school civic education teacher to give me an example of an activity she used in the classroom, she immediately began describing the changes from the old curriculum to the new curriculum introduced during the training sessions:

> In the previous curriculum we were more concentrated on content. So we are now aiming for competencies and expecting results, so we need to be more pragmatic, more like practitioners. We are not so concerned with content, but with the behavior, with the action.

Training sessions on the new competency-based curriculum had shifted educators' thinking away from teaching content and more towards measuring results. According to one teacher, training sessions focused on helping teachers to map out how they were going to achieve the competencies using language such as 'benchmarks', 'continual assessment' and 'grade assessment'.

Many teachers felt that while in implementing the competency-based curriculum there was an emphasis on standards and assessment, the actual substance of this new curriculum was not much different than the old curriculum. Half of the teachers interviewed argued that learning the new curriculum was about learning different terminology. One teacher told me that he had reservations about the curriculum training because he felt that he was not learning anything new; it was a new way of packaging old thinking. Another veteran teacher from a pilot school described the new curriculum as such:

[I] don't think that it's very different because we had the same things in the previous curriculum but they were explained as results but now we call them objectives .... Before the war teachers thought they had these objectives; three part teaching hour (introduction, session and reflection) which is now with these new methodologies for reading and writing in critical thinking. A good teacher did this before. Now they should try to adopt the terminology.

Training sessions were considered instrumental to learning the terminology of the competency-based curriculum. While the curriculum designers and members of the ministry attended trainings outside of Kosovo, teachers and administrators from pilot schools were mandated to attend trainings in their local communities. One of the teacher coordinators from a pilot school said that during the first year they had to attend 40 hours of training for the new curriculum, but after the first year they realised that 40 hoursw was not sufficient so the next year the Pedagogical Institute of Kosovo extended the training to 104 hours. Even with the increased training hours for teachers, 9 out of 12 ministers and NGO workers who were interviewed talked about the need for *more* training. Yet it was not just any type of training. The successful execution of the curriculum relied upon the expertise knowledge provided by institutions from outside of Kosovo. According to a top-level ministry official, in-service training provided by experts from the development sector were considered more beneficial than pre-service (college) training:

The in-service, seems to be more guided and directed to teachers' needs in supporting the curriculum and supporting new teaching methodologies, whereas pre-service tends to be not well developed and up-to-date with the new requirements, so questions about planning, lesson planning, curriculum planning, teaching methodology, um, if when the new teachers come into the system sometimes, in a lot of cases, they are so behind with teachers in the system that have gone through various, various in-service trainings.

Ministry officials and NGO workers correlated the success and failure of the new curriculum with training teachers in new methodologies, approaches and terminology. One NGO worker told me that many teachers used outdated methodologies that would not be appropriate for developing the competencies of the responsible citizen:

Only a few teachers know about new methodologies and implement it during their courses, but a majority of them are still teachers who are lecturing in a traditional way so, umm, those teachers need to enrol in courses sponsored by NGOs.

Teachers and some NGO workers, however, were quick to point out that simply training teachers was not the answer. The biggest complaint from teachers centred on the lack of up-to-date textbooks to accompany the curriculum. The lack of adequate resources was the biggest problem teachers cited, but they also complained about lack of institutional support in implementing the curriculum, the difficulties of collaborating with other teachers on curriculum issues and the amount of time spent in both training and implementing the curriculum. Yet, even though teachers cited these difficulties, the training sessions did not provide any guidance and assistance for the lack of resources and institutional support.

Discussion

When asked to describe the attitudes, behaviours and values of the responsible citizen, interviewees had a difficult time articulating what actually was being taught in schools. The difficulty in responding did not imply that ideals attached to the responsible citizen were not important, but rather the ideals of human rights, democracy, tolerance and so on were complex. Yet the moral, cultural and political complexity of the citizenship competency was not reflected in the implementation process. Neither the curriculum text nor the curriculum training provided definitions, explanations or discussions of the content. The implementation of the curriculum created a paradox: while the intention of the curriculum policy represented a solution to social problems, it seemed in execution that the new curriculum allowed for the perpetuation of the conditions creating fragility. The enactment of the curriculum made it such that the content was not given serious consideration in a meaningful way. Without serious discussion of the citizenship competency content, educators could not tackle the conditions of ethnic divisions, political corruption and economic disparity that justified Kosovo's classification as a fragile state.

Kosovo's reform process was entrapped in a cyclical rationale whereby the reform's intentionality of addressing poverty, insecurity and lack of governance was unable to come to fruition, which continued to encapsulate Kosovo as a fragile state creating the need for more reform efforts. The Kosovo government and development institutions identified the need for citizenship education curriculum based on the European competency-based model. The solution was to utilise experts to build the capabilities of the teachers through in-service training. The training sessions required teachers to learn new and different teaching approaches, instructional language, measurement assessments and planning techniques. While these requirements were arguably important in teacher professional development, they created an unintended consequence. Focusing on the methods, standards and accountability measures of the curriculum made citizenship education, which was not technocratic in nature, technical. Political, economic and social questions regarding the relationship between citizenship and the polity had either been ignored or repositioned as technical problems during the training sessions. By 'rendering technical' (Li 2007) the citizenship competency, it made it easier and more manageable to plan, measure and disseminate the production of the democratic citizen without ever discussing what this citizen actually looked like.

While citizenship education is itself political, the technocratic focus of implementing the responsible citizen competency rendered it non-political. Even though people spoke openly and passionately about the social problems of high unemployment and political corruption, they did not bring them into the realm of citizenship education. Trainings were not centred on conversations about political and economic issues that could connect the citizen to deeper political processes. Moreover, the training sessions did not help prepare educators to address social cohesion objectives as intended. Problems of ethnic divisions were not discussed nor were spaces for reflection provided during the implementation process that could help teachers speak to the Albanian or Serbian nationalist perspectives of history, which are deeply connected to citizenship (Weinstein, Freedman, and Hughson 2007).

Even though training was not centered on content, teachers were still expected to impart values of tolerance and acceptance as well as fostering critical thinking and interactive skills among learners as these competencies were considered critical for Kosovo's accession into the EU. These expectations, however, created tensions between the teachers and ministry officials and NGO workers. Teachers felt they lacked up-to-date textbooks, resource materials and institutional support to effectively achieve the curriculum teaching goals. Ministry officials and NGO workers, while recognising these problems, spoke more about the attitudes and behaviours of teachers as the primary concern. When talking about the implementation process, NGO workers and Ministry officials conceptualised teachers as representing a past that stymied the progress of modernity. Teachers were talked about as having a cliché understanding of democracy and clinging to outdated teaching practices. Non-governmental organisations and ministry officials often viewed teachers as embodying attitudes and behaviours reflecting the communist past, which was understood to contribute to the conditions of fragility. Therefore, the solution offered was to modernise the teacher to achieve the imagined future. The implementation of the curriculum exposed how teachers were entrapped in a binary way of thinking that Bacevic (2014) called the communist-legacy versus Europeanisation process.

Not only were educators blamed for social malfunctioning within Kosovo, but they were also disempowered in the political process of policy-making. Interviews revealed that most teachers and administrators felt they did not have a voice in creating the curriculum and, as Tawil and Harley (2004) argued, without including multiple voices in designing and implementing curriculum, conditions that create fragility cannot be fully understood. More importantly, the technocratic nature in which the curriculum was implemented undermined the lived realities of those in schools. The day-to-day power and agency that teachers have in effectively building cohesion were not recognised. While I interviewed and observed teachers who were engaged in classroom and community citizenship projects with their students, these experiences were not brought into discussions of the new curriculum. The new curriculum represented something that remained outside of their teaching experiences and instead became a tool for them to talk about new measurements and standards. In this sense, the policy reform repositioned the teacher in their understanding of and participation to change. This effect disempowered teachers from addressing issues that they saw, felt and knew and, by silencing and/or sidelining teachers' voices, limited their possibilities to affect change, both inside and outside of the classroom.

Implications

The aim of my research is not to judge the Kosovo curriculum framework as a success or a failure. By looking at the curriculum goals of providing 'quality and equitable educational services for all students' (Boshtrakaj et al. 2010, 6), it can be argued that the designers of the curriculum framework had positive intentions when creating the document. Yet, what is envisioned on paper often looks different in practice. Translating education reform into school practice can be problematic, and this is especially true in fragile contexts. As Bush and Saltarelli (2001) illustrated, there are 'two-faces' of education in fragile settings. Education reform seeking to mediate and negate conditions of fragility can actually perpetuate them (Davies 2011; Novelli and Cardozo 2008; Rose and Greeley 2006; Smith 2005).

In aligning with European-competency model, the Kosovo's citizenship education competency intention was to focus on issues of human rights, democratic processes and general public issues as part of the peacebuilding and state building efforts (Ministry of Education Science and Technology 2011). Yet in implementing the citizenship education competency, the focus centred on the technocratic elements – standards and measurements. Talk of standards and measurements replaced conversations about social, economic and political issues causing fragility. By sideling curriculum content, the teachers' experiences with and knowledge of societal problems were also ignored. By displacing the teachers' social, cultural and moral realities and replacing it with the imperatives of learning outcomes, policy-makers limited possibilities for effective change. In the case of Kosovo, the curriculum reform became more about changing teachers than changing societal problems. As practioners and scholars in citizenship education, the Kosovo example should offer a moment of pause. As education reform is increasingly being used as a panacea for social ills in fragile contexts, we have to recognise how the implementation of policy might not yield the desired results and, more importantly, how they might exacerbate the problem we are trying to solve.

Disclosure statement

No potential conflict of interest was reported by the author.

References

"About Kosovo." 2015. *UNDP in Kosovo*. http://www.undp.org/content/kosovo/en/home/countryinfo.html.

Bacevic, Jana. 2014. *From Class to Identity: The Politics of Education Reform in Former Yugoslavia*. Budapest: Central European University Press.

Ball, Stephen J. 1990. "Management as Moral Technology." In *Foucault and Education: Disciplines and Knowledge*, edited by S. J. Ball, 153–166. London: Routledge.

Ball, Stephen J. 1994. *Education Reform: A Critical and Post-Structural Approach*. Buckingham: Open University Press.

Boshtrakaj, Lindita, Luljeta Demjaha, Eda Vula, and Richard Webber. 2010. "Kosovo Curriculum Framework Curriculum Writers' Handbook." EU Education Swap Project, July.

Brinkerhoff, Derick W. 2007. *Governance in Post-Conflict Societies Rebuilding Fragile States*. London; New York: Routledge.

Bush, Kenneth D., and Diana Saltarelli. 2001. *The Two Faces of Education in Ethnic Conflict: Towards a Peacebuilding Education for Children*. Florence, Italy: UNICEF.

Carment, David, Yiagadeesen Samy, and Joe Landry. 2013. "Transitioning Fragile States: A Sequencing Approach." *The Fletcher Forum of World Affairs* 37: 125–151.

Castles, Stephen, and Alastair Davidson. 2000. *Citizenship and Migration: Globalization and the Politics of Belonging*. New York: Routledge.

Cerami, Alfio, and Paul Stubbs. 2011. *Post-Communist Welfare Capitalism: Bringing Institutions and Political Agency Back in*. Zagreb: Ekonomski institut.

Council of Europe. 2005. *European Year of Citizenship through Education 2005: Learning and Living Democracy (Concept Paper)*. Accessed October 5, 2006. http://www.coe.int/T/E/Cultural_Cooperation/education/E.D.C/Documents_and_publications/By_subject/Year_2005/Year_concept_paper.PDF

Counts, George S. 1969. *Dare the School Build a New Social Order?* New York: Arno Press.

Davies, Lynn. 2011. "Learning for State-Building: Capacity Development, Education and Fragility." *Comparative Education* 47 (2): 157–180. doi:10.1080/03050068.2011.554085.

Davies, Lynn, and European Training Foundation (Italy). 2009. *Capacity Development for Education Systems in Fragile Contexts*. Working Paper.

Dewey, John. 1916. *Democracy and Education: An Introduction to the Philosophy of Education*. New York: Macmillan.

Dreyfus, Hubert L., and Paul Rabinow. 1983. *Michel Foucault: Beyond Structuralism and Hermeneutics*. Chicago: University of Chicago Press.

Fagerlind, Ingemar, and Lawrence Saha. 1983. "Education, Political Mobilization and Development." In *Education and National Development: A Comparative Perspective*, edited by Ingemar Fagerlind and Lawrence Saha, 123–142. New York: Pergamon Press.

Ferguson, James. 1994. *The Anti-Politics Machine: 'Development,' Depoliticization, and Bureaucratic Power in Lesotho*. Cambridge [England]; New York: Cambridge University Press.

Foucault, Michel. 1991. "Governmentality." In *The Foucault Effect: Studies in Governmentality*, edited by Graham Buchell, Collin Gordon, and Peter Miller, 87–104. Chicago: University of Chicago Press.

François, Monika, and Inder Sud. 2006. "Promoting Stability and Development in Fragile and Failed States." *Development Policy Review* 24 (2): 141–160. doi:10.1111/j.1467-7679.2006.00319.x.

G7+. n.d. "A New Deal for Engagement in Fragile States.Pdf." Accessed January 11, 2018. http://www.g7plus.org/sites/default/files/basic-page-downloads/A%20New%20Deal%20for%20engagement%20in%20Fragile%20States.pdf

Grimm, Sonja, Nicolas Lemay-Hébert, and Olivier Nay. 2014. "'Fragile States': Introducing APolitical Concept." *Third World Quarterly* 35 (2): 197–209. doi:10.1080/01436597.2013.878127.

International Institute for Educational Planning (IIEP). 2011. *Understanding Education's Role in Fragility Synthesis of Four Situational Analyses of Education and Fragility: Afghanistan, Bosnia and Herzegovina, Cambodia, Liberia*. Paris: IIEP Publishing. http://unesdoc.unesco.org/images/0019/001915/191504E.pdf

King, Iain, and Whit Mason. 2006. *Peace at Any Price: How the World Failed Kosovo*. Ithaca, N.Y.: Cornell University Press.

Kirk, Jackie, Karen E. Mundy, and Sarah Dryden-Peterson. 2011. *Educating Children in Conflict Zones: Research, Policy, and Practice for Systemic Change: A Tribute to Jackie Kirk*. New York: Teachers College Press.

Li, Tania. 2007. *The Will to Improve: Governmentality, Development, and the Practice of Politics*. Durham: Duke University Press.

McCowan, Tristan, Elaine Unterhalter, and Bloomsbury Publishing. 2016. *Education and International Development: An Introduction*. London [etc.: Bloomsbury Academic, an imprint of Bloomsbury Publishing.

Ministry of Education Science and Technology. 2011a. *Curriculum Frameworks: For Pre-University Education in the Republic of Kosovo*. Pristina, Kosovo: Government of Kosovo. http://www.ibe.unesco.org/curricula/kosovo/kv_alfw_2011_eng.pdf

Ministry of Education Science and Technology. 2011b. *Kosovo Strategic Education Plan: 2011–2016*. Pristina, Kosovo: Government of Kosovo. http://www.herdata.org/public/KESP_2011_2016.pdf

Mitchell, Timothy. 2002. *Rule of Experts: Egypt, Techno-Politics, Modernity*. Berkeley, CA: University of California Press.

Montanaro, Lucia. 2009. *The Kosovo Statebuilding Conundrum Addressing Fragility in a Contested State*. Madrid: FRIDE.

Mundy, Karen. 1998. "Educational Multilateralism and World (dis) Order." *Comparative Education Review* 448–478.

Musliu, Vjosa. 2015. "Mapping Narratives on Failed States: The Case of Kosovo." In *States Falling Apart? : Secessionist and Autonomy Movements in Europe*, edited by Eva Maria Belser, Alexandra Fang-Bär, Nina Massüger, and Rekha Oleschak Pillai, 369–382. Bern: Stämpfli Verlag.

"National Democracy Education Action Plan for Repubic of Kosovo." 2014. Accessed October 13, 2015.http://www.academia.edu/12879146/National_Democracy_Education_Action_Plan_for_Repubic_of_Kosovo

Novelli, Mario. 2010. "The New Geopolitics of Educational Aid: From Cold Wars to Holy Wars?" *International Journal of Educational Development, the New Politics of Aid to Education* 30 (5): 453–459. doi:10.1016/j.ijedudev.2010.03.012.

Novelli, Mario, and Mieke T. A. Lopes Cardozo. 2008. "Conflict, Education and the Global South: New Critical Directions." *International Journal of Educational Development* 28 (4): 473–488. doi:10.1016/j.ijedudev.2008.01.004.

OECD. 2003. *Reviews of National Policies for Education: South Eastern Europe*. (vol. 1). Paris, France: OECD.

OECD. 2015. *States of Fragility 2015: Meeting Post-2015 Ambitions*. Paris, France: OECD Publishing, Paris. doi:10.1787/9789264227699-en.

"Open Data Kosovo - The Home of Kosovo's Open Data." 2016. *Open Data Kosovo*. Accessed January 10. http://opendatakosovo.org.

Parker, Walter. 2003. *Teaching Democracy Unity and Diversity in Public Life*. New York: Teacher's College Press.

Parker, Walter. 2005. "Teaching against Idiocy." *Phi Delta Kappan* 86 (5): 344–351.
Popkewitz, Thomas S. 1991. *A Political Sociology of Educational Reform: Power/Knowledge in Teaching, Teacher Education, and Research*. New York: Teachers College.
Putnam, R. 2004. "Education, Diversity, Social Cohesion and 'Social Capital.'" Meeting of OECD Education Ministers, Dublin.
Rose, Nikolas S. 2005. *Governing the Soul the Shaping of the Private Self*. London [u.a.]: Free Association Books.
Rose, Pauline, and Martin Greeley. 2006. "Education in Fragile States: Capturing Lessons and Identifying Good Practice." *DAC Fragile States Group*. http://toolkit.ineesite.org/resources/ineecms/uploads/1096/Educ_Fragile_States_Capturing_Lessons.PDF.
Rose, Nikolas, and Peter Miller. 1992. "Political Power beyond the State: Problematics of Government." *The British Journal of Sociology*. 61: 271–303.
Saldaña, Johnny. 2013. *The Coding Manual for Qualitative Researchers*. Los Angeles [i.e. Thousand Oaks, Calif]: SAGE Publications.
Shah, Ritesh. 2012. "Goodbye Conflict, Hello Development? Curriculum Reform in Timor-Leste." *International Journal of Educational Development* 32 (1): 31–38. doi:10.1016/j.ijedudev.2011.04.005.
Shah, Ritesh, and Mieke Lopes Cardozo. 2014. "Education and Social Change in Post-Conflict and Post-Disaster Aceh, Indonesia." *International Journal of Educational Development* 38 (September): 2–12. doi:10.1016/j.ijedudev.2014.06.005.
Shah, Ritesh, and Mieke Lopes Cardozo. 2015. "The Politics of Education in Emergencies and Conflict." In *Education and International Development: An Introduction*, edited by Tristan McCowan and Elaine Unterhalter, 181–200. London [etc.]: Bloomsbury Academic, an imprint of Bloomsbury Publishing.
Shore, Cris, and Susan Wright, eds. 1997. *Anthropology of Policy: Critical Perspectives on Governance and Power*. New York: Routledge.
Smith, Alan. 2005. "Education in the Twenty-First Century: Conflict, Reconstruction and Reconciliation1." *Compare: A Journal of Comparative Education* 35 (4): 373–391. doi:10.1080/03057920500331397.
Sommers, Marc and Peter Buckland. 2005. *Parallel Worlds: Rebuilding the Education System in Kosovo*. IIEP.
Stambolieva, Marija. 2015. "Welfare State Change and Social Citizenship in the Post-Yugoslav States." *European Politics and Society* 16 (3): 379–394.
Tawil, Sobhi, and Alexandra Harley. 2004. *Education, Conflict and Social Cohesion*. Geneva: International Bureau of Cohesion.
Tikly, Leon. 2004. "Education and the New Imperialism." *Comparative Education* 40 (2): 173–198.
Turrent, Victoria, and Moses Oketch. 2009. "Financing Universal Primary Education: An Analysis of Official Development Assistance in Fragile States." *International Journal of Educational Development* 29 (4): 357.
UNICEF Kosovo. 2001. "The New Kosovo Curriculum Framework - White Discussion Paper." Accessed September 2, 2015. http://www.academia.edu/2912975/The_new_Kosovo_Curriculum_Framework_-_White_Discussion_Paper
Weinstein, Harvey M., Sarah Warshauer Freedman, and Holly Hughson. 2007. "School Voices: Challenges Facing Education Systems after Identity-Based Conflicts." *Education, Citizenship and Social Justice* 2 (1): 41–71.
Winthrop, Rebecca, and Elena Matsui. 2013. *A New Agenda for Education in Fragile States*. Center for Universal Education at Brookings. http://ww.protectingeducation.org/sites/default/files/documents/brookings_education_agenda_fragile_states.pdf

Index

Note: Page numbers in *italics* refer to figures
Page numbers in **bold** refer to tables
Page numbers followed by 'n' refer to notes

active citizenship 5, 6, 46, 99–102
Adinkra symbols 27–29, *28*, 35
Africa, indigenous knowledge of 14–15; *see also* South Africa; West Africa, indigenous knowledge/practices of
African Charter on the Rights and Welfare of the Child 25
African Renaissance 14–15, 16
Akan: Adinkra symbols of 27–28, *28*, 35; notion of personhood 28–29
Akar, Bassel 6, 76
Al-Ghazālī 84
Al-Jirari, Abbas 88
Al-Nakib, Rania 79
Andreotti, Vanessa 61, 97
Apple, Michael W. 104
autonomous citizens 11, 13, 14, 21
Auyero, Javier 47

Bacevic, Jana 118, 125
Ball, Stephen J. 115
Banks, James A. 45, 61–62
Bellino, Michelle J. 5–6, 41
benevolence, and citizenship 88, 89
Berlin Wall, fall of 95
Bermudez, Angela 1, 2
Bhabha, Homi 13, 16
Bhengu, Mfuniselwa John 18
bidūn 84
'big P' politics 96
Bleck, Jaimie 26
Brazil: Citizen School project 104; *Landless Workers' Movement* (MST) 104; *see also* Latin America, citizenship education discourses in
buen vivir 105–106
Bush, Kenneth D. 117, 125

Canada: global citizenship education in 59–60; young people's conceptualizations of citizenship in 81

Cardozo, Mieke Lopes 117
Carretero, Mario 1, 2
Castro-Gómez, Santiago 97
Chatterjee, Partha 13
China, global citizenship education in 62
citizen participation, pedagogies of 104–105
Citizen School project (Brazil) 104
citizenship: according to young people 79–81; competences 100, 121; conceptualizations 95–96; cosmopolitan 95; defining 25, 83, 84; reactionary-conservative concern with 95; in South Africa 20; status, feeling, and practice 30–31, 84, 85; Western construction of 13; *see also* young people, conceptualizations of citizenship
citizenship education 95–96; according to young people 79–81; globalisation/localisation of 96–98; as a global issue 95; school-based 26; studies 1; theories 95–96; Western construction of 12–13
citizen-subject binary 13
Civic Education Study (CivEd) 31, *32*, 76, 77, 78
civic efficacy 46, 47
civic engagement 2, 46, 54, 96, 101
civic participation 24; in Guatemala *see* Guatemala, youth civic development in; and Liberian traditional justice systems 34, 35
civil society 13, 47, 48, 51–52, 55, 87
cognitive competence 100
Cohen, Aviv 63
colonialism: and Africa 15; and African diaspora 26; and democracy 12–14, 19; in Liberia 31; in South Africa 19; *see also* post-colonial theory
communicative competence 100
community(ies): and construction of citizenship 86–87; engagement 104–105; and individuals 11, 18, 27–29, *28*, 35; West African 27–29, *28*, 35
comparative education 1, 2, 4, 12
Connell, Raewyn 2
Constitution and Human Rights (CHR) 79

context, and citizenship education 3, 25–26, 30
convivencia, citizenship as 102–103
Cortina, Adela 100
Council of Europe Charter on Education for Democratic Citizenship and Education for Human Rights 121
courts *see* traditional justice systems, Liberian
critical democratic citizenship education 19–21
critical pedagogy 95, 96, 104
Crossley, Michael 14
Crow, David 96
cultural hybridity 5, 11, 13–14
culture 5, 11, 27; and conceptualisations of citizenship 78, 82, 83, 84; and democracy 15–17, 18, 21; difference 13; interculturality 105–106; of violence 46–47; and Western construction of democracy 13
curriculum: global citizenship education in *see* global citizenship education (GCE); in Guatemala 41; in Kosovo *see* Kosovo, citizenship education reform in; in Latin America *see* Latin America, citizenship education discourses in; in Lebanon 79; policies, in post-conflict states 117–118; quality, improving 102; and state building 117

Davies, Lynn 61, 62
decolonial pedagogies, in Latin America 105–106
decolonial theory, from Latin America 96–98
deliberative democracy 95, 96, 100
democracy: critical pedagogy and social justice education theories 95, 96; and culture/globalisation 15–17; deliberative 95, 96, 100; epistemological binaries in Western constructions of 12–14; ethnic 63; immaterial space of 12; indigenous 19; liberal 13, 14, 95, 99, 100, 113; material space of 12; non-liberal 63; non-Western constructions 14–15; poststructuralist theories 95–96; Xhosa teachers' constructions of 17–19
democratic citizenship, epistemological influences on 11–12; African IK and non-Western democratic constructions 14–15; binaries in Western constructions of democracy 12–14; critical democratic citizenship education 19–21; culture and globalization 15–17; Xhosa (South Africa) 17–19
Department for International Development (DfID), UK 116, 117
Dill, Jeffrey S. 61
Dillabough, Jo-Anne 81
Durham, Deborah 46

economic globalisation 54, 67
Educational Goals 2021 (OEI) 102
Education for All (UN) 102, 117
education policy, in fragile states 114, 116–118; *see also* Kosovo, citizenship education reform in
El Salvador, youth in 45

emigration, and Israeli global citizenship education 67–68
epistemological influences *see* democratic citizenship, epistemological influences on
ethnic democracy 63
ethnicity: and citizenship 81; and cultural identity 16; divisions, in Kosovo 119, 124; indigenous, in Liberia 31; and urban-rural binaries 13; in Yugoslavia 118
ethno-nationalism 63, 71
European Commission 119
European Union (EU) 31, 119, 120
expertise, politics of 116

failed citizens/citizenship 45
failed states 114
Feldman, Jackie 67
Fincham, Kathleen 79
Firer, Ruth 63
Foucault, Michel 115
Fox, Jon E. 82
fragile states: definition of 114, 117; education policy in 114, 116–118; humanitarian assistance to 114; *see also* Kosovo, citizenship education reform in
Freire, Paulo 104, 105
Fukuyama, Francis 95, 99
funds of knowledge, youth civic 36
funtunfunefu denkyemfunefu (Adinkra symbol) 27, 28, 35

Gandin, Luis A. 104
Garuba, Harry 13
German Technical Cooperation Agency 120
Gill, Scherto 61
global citizenship education (GCE) 24, 35, 59–60, 96–97; advocacy mode of 61, 71; in conflict-ridden *vs.* post-conflict societies 71–72; cosmopolitan mode of 61, 71; definition and models of 61; differing justifications for 62; as education for peace 61–62; global competencies approach 61; global consciousness approach 61; humanistic models of 60; in Israel *see* Israel, global citizenship education in; meaning of 60; pragmatic and instrumental approaches to 70; theoretical orientation 60–64
globalisation 27, 97; alternative 105; of citizenship education 95, 96–98; and democracy 15–17; economic 54, 67; and knowledge 14
Gordon, Neve 69
Goren, Heela 6, 59
Green, Lesley J. F. 15
Greene, Maxine 18
Guatemala, youth civic development in 5–6, 41–43; anger and frustration toward the state 51; anti-corruption spring 51–52; authenticity and enduringness of change 51–52; citizenship education in schools 55; civic efficacy 46, 47; collective action 50–51; costs and benefits of

both action and inaction 48–50; democratic disjuncture and citizenship 43–46, 50; elections, participation in 51; ethos of pessimism 52; everyday negotiations 47–52; feeling of exclusion 48, 49; gang graffiti clean-up project 50–51; gaps in civil contract 44; institutionalisation of state violence 47; lack of public interest in justice movements 49; liminality 42, 50; mega-development projects, resistance against 48–49; mob violence 49; *ninis* 44; patience 47, 52, 53; postponing democracy 53–54; post-war challenges 43–44; powerlessness 47, 49; risks and benefits, calculation of 48, 49; structural constraints 44, 47, 48, 49, 53, 54, 55; structural reforms 55; value of participation in civil society 50–51; wait-citizenship 42–43, 47, 49, 50, 52, 53, 54; youth agency and apathy 46–47; youth as problem 44
Gyekye, Kwame 28–29

Habermas, Jürgen 100
Hanna, Helen 63, 69
Harley, Alexandra 125
Haste, Helen 1, 2
hegemonic discourses 94, 95, 98
Hill, Thomas 20
Hobsbawm, E. J. 82
Holocaust 66, 67
Holy Qur'ān 84
Hoskins, Bryony L. 77
humanness *see* ubuntu (humanness)
human rights 25, 61, 68–69, 71, 84, 88, 100, 121
Huntington, Samuel 95, 99
hybridity, and epistemological influences 13–14, 20, 27; *see also* cultural hybridity

indigenous democracy, in South Africa 19
indigenous knowledge (IK) 2, 3–4, 5, 26; African 14–15; definition of 14; West African *see* West Africa, indigenous knowledge/practices of; and youth civic funds of knowledge 36
individualism 95; and communalism 11, 18, 27–29, *28*, 35; and global citizenship education 70
Inglehart, R. 77
instrumentalism 16, 70
Instrument for Pre-accession Assistance (IPA) 119
Inter-American Democratic Charter 102
Inter-American Development Bank (IDB) 98, 99–100, 107n1, 107n2, 107n4
interculturality, in Latin America 105–106
International Association for the Evaluation of Educational Achievement (IEA) 76, 77; Civic Education Study (CivEd) 31, *32*, 76, 77, 78
International Baccalaureate Organization 61
International Bureau of Education 119
International Civic and Citizenship Study (ICCS) 31, *32*, 44, 76–77

Islam 84
Israel 62; citizenship education in 63; as Jewish and democratic state 63; national conflict and internal divisions 62
Israel, global citizenship education in 6, 63; bridging gaps within Israeli society 69–70, 72; demographic challenges and discourse of betrayal 67–68; disputed global norms 68–69; emigration 67–68; Holocaust 66, 67; human rights and universalism 68–69; individualism, fostering 70; Israeli-Palestinian conflict 6, 62, 63, 65–66, 70, 71; nationalism 65–66, 71; obstacles and opportunities 71; paradox within education system 67; potential benefits of GCE in a conflict-ridden state 69–70; research methodology 64–65, **64**; research study 63–64; school trips and annual youth delegations 67; 'us *vs.* them' narrative 6, 71

Jamaica 25–26
justice *see* traditional justice systems, Liberian

Kahne, Joseph 96
Kant, Immanuel 20
Kennedy, K. 78
Kennelly, Jacqueline 81
Khaldūn Ibn 84
Khātami, Mohammad 88
kinship, and citizenship 83–84, 86, 89
Kohlberg, Lawrence 100
Kosovo, citizenship education reform in 7, 114–115, 118–119; attitudes and behaviours of teachers 125; cheating in school system 122; curriculum reform process 119–120; difference between new and old curriculum 122–123; disempowerment of educators 125; fragile context 118; implementation of curriculum 119, 120, 122, 123, 124, 125; implications 125–126; in-service training 123; lack of resources 123; rendering technical of curriculum 115, 121–123; research methodology 120–121; responsible citizen competency 120–124; teaching methodologies 123; training sessions 122, 123, 124
Kovalchuk, Serhiy 1
Kubow, Patricia K. 4, 11, 13
kurontire ne Akwamu (Adinkra symbol) 27–28, *28*
Kuwait, young people's conceptualizations of citizenship in 79

Landless Workers' Movement (MST) 104
Latin America, citizenship education discourses in 6–7, 94–95; alternatives to the Western citizen 103–106; citizenship as *convivencia* and slippery slope to securitisation 102–103; citizenship conceptualizations and citizenship education 95–96; community engagement 104–105; critical pedagogy 104; decolonial pedagogies, interculturality and *buen vivir* 105–106;

decolonial theory and globalisation/localisation of citizenship education 96–98; multilateral institutions' discourses of citizenship education 99–103; pedagogies of citizen participation 104–105; re-creation of pedagogical imaginaries in comparative perspective 106–107; students' strikes 101; vertical comparisons, multilateral institutions' discourses as 98–99; Western cosmopolitan man 100–101; youth (dis) engagement and active (responsible) citizenship competences 99–102
Lave, Jean 36
Lebanon, young people's conceptualizations of citizenship in 79, 85–86; and good manners 88; influences 87; maximal and communitarian construct of citizenship 86–87; universalities, knowledge and participation 87–88; willingness to participate for change 87
Lederach, John Paul 52
Lee, Nam-Jin 96
Lemish, Peter 70
Lennon, John 68
Levinson, Meira 46
Li, Tania 116
liberal democracy 13, 14, 95, 99, 100, 113
Liberia: global citizenship education in 60; one-man-one-vote principle in 26; traditional justice systems 5, 30–35, *32*, *33*, **34**
liminality 42, 45, 50, 54
Lincoln, Yvonna 83
Lister, Ruth 80
'little p' politics 96
local knowledge *see* indigenous knowledge (IK)

Magna Carta (1215) 29
Mali 26, 30
Mande Charter (1222) 29–30, 35
Mandela, Nelson 14
Mbeki, Thabo 14
methodologies, research 4
Metz, Thaddeus 14
Millei, Zsuzsa 3
Millennium Development Goals 117
Miller-Idriss, Cynthia 82
Mitchell, Timothy 116
Morales, Jimmy 52, 55n1
Morris, Paul 61
multicultural education 61; *see also* global citizenship education (GCE)
multilateral institutions' discourses, in Latin America 7, 94, 99–103; citizenship as *convivencia* and slippery slope to securitisation 102–103; as vertical comparisons 98–99; youth (dis)engagement and active (responsible) citizenship competences 99–102
Mutua, Makau 25

National Democracy Education Action Plan (Kosovo) 119

nationalism: and Israeli global citizenship education 65–66, 71; and young people's conceptualizations of citizenship 81
negative rights 29
neoliberalism 45, 54, 70, 99, 101
Niens, Ulrike 61, 70
Nieto, Diego 6–7, 94
non-liberal democracy 63
Norris, P. 78
North Africa, constructions of citizenship in 83, 84, 88
Northern Ireland, global citizenship education in 60, 62, 66, 69, 70, 71–72
Novelli, Mario 103

Odora Hoppers, Catherine 14
okra 29
one-man-one-vote principle 26
Organization for Economic Co-operation and Development (OECD) 107n1
Organization of American States (OAS) 99, 102, 107n1
Organization of Iberoamerican States (OEI) 98, 102, 107n1, 107n4
Osler, Audrey 30, 80, 84
O'Toole, Therese 79, 81
Otting, Jennifer 7, 113
Oxley, Laura 61

Palestinian-Israeli conflict 6, 62, 63, 65–66, 70, 71
particularism 6, 63, 68, 71
peacebuilding 46, 114, 115, 116, 117
peace education, global citizenship education as 61–62, 69
pedagogy: of citizen participation 104–105; critical 95, 96, 104; decolonial, in Latin America 105–106; socialist 3
Pedahzur, Ami 63
Pérez Molina, Otto 51–52
personal freedom, *vs.* relational freedom 29
personhood, Akan notion of 28–29
person-human duality 29
Piattoeva, Nelli 3
policy, as technology of governing 115–116
political discourse analysis 94, 98
political participation 5, 27, 80, 81; and contextual information 26; and traditional justice systems 31; of youth, in Latin America 101
political practices, and democracy 18
popular education 104
post-colonial theory 5, 25, 26, 27, 30–31
post-Soviet countries: qualitative research in 4; socialist pedagogy 3
poststructuralist theories 95–96
power 83, 97, 103, 105; and citizenship education 25, 30, 31; and democracy 12, 95; and incorporation of indigenous knowledge 35, 36; and policy processes 115
primordialism 16

qualitative research methodologies 4
Quaynor, Laura 5, 24
Qur'ān, Holy 84

Raditlhalo, Sam 13
Rapoport, Anatoli 1
Reilly, Jacqueline 70
relational freedom, *vs.* personal freedom 29
relativism, and indigenous knowledge 16
religion: and citizenship 79, 83, 84; and democratic participation 26
Resnik, Julia 63, 71
respect, and democracy 18, 19, 20, 21
responsibility, and democracy 18
rights 119; and democracy 18, 19, 21; human rights 25, 61, 68–69, 71, 84, 88, 100, 121; Mande Charter (1222) 29–30, 35; and state fragility 53
Rosario, Melissa 101
Rwanda, youth in 45

sacrifice, and citizenship 86, 89
Saldaña, Johnny 121
Saltarelli, Diana 117, 125
Santos, Boaventura de Sousa 97
Schattle, Hans 61
Schugurensky, Daniel 105
securitisation 102–103, 117
Shah, Ritesh 117
Silova, Iveta 3
Smooha, Sammy 63
Sobe, Noah W. 2
social constructionism 82–83
social constructivism 6, 82–83, 85
socialist pedagogy 3
social justice education 95
socio-emotional competence 100
solidarity, and citizenship 86, 89
Sommers, Marc 45
South Africa 5, 11–12; critical democratic citizenship education 19–21; culture as tool of struggle and resistance in 16; post-Apartheid, youth in 45; *ubuntu* (humanness) 5, 12, 14, 15, 18–19, 20; Western construction of citizen in 13; Xhosa teachers' constructions of democracy 17–19
Spain, global citizenship education in 60
Stambolieva, Marija 118
Starkey, Hugh 30, 80, 84
state building: and education 113; and education policies 117; and fragile states 114; *see also* Kosovo, citizenship education reform in
student strikes, in Latin America 101
Sunjata Keita 29
Sustainable Development Goals (2015) 114
Swanson, Dalene 15
symbols, Adinkra 27–29, *28*, 35

Tarlau, Rebecca 104
Tawil, Sobhi 125

Tereshchenko, Antonina 80
traditional justice systems, Liberian 5, 30–35; IEA CivEd and ICCS items *32*; responses by gender 32, 34, **34**; responses by parental education level 32, 34, **34**; and social status 34; survey questions *33*
Turner, Bryan 13
Turner, Victor 42
Tutu, Desmond 15

ubuntu (humanness) 5, 12, 14, 15, 18–19, 20
Ukraine, young people's conceptualizations of citizenship in 80–81
UNESCO 35, 61, 102, 103, 117, 119
UNICEF 119
United Kingdom, young people's conceptualizations of citizenship in 79–80
United Nations 36; Charter of Human Rights 25; Education First initiative 24; Education for All 102, 117
United Nations Convention on the Rights of the Child 25, 83
United Nations Development Programme (UNDP) 77, 103, 107n1
United Nations Mission in Kosovo 119
United Nations Relief and Works Agency for Palestine Refugees in the Near East (UNRWA) 84
United States: democratic education programmes in 96; global citizenship education in 60, 62, 66; young people's conceptualizations of citizenship in 80
universalism: of global discourses 97; and indigenous knowledge 16; and Israeli global citizenship education 68–69, 71
urban-rural binary 13
USAID 31, 116, 120

vertical comparisons 98–99
Veugelers, Wiel 61
victims, of failed citizenship 45
violence: culture of 46–47; mob 49
voting: and democracy 26; in Guatemala 51

Waghid, Yusef 20
wait-citizenship 5–6, 42–43, 45, 47, 49, 50, 52, 53, 54
Walsh, Catherine 105
wa Thiong'o, Ngũgĩ 15
'way of living' approach *see* poststructuralist theories
Weber, Max 11, 13
Weinstein, Harvey M. 117
Weller, Susie 80
Wenger, Etienne 36
West Africa, indigenous knowledge/practices of 5, 24–25; Adinkra symbols and political knowledge 27–29, *28*, 35; Liberian traditional justice systems 30–35, *32*, *33*, **34**; Mande

Charter (1222) 29–30, 35; need for new paradigms 25–26
West Asia, constructions of citizenship in 83, 84, 88
Westheimer, Joel 96
Williams, Dierdre 25–26
Wingo, Ajume 29
Wiredu, Kwasi 28–29
wonsa (Adinkra symbol) 27, *28*, 35
World Bank 44, 107n1, 107n2, 116, 120

Xhosa township (South Africa), teachers' constructions of democracy in 17–19, 20, 21

Yemini, Miri 6, 59
Yonah 63
young people, conceptualizations of citizenship 6, 76–81; context-specific variables 81; dimensions of citizenship 83–84; epistemological approaches 78; geographical perspective 80; and income 81; indicators of citizenship 83; influences 87; inside-out approach 81–82, 83, 88, 89; Lebanon 85; maximal and communitarian construct of citizenship 86–87; normative construction of citizenship 77–78; operationalising citizenship 83; qualitative-based methodologies 81, 89; socially constructing knowledge as a view of the world 82–83; status, feeling, and practice 84, 85; studies 76–77; universalities, knowledge and participation 87–88; wide-ranging framework of citizenship for inquiry 84–85, 88, 89
youth agency, in Guatemala 46–47, 53
youth apathy, in Guatemala 46–47, 49
youth civic development *see* Guatemala, youth civic development in
youth engagement, in Latin America 99–102
youth mobilisations, in Latin America 101

Zaalouk, Malak 45
Zionism 63, 66, 67, 68, 69